Prayers that Restore My Soul

Carlotta P. Waldmann, M.A.
with Kay Flowers

Copyright © 2018 - Cross Walk Life, Inc.

This book is protected by the copyright laws of the United States of America. All rights reserved, including the right to reproduce this book or portions thereof in any form or by any means, electronic or mechanical, without permission from the author.

Inquiries should be addressed to:
Carlotta Waldmann
PO Box 2334
Santa Rosa Beach, FL 32459

ISBN 978-1-7325703-2-0

Most of the scriptures in this book are from these versions.
AMP – the Amplified Bible
KJV – King James Version
NKJV – New King James Version
NAS – New American Standard
NASB – New American Standard Bible
NIV – Holy Bible, New International Version

CONTENTS

Foreword	
Endorsements	
Acknowledgments	
Introduction	8
Part I: Understanding the Underlying Patterns in Your Soul	10
Restoration, Remorse or Repentance?	11
Strongholds and Doors of Access	11
Ungodly Beliefs	14
Sowing and Reaping	15
Ungodly Soul Ties	16
Bitter Root Judgments	17
Fleshly Strongholds	17
Accepting Our True Identity in Christ	18
Fleshly Inner Vows	19
Bitter Expectations	19
Integrated Prayer Ministry versus Secular Analysis	20
Self-Directed, Christ-Directed or Christ Controlled?	22
Being Born Again?	23
Knowing the Power of Forgiveness	27
The Cross Walk Prayer	29
Part II: Insights and Prayers	32
Abortion and PAS	33
Addictions and Sexuality	36
Anger Management or a Spirit of Anger?	37
Breaking the Power of Word Curses or Negativity	42
Burnout	45
Captive Spirit	49
Deliverance after Integrated Ministry	53
Depression, Discouragement, and Hopelessness	57
Destiny Blockages: God's Unfulfilled Plan for You	62
Eating Disorders	66
Emotions: Destructive or Negative	70
Faith or Fear Faith	74
Fatherhood Issues	77
Fear and Doubts about God	81
Financial Issues	85
Heart of Stone/Inner Vows	88
Illegitimacy, Prenatal or Early Childhood Wounds	92
Illicit Sex, Immorality and Sexual Sin	96
Illnesses and Infirmity: Spiritual Roots	100

Judgmental or Critical Attitude	109
Legalistic Thinking	112
Lonely, Unloved or Rejected	116
Love, True or False?	120
Marriage Issues	123
Men: What Do They Want?	127
Nurturing Your Personal Inner Spirit	130
Performance Orientation	135
Pride	140
Rape and It's Effects	144
Rebellion: My Way or God's Way	148
Roots of Bitterness	155
Self-Image Issues and True Identity	158
Slumbering Spirit	164
Strongholds: Corporate and Personal	168
Suicidal Intents	172
Unforgiving Attitudes	175
Why Do We Train Restoration Prayer Teams?	177
Part III: Exhibits and Opportunities	**178**
Cross Walk Prayer	179
Favorite Tools, Prayers and Handouts	180
Opportunities and Resources	184
Bibliography	189

FOREWORD BY BISHOP BILL HAMON

Prayers that Restore My Soul

Carlotta has put together some truth principles that, if practiced, will transform your life. The truths she presents were not learned just by book knowledge but also by life experiences. They have been proven to be workable in her life and the numerous people she has counseled and mentored over many years.

For every negative and hurtful thing in life there is a principle in God's Word that will uproot it and bring deliverance and transformation. The sin of unforgiveness is found to be the root problem in human relationships and many mental and physical ailments. This just may be the book that will bring deliverance and wholeness to your life. It is no accident this book came into your possession. Read it with an open mind, faith and a willingness to practice the truths presented.

Bless you Carlotta for allowing God to transform your life and then put in this book those truths that will transform those who read this book.

By: Bishop Bill Hamon
Bishop: Christian International Apostolic-Global Network

Author: The Eternal Church, Prophets & Personal Prophecy, Prophets & the Prophetic Movement, Prophets, Pitfalls, & Principles, Apostles/Prophets & the Coming Moves of God, The Day of the Saints, Who Am I & Why Am I here, Prophetic Scriptures Yet to be Fulfilled (3rd Reformation), 70 Reasons for Speaking in Tongues, How Can These Things Be? and God's World War III

It was my honor to meet Bishop Bill Hamon at Christian International in 1993 at the International Gathering of Apostles and Prophets at Santa Rosa Beach, FL. My whole Christian world view was changed! In 1996, I resigned from my 25 year career as a nurse and enrolled in his ministry training college. My first ministry trip was with Bishop and that was the first day of the rest of my life!

Bishop Hamon and Christian International have ordained over 4,000 prophetic ministers including my husband, Louis, and I. Over 400,000 believers have been activated in their spiritual gifts and prophecy. We are blessed beyond measure to have him as our neighbor and oversight for our ministry, Cross Walk Life, Inc. Bishop is an awesome example to us and never passes us without speaking. We call him our spiritual father and the founder of the prophetic movement.

Endorsements

Believe me, you will want to read this book! Each of us need to hear this message of soul-restoration and how to unlock the reservoir of God's lovingkindness and healing power. Life pours out of the pages of Carlotta Waldman's book, *Prayers that Restore My Soul*! You will feel God's presence as you read. Discover the keys of soul healing prayer. Delight yourself in getting answers you've waited year to hear. God will do a beautiful thing in your life as you read. Enjoy!

Dr. Brian Simmons
The Passion Translation Project
Passion & Fire Ministries

Carlotta Waldmann's "Prayers That Restore My Soul" is far more than just another prayer guide; it is an in-depth look at the mysterious correlations between sin and sickness and sowing and reaping. We often find it difficult to receive our healing simply because we do not understand the direct connection between these two. This book is a systematic examination of their "cause and affect" relationship. This approach to healing prayer has long been neglected, but greatly needed in the Body of Christ.

Ira Milligan
Author of "Understanding the Dreams You Dream"

Acknowledgments

No one has succeeded entirely on their own efforts. Father God was faithful to bring alongside inspiring leaders and behind the scenes supporters who believed in us. Years ago I was encouraged to believe a godly belief, "God will bring people alongside you who not only believe in you but are honored to invest in your vision, your training and in fulfilling your mission." I couldn't imagine it but God honored my faith declarations and decrees.

I want to express my profound appreciation to my husband, Louis F. Waldmann III, for doing everything possible to support me as a person, a woman in ministry and all that God wants to do through me.

This book is only possible because of my dear friends and excellent editing and publishing team: Kay Flowers, Patricia Brown and Rebecca Francis, who worked tirelessly with us for the Kingdom's sake.

I cannot express how grateful I am for Chester and Betsy Kylstra who wrote *Restoring the Foundations* and mentored me. We are forever in debt to John and Paula Sandford who wrote *Transformation of the Inner Man* and the manuals for the *Elijah House Training for the Ministry of Prayer Counseling*. Their teachings and training not only restored me but are strong pillars in my life message.

We are especially grateful to Bishop Bill Hamon and all the dedicated faithful Christian International ministers and members who have poured into our lives and have interceded for us.

We want to bless all the pastors, ministry leaders and lifelong friends, who share our vision to make these insights and training available to all churches, all cultures and all nations.

We are also greatly in debt to those to whom we have ministered, our prayer receivers, who have also taught us so much about the strategies of the enemy and our triumphant deliverer, the Lord of Hosts.

Thank You, Holy Spirit our tutor. We could never begin to write these books if we were depending on our own ability to say it just right. We trust You Holy Spirit to touch each reader where they need healing and restoration like only You can do! You are the One who restores our souls.

Introduction

I was highly motivated to help others find healing and freedom in Jesus because lies and deceptions had blocked me from fulfilling my destiny for decades. After years of experience as a mental health nurse, a Bachelor's degree in theology, being ordained as a Minister of Counseling, and receiving more training in restoration prayer ministry, I thought surely I was ready to pray for people. The Bible warns us not to release a novice into ministry too quickly, but I had been doing "Christian counseling" for years and thought I was prepared. Little did I know "how little I did know" in natural knowledge or in spiritual discernment.

My first trusting friend came for several days of restoration prayer. Wanting to be a good hostess, I rented a movie to help us relax after her trip. Back then, I was too green to understand why the movie *Ghost* was not a good Christian spiritual choice. (It contains astral projection, divination by a medium and explicit sexual content.) Early in the movie, one character is shot and killed, dying in his girlfriend's arms. At this point, my friend jumped to her feet, screaming in horror and grief. Too late, I realized my mistake. Her late husband had also been shot and had died in her arms! What a mistake! Thank God, He is able to redeem everything, and He brought great healing in spite of our rough start.

I hope my books will help you avoid similar rough starts! I birthed my first book, *Restoration Prayer Ministry Manual One,* out of my passion to help prepare you to minister restoration to yourself and to others. I encourage you to read Manual One first and build a strong foundation of understanding how to trace issues from fruit to root, how to discern root causes from surface symptoms and how to pray more effectively using restoration prayers. Manual One will help prepare you to minister to yourself and others more effectively whether you are a lay minister, a licensed mental health professional, a caring intercessor or a pastor in need of a spiritual handbook for pastoral counseling.

This my second book, *Prayers that Restore My Soul*, will provide you with more resources, prayers, handouts and tools in your ministry tool belt. It will guide you in praying for troubled believers who have different underlying patterns of behavior, with just as many different reasons for those behaviors. Perhaps the person you most want to help first is yourself. Either way, as you seek the guidance and wisdom of the Holy Spirit, you will gain knowledge and discernment of these patterns.

You will learn to do active listening on several levels at once and to listen for "roots" as troubled believers share their circumstances. You will also learn to listen to the Holy Spirit at the same time, as He shares His strategy to heal. He will guide you to not only identify the surface symptoms but also to form your healing prayer to include faith to break the power of the root causes.

I went to many wannabe Christian counselors who were caring but knew little more than to pray surface prayers over surface issues. I realized the great need to teach ministers how to minister in the power of the Holy Spirit. I hope that you will learn how to use your spiritual power and authority to set the captives free. As you learn to effectively partner with the Holy Spirit, you can expect many darts from God's enemy. Satan will throw numerous roadblocks in the pathway to healing and "hooks," which will dig into one of the biggest roadblocks, your own fleshly baggage. Your mind and flesh will constantly resist what can only be done by the Spirit.

In this book, you will understand how to guide believers (and yourself) into a renewal of mind and heart, and how to pray for cleansing and spiritual healing. You will learn the power of forgiveness as you lead wounded lives to seek forgiveness five essential ways. Transformed by the Cross of Christ, hearts will be changed as people come to the end of trusting in themselves, in their own righteousness or in their own fleshly strength, and learn to enter into God's rest as promised in Hebrews 4:9-10, redeeming all the rewards and blessings and missed opportunities for spiritual growth. You will witness the miracle of the influence of the Holy Spirit on believers who were once powerless and hurting, now set free for heavenly service, empowered by the grace of our amazing God.

IinHimHeinme, Carlotta Waldman

Brief Bio: Carlotta P. Waldman is the founder of Cross Walk Life, Inc., a ministry outreach and website that includes over 200 articles. Filled with the Holy Spirit and endowed with strong spiritual gifts, Carlotta has seen God use her as a Bible College educator, seminar speaker, former mental health nurse and an ordained Minister of Counseling. She is known for her insights on how to break strongholds in the lives of believers, setting them on fire for service to Him. NowFaith.TV is an online 4-year video/audio ministry training school that reaches thousands every month in over 175 countries. In 2005, Carlotta began hosting Cross Walk Talk, a Christian talk radio show which invites callers to call in for ministry on the air. Carlotta has a Masters in Biblical Studies with an emphasis in Christian Counseling and was ordained by Christian International Ministries. You can find out more about applying for Restoration Prayer Ministry, mentoring, online education, training, consultation or ministry to survivors at www.RestorationPrayerMinistry.com

To apply	http://www.RestorationPrayerMinistry.com
Home site	http://www.CrossWalkLife.com
Online school	http://www.NowFaith.TV
YouTube	http://www.youtube.com/user/NowFaithTV
Radio archives	http://www.blogtalkradio.com/Cross-Walk-Talk
For survivors	http://crosswalklife.com/Recovery-for-survivors-home.html

Part I:
Understanding the Underlying Patterns in Our Souls

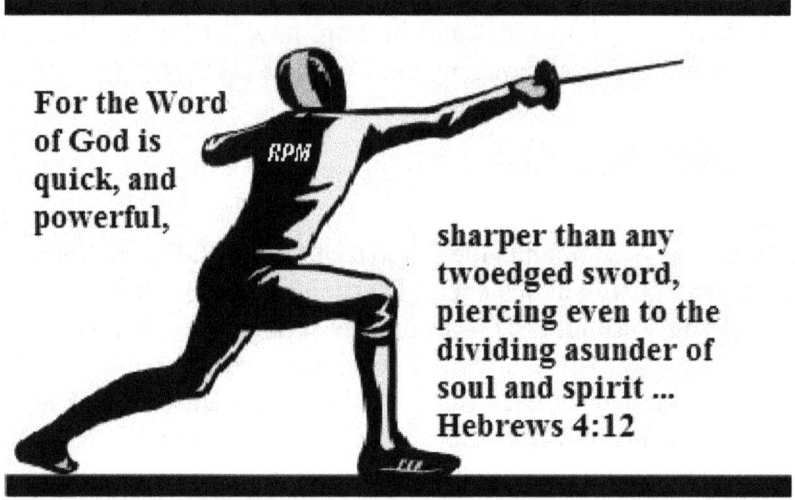

Understanding the Underlying Patterns in Our Souls

Restoration, Remorse or Repentance?

Did you ever feel like a hurtful conflict was still unresolved even though you had sincerely forgiven those involved? Did you sense they had no grasp of how badly they had hurt you? Did you think trying to reconcile was almost hopeless, because they had made little or no effort to rebuild the trust they had crushed?

Your perceptions may be right! There is a huge difference between true repentance and simply showing remorse for what happened. The repentant one is honestly sorry for any hurtful words or actions and is willing to make restitution. The one who merely shows remorse may only be sorry they got caught and have no intention of owning responsibility for their own sinful responses or accountability for damages.

True godly repentance comes from a godly grief about sinning against God first of all, and secondly understanding how badly our words or actions have hurt others. It is a broken heartedness about what was done without making excuses, blaming others or presenting half-truths. A repentant attitude shows genuine concern by asking forgiveness for the hurt done.

While it is easy to focus on their fault in the matter, Holy Spirit may convict us that we are partially at fault too. Regardless of how guilty the other party was, it is no excuse for us to indulge in sinful reactions and behaviors toward them. Holy Spirit may ask us to repent of our judgmental, critical attitudes and behaviors. If we repent of our own sinful reactions, we are then able to invite Jesus to heal our hearts, restore our souls, and take the guilt, pain and shame on Himself. However, if we excuse these sinful reactions, we are falling for the bait of Satan to take offense and are giving him permission to erect strongholds in our lives.

Satan wants to create open doors of access and strongholds in our lives

"For the weapons of our warfare are not carnal, but mighty through God to the pulling down of strongholds, casting down imaginations and every high thing that exalts itself against the knowledge of God and bringing into captivity every thought to the obedience of Christ" (II Corinthians 10:4-5).

A personal stronghold is an automatic, practiced and habitual way of thinking and behaving that we know is not godly but we feel hopeless to change. Common personal strongholds are related to illness, bitterness, anger, separated thinking, jealousy, doubt, unworthiness, self-pity, performance based acceptance, rejection, fear, intimidation, accusation, witchcraft, religious control and pride.

A stronghold often begins when we react sinfully to personal hurt or trauma. God created us with lives and wills of our own, but the automatic sinful reactions that we create also have lives of their own. This is manifested in habits, fantasies, addictions and wrongful ways of thinking. The strongholds and sinful reactions that we developed before we knew Jesus can resurrect and maintain lives of their own even after we receive Christ into our lives.

Satan's plan is to set us up to have sinful reactions and behaviors so he will have an opening to separate us from others, from God and even from ourselves. He isn't content just to set us up to be hurt and wounded. He wants us to react sinfully so he can build sinful strongholds in our souls. When we defend our right to take offence or to behave sinfully, we are beginning to build a stronghold. This stronghold will block our efforts to get healing and restoration in our souls. When we repent of our sinful reactions and behaviors, we also give Jesus access to heal our souls, take the pain, remove the shame and leave us with His wisdom.

Sometimes, we discover that we not only need healing but we also need to do some "deep cleaning." Through God's Word, we know how to apply Christ's blood to receive forgiveness of sins, but we do not necessarily understand how to bring every block, sin or fleshly (self-powered) structure in our lives to the Cross to be crucified. We will either believe that we will go through the Christian life asking for forgiveness of sin after sin, or we will learn how to live the victorious life, bringing ungodly patterns (sinful actions or reactions) to the Cross once and for all. We will either learn how to bring our soul hurts to Jesus for healing or carry on as victims indefinitely. Thank God, Jesus Christ came to restore our souls and to heal the brokenhearted.

You can't heal your heart with your head

The world's viewpoint is usually in direct opposition to the Word of God. Some psychologists tell us we can simply re-decide and make better choices with positive thinking. Motivational speakers tell us we can do anything we set our minds to accomplish. Personal life coaches instruct us to overcome our weaknesses with a powerful new self-image. In the Bible, however, we find different keys to victorious living.

God's Word teaches us that we need to come under His training, to accept what He knows is best for us. As we grow in faith, He creates opportunities for us to trust Him even more, to become radical lovers who are unfettered in our passion for Him and our compassion for others. In order to walk through these open doors of opportunity, we have to choose to die to our self-centeredness and to live in Christ. Patterns of sinful reactions and sinful behaviors have to be brought to the Cross for Jesus to bring them to death. Instead of defending our strongholds by tolerating, excusing or minimizing our sin, we must choose to allow God to circumcise our hearts (purify our motives). Jesus died to break the power of sin in our lives (Romans 6).

We must discern the difference between eternal versus temporary motivations and spiritual versus fleshly sources. Was it just me or Jesus Christ through me? 1 Corinthians 3:11-13 says, "For no other foundation can anyone lay than that which is laid, which is Jesus Christ. Now if anyone builds on this foundation with gold, silver, precious stones, wood, hay, straw, each one's work will become clear; for the Day will declare it, because it will be revealed by fire; and the fire will test each one's work, of what sort it is." We should ask ourselves, "Was I reacting with sinful reactions or responding out of the mind and heart of Christ in me?"

Why does God allow adversity in our lives?

Jesus said He came to destroy the works of the enemy and to heal the brokenhearted. Psalm 107 says God will deliver us out of all of our distresses, whether they were due to our own poor choices, wounds from others, natural disasters or just happened. Sometimes, we have to learn how to renounce the lies and word curses spoken by others or by ourselves recently or in the past, and replace them with God's truth. We travel through "adverse-city," but we definitely don't want to get stuck living there.

When we cry out for a transfer from "adverse-city," the Holy Spirit, our personal tutor, will give the revelation: the key is to repent of wanting pity for our problems and to speak His truth about our powerful potential.

As we abide in Jesus, we learn a lifestyle of focusing on Jesus rather than on problems. We choose to partner with God. Instead of focusing on disease, we focus on the opportunity to receive or minister healing. As we live by faith and walk by faith, we don't focus on lack or poverty, but we speak God's abundance and provision into existence for all that He wants done. We learn that every apparent problem is simply a stage set for us to agree with God, to declare and to decree His miracle-working power. We live by His supernatural power, not our natural power.

For many believers, this is radical thinking. They are afraid to step out and allow God to activate them in supernatural power because they know their hearts are not pure. They are afraid to speak blessing and miracles into existence because they know they have also used their words to harm others. James 3:10 says, "From the same mouth come both blessing and cursing. My brethren, these things ought not to be this way." They recalled that in the past, they had spoken judgments against others, dishonored authorities and have doubted God. While they may have been able to modify their behavior, it is not enough. Their hearts still need to be purified.

If you have Jesus Christ in side you, you already have it all.

If you have Christ in you, you have everything you need to fulfill your destiny in Christ, but most people may not know how to release this life-changing power. Believers in Jesus Christ as Lord have been called from the foundation of the earth and have His unlimited power within to be all He has called them to be. He has made unique deposits into each believer's life and has been preparing individuals for a unique gifting, a unique calling and a unique anointing.

It is God's pleasure that believers experience blessing and undeserved favor to fulfill their God-given destiny. If asked, He will give personal revelation about spiritual principles that will allow believers to pinpoint their destiny, to identify the blocks to that destiny and to be released to fulfill it. What excitement, to be able to lead believers in effective prayer leading to the fulfillment of their God-given purpose in Christ!

Patterns that can block restoration and healing.

What are fleshly structures or patterns? Everyone has fleshly, self-centered reactions, whether they are a born-again believer or not. Pediatricians would say that babies are born with preferences, fears, dislikes, likes, opinions or even addictions that were formed during prenatal experiences. For instance, an unborn baby who was subjected to physical, verbal or mental abuse in the womb will form reactions to the abuser and will react if that person tries to hold them in the labor room. Anxious mothers-to-be may give birth to colicky, fearful babies. Early childhood wounds cause children to have fleshly reactions and fleshly behaviors before they understand the difference between spiritual responses and fleshly reactions.

Romans 7 describes the struggle that every believer experiences, as our self-centered, fleshly lusts war for dominance over our spirit-led desires. Even though we can be assured that our old nature is dead, as Christ died once for all (Romans 6), our flesh still remembers the self-life and wants to be in control.

Romans 7:1-6 says the secret is to die to our "old husband" of keeping the law in our strength and to be married to another, our new Bride Groom in the Spirit, Jesus Christ. Out of this union, life is conceived and lasting fruit is born. We have died to living by the letter of the law and live out of our new, personal spirit, which actually can be one with Holy Spirit. (1 Corinthians 6:17)

Ungodly Beliefs

Many believers go through their entire lives like hungry passengers on a cruise ship, unaware that fabulous meals are included in the fare. They continually beg God to give what He has already given. They may know that God's Son has already paid the price for the fare, but they are blocked from further knowledge of the contents of the dining room—or even how to find it. They may read words in the first chapter of Ephesians like "holy and without blame" but they don't really believe all these blessings, benefits, and privileges belong to them. If you try to share that they already have been given everything they need for life and godliness, they may stare at you like a cow looking at a new gate: "If I go through this new gate, where will it lead?"

There are many reasons Christians don't seem to live the victory Christ has promised. The main reason is that God's enemy (and ours) is constantly seeking to undermine the abundant life God offers so that Christians will not enter into God's fullness. First, we must choose to believe that walking in the fullness of the Holy Spirit in victory is a "mission possible" because Jesus died that we might be free from the law of sin and death. (Romans 7:1-6)

Satan is out to destroy believers and their hope that Jesus Christ would want to live His life through them in love and power. God's plan is to empower us to love Him, ourselves and others. Satan's master plan is to separate us from God, ourselves and others. Satan sets up circumstances so that believers feel separated and isolated, alone in their struggles and sure that no one understands them. Yes, Christians can certainly feel brokenhearted, despondent, and inconsolable, but to remain in that state is a trick of the devil, who may have worked for decades to plant the seeds of condemnation, expectations of failure or word curses handed down from previous generations.

Satan is out to strangle faith ,and he will go to any extent to intimidate, sidetrack, mislead and render believers powerless. He will use events of hurt and trauma to sow ungodly and untrue beliefs about God, others or themselves and build fleshly, reactive behaviors on the foundation of these false beliefs. As Christians come to wrong conclusions about themselves, others and God, Satan hopes to use these wrong conclusions to keep believers weak and ineffectual for a lifetime.

God is delighted that you are willing to partner with His Holy Spirit to identify and destroy Satan's strategy. For some reason, God usually limits Himself to working through human beings. We are hurt in relationships, but we are also healed in relationships when we allow others to minister restoration to our souls.

The Bible says that we determine our future by the "fruit of our own lips," or you might say, "We get what we speak." We also get what we believe for; faith works, whether negative or positive faith. There are spiritual laws that are just as sure as natural laws like gravity. We don't break the law of gravity, it breaks us. A spiritual law that has everything to do with healing, freedom and restoration is the law of sowing and reaping.

Sowing and Reaping

Another reason for lack of vibrant Christianity is the pattern of sowing and reaping. Many people today do not understand cause and effect; they think that even long-term patterns in their lives just come out of nowhere. If there is a long-term negative pattern or curse in their lives, they need to run to ask God for the root cause because Proverbs 26:2 says it is not there without a cause. Patterns don't develop spontaneously. They are constructed bit by bit over time.

Anytime someone comes complaining of reaping more than their share of trouble or of an ongoing pattern, one has to ask God how they sowed the bad seeds they are now reaping and how to break the power of the cause. **The rule of cause and effect** (or sowing and reaping) applies to everyone, including believers. For example, a sinful reaction to godly authority sows a grudging attitude that will reap a harvest of discontent and disrespect, especially if that person becomes an authority themselves.

Sowing and reaping, like gravity, is an impartial law. Whatever seeds we sow, whether good or bad, we will reap what we sow, later than we sow and more than we sow. No amount of counseling can make this reaping pattern go away, and no amount of counseling can cause the receiver to be immune to God's natural and spiritual laws, like sowing and reaping. As Galatians 6:7 says, "Do not be deceived: God is not mocked, for whatever one sows, that will he also reap" (ESV).

For example, if a man sows one kernel of corn, he will reap about 7-800 kernels per ear, no matter what he believes. The negative or sinful seeds that we have sown in the past do not expire even if we do not remember sowing them. We must repent and renounce them to break the power of the sowing and reaping cycle.

Ungodly Soul Ties

Ungodly soul ties develop when we enter into an ungodly covenant with another person, group or institution. It is important to formally break the ungodly part of our ties and to keep the godly ties. The fruit of the transference of spirits, ungodly beliefs, bitter expectations, inner vows, and word curses spoken by them or us will affect our lives until we renounce and break the power of our ungodly agreements with them. God is a covenant keeping God and honors the covenants we have made until we break them. We must identify and cut the ungodly soul tie by praying a prayer of agreement with someone with spiritual authority.

Soul ties can be made in many more relationships than just sexual ones. People will come for prayer ministry to rid themselves of the residue of personal relationships; ties with denominations; error taught in books; wounds from business contracts, employers, church leadership, teachers, or coaches; blood packs; vows with secret organizations; domineering or abusive relationships; or even from the control of people who have already passed away. Soul ties must be broken with the power of agreement with someone with spiritual power and authority. I had been teaching about soul ties for years before I realized the power of them in my own life.

Thirty-three years after I was separated from my high school sweetheart (because my family moved to another state), he appeared in my doorway. My heart was leaping for joy, believing that I would finally have the true love I had always wanted. This powerful tie had been lying dormant for thirty-three years. I was single and available! But after three weeks of calls and emails, I had to admit that I was now Spirit-filled with spiritual gifts, and he was not. My poor heart had to give him up AGAIN! After five weeks of tears, a pastor prayed with me to break the power of the soul tie, and I was finally free to take my heart back. Good thing too…because I met my husband, Louis, the next week!

Bitter Root Judgments

Hebrews 12:15 says to look "carefully lest anyone fall short of the grace of God; lest any root of bitterness springing up cause trouble, and by this many become defiled" (NKJV). A bitter root of judgment from an offense or wound in the past is one of the most common spiritual roots of current negative patterns. The more we meditate on scriptures, the more these bitter roots are brought to light, so that the sowing and reaping cycles can be broken.

If there is bad fruit on your tree, the bad root is on your tree. Believers need to take a good, long look at their lives and their sinful reactions to hurts and wounds. Are they exhibiting the good fruit of the Holy Spirit or some other kind of fruit? Where there is lots of bad fruit, there is a bad root—often a root of bitterness caused by a judgmental attitude, resentment, or repressed anger, grief or guilt not completely dealt with, or even a hardened attitude of unforgiveness.

Bad fruit on MY tree is from MY own sinful reactions and hidden roots on MY tree ... not their tree!

Bitter judgments are like negative faith, and faith works whether it is positive or negative. We have all been hurt by bitter roots, when someone refused to forgive us and expected us to continue to fail. When believers judge with condemnation, they are helping Satan put prison bars around the other and their sin, making it harder for them to experience the freedom from sin that is needed. This bitter root will grow and fester within hearts and lives, so that Christians begin to believe in a twisted sense of God's truth, inhibiting their own spiritual maturity and tainting the lives of everyone around them.

The good news is that the Holy Spirit is able to show us how to pray, whether we are tracing the pattern from bad fruit to bad root or from a bad root to bad fruit. Even if the fruit has not yet fully blossomed, we can renounce our bad roots and avoid reaping crop after crop of bad fruit in the future. Luke 6:46-49 exhorts us to dig deep and to see if our foundation is built upon the "rock" which cannot be shaken.

Fleshly Strongholds

Strongholds are areas of fleshly resistance in our lives that we know are against the will of God but seem impossible for us to change. The Holy Spirit will try to convict us of sinful thoughts and behaviors, but if we resist, we are in danger of developing strongholds in our lives.

Often they begin when we have reacted sinfully to hurts and have begun to tolerate sinful thoughts, followed by excusing sinful behaviors and the development of new sinful beliefs, behaviors and expectations. When we defend all these sinful reactions instead of repenting of them, we are then defending our fleshly stronghold.

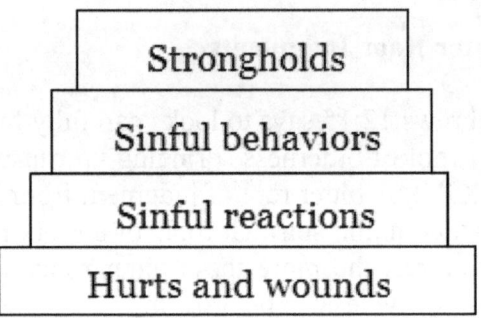

When strongholds are operating in our lives, we tend to judge others and ignore our own blind spots. Strongholds give us a false identity and we begin to agree with it saying, "I am angry" or "I am fearful" or "I am rejected" or "I am jealous." Even though we know that this is not God's higher truth about us, we feel that it is hopeless to change. Satan's original goal was to damage our identity.

Over time, strongholds are slowly built in our lives until we resist any kind of ministry and claim our rights to react sinfully. For instance, we don't decide to have a stronghold of bitterness; we decide that because of what "they" did to us, we then have a right:

- to refuse to forgive the offender until "tomorrow"
- to resent them for today and review our record of wrongs
- to judge them with condemnation, attack or avoid them
- to imagine how we could even the score or retaliate
- to allow ourselves to rage or express our wrath to others
- to choose to hate them, not just their actions
- to imagine how to eliminate them from our world
- to entertain murdering them through words or violence

When I began to pray scriptures against each stronghold in my own life, I was healed of twenty-four illnesses. They were documented illnesses, but physicians could only treat the symptoms. It was humbling to realize that praying scripture defeated my own personal strongholds and I was healed.

Praying the Word of God in agreement with other Christians will break the stronghold's power to hold us and will show us how to come into agreement with God's truth about who we are in Christ. Praying scripture helps us to discern Satan's plan to cause separation between us and God, others and even within ourselves. Our eyes are opened to see God's plan to enable us to love Him, others and ourselves. When we pray scriptures, angels rush to perform the Word of the Lord!

Accepting our True Identity in Christ

The Bible has much to say about us that may sound hypocritical when we try to declare these truths over ourselves. I would say a hypocrite is someone who pretends to be someone he or she is not. But I am commanded to believe that I am holy, blameless, righteous, totally forgiven and unconditionally loved and accepted, completely apart from my performance. If God says this is who I am, because Jesus died and took my sins upon Himself, am I a hypocrite to say this is who I am or a hypocrite to pretend I am not who God says I am?

Some of us are particularly prone to base our identity on our performance or lack of it. It is difficult for us to understand that our new identity is based on the true reality of who Jesus says we are: since we have exchanged our old nature for our new one. Choosing to walk as a new creature in Christ (old things having passed away and all things made new) is the first step to accepting our new identity in the true reality, God's reality. (2 Corinthians 5:17)

The Bible is clear that our old man has died, and we have been raised to newness of life. Romans 6:6-11 says, "Knowing this, that our old man was crucified with Him that the body of sin might be done away with that we should no longer be slaves of sin. For he who has died has been freed from sin. Now if we died with Christ, we believe that we shall also live with Him, knowing that Christ, having been raised from the dead, dies no more. Death no longer has dominion over Him. For the death that He died, He died to sin once for all; but the life that He lives, He lives to God. Likewise you also, reckon yourselves to be dead indeed to sin, but alive to God in Christ Jesus our Lord." NKJV

Fleshly Inner Vows

Fleshly inner vows are promises or vows to ourselves in the power of our own strength: "I will never..." or "I will always…" These vows are powered by the power of the flesh, are not Spirit-led and should be renounced utilizing the power of agreement with someone who knows their spiritual power and authority. In the Bible, we are commanded to simply let our "yes" be "yes" and our "no" be "no" without swearing. In order to break the power of a fleshly inner vow, we must ask someone with spiritual authority to pray in agreement with us in the Name of Jesus Christ. The most common fleshly inner vow that I know of is "I will not talk, tell, share, feel, be real or ask for what I want." This vow can seriously limit your future.

Fleshly inner vows such as "I will never grow up" or "I will never marry" or "I will never have children" have actually prevented the person from developing physically, or having a successful marriage or delivering a live child. Once renounced in agreement with someone who knows their spiritual power and authority, people were suddenly able to mature physically, enjoy a successful marriage or deliver a live child.

Bitter Expectations

Bitter expectations are almost as powerful as bitter roots of judgment. When we expect others to fail, we are agreeing with the enemy and defiling others. While it is easy to expect others to continue to act like they have in the past (or the present), it is godly love and obedience to believe the best and to agree with God for their healing and deliverance from sin. (When we continue to expect others to fail us, and they do, we may also develop bitter roots of judgment.)

Although it's easier to feel like the innocent victim and blame others, people who truly want deliverance for themselves need to be held accountable for their ungodly reactions to the failings of others. Dishonoring or judging others for their failures or their sins may seem like a normal reaction or an easy out, but playing the "blame game" allows people to avoid responsibility for their own actions, reactions or overreactions. Until they face the reality of their own possible contribution to the problem, whether conscious or unconscious, healing from the pain and consequences of past mistakes will not be complete.

I learned this the hard way. I had judged my father for being distant even though he had to travel for a living. Then I began to judge my tenant and spiritual leaders for being distant too. But when I repented of judging my father for being distant, I noticed an immediate change in my father, spiritual leaders and tenant, who suddenly wanted to spend time with me. I realized I was reaping the judgments that I had sowed. But is it enough to identify the root problem? What is restoration?

Restoration Prayer Ministry (RPM) is not just identifying, analyzing or talking root issues to death. It is not presuming that we can use the steps that worked yesterday. It is not telling Jesus how to heal a person or telling the person what to imagine or visualize. It is not just praying that they will forget the pain, leave the past behind or even that they will not hurt anymore. It is not deliverance or healing alone. My friend, Cheryl Dely, sent an article describing why we need restoration.

Integrated Prayer Ministry versus Secular Analysis
Submitted by Cheryl H. Dely, M.S.W.

Scripture declares we are to *"work out our salvation with fear and trembling"* (Philippians 3). The root word for salvation means *"to become whole; to become healed."* Wholeness and healing encompass much more than a surface assessment of current pain and/or dysfunction. Forgiveness and comfort have long been the standard for ministering healing.

While they are important and appropriate, standing alone, they are incomplete. We have been guilty of *"Healing the wound of my people lightly, saying peace, peace when there is no peace" (Jeremiah 6:14, 8:11).* We must ask ourselves do we want the *"balm of Gilead"- a long-term change agent*. Or will we be satisfied with a *salve – a temporary remedy*? If we are going to *"lay the axe to the roots"* (Luke 3:9) and go after deep level causes of our pain, we must be willing to go the heart of the matter.

We need to uncover structures, patterns, habits, perceptions and thinking that underlie and motivate current behaviors. These deeply imbedded structures have developed over time and may have their origins in early childhood, generational sins/curses, emotional hurts and wounding, various ungodly beliefs (inner vows, bitter root judgments/expectations) or even demonic oppression, not to mention our own sin nature.

If we truly desire to lay claim to what is promised in scripture, mere awareness is not enough.
- *"recover our sight" (John 9:25)*
- *"be set free…be transformed" (Colossians 3:5)*
- *"forgive and you will be forgiven" (Luke 6:37)*
- *"see to it no root of bitterness springs up" (Hebrews 12:5)*
- *"first clean the inside of the cup" (Matthew 23:25)*
- *"judge not that we should not be judged" (Luke 6:37)*
- *"not be put to shame" (I Peter 2:6)*
- *"honor father and mother, so it may go well with us" (Exodus 20:12)*

Cognitive approaches that enlighten our understanding illumine the problem. A problem-centered approach ignores the fact that sin, ours and others, is the root of the problem – not hurts, wounds or shame. We must be willing to submit our hearts to a process that is open to conviction, facilitates forgiveness, death of these inner structures on the Cross and rebirth by the regenerating power of God's Holy Spirit.

After all, the Bible says our primary focus is to know and glorify God. It is quite natural to want pain relief for ourselves and others. The temptation is to look at God as a way to put our lives in order - the way we want it! If counseling is really one aspect of sanctification, what is the purpose of sanctification – to get over our problems, or be a reflection of God in the middle of them?

If the heart has <u>not</u> been effectively dealt with from a comprehensive and integrated approach as described above, true sanctification has been short-circuited. Deeply rooted inner structures escape the deathblow of the cross of Christ, and we continue as a people who desire temporal solutions more than we desire God.

Transformation comes through brokenness. The bread that fed the multitudes first had to be broken before it could be shared. Our personal experience of ministry received reflects a law of life. Can a stalk of corn produce an ear unless it first receives life from the parent seed? It's the principle of abiding, love absorbed and healing received. As we have our soul-hunger satisfied, then we can go forth with a full basket.

As we are talking to others about their story, we are forced to look at our story and realize they are parallel in deeply meaningful ways. Sometimes you are addressing issues not yet addressed in your life. Through it, we come to know we aren't healers or fixers, just fellow strugglers who join with others in the pursuit of God.

Self-Directed, Christ-Directed or Christ Controlled?

You can see that Satan has lots of tricks up his slippery sleeve, and he has used these same traps with generations of believers who keep on falling into them. However, the good news is that when people do admit they are part of the cause, they also have power to be part of the solution. In agreeing with God that their attitudes and actions are sinful, believers can be led into the healing presence and power of Holy Spirit to be set free to live in victory, with vitality and purpose.

Romans 12 says that we need to present ourselves as living and holy sacrifices, allowing our minds to be renewed. In Luke 9:23 Jesus said, "If anyone wishes to come after Me, let him deny himself, take up his cross daily, and follow Me." In Galatians, Paul teaches that those who belong to Christ are to crucify fleshly passions and lusts. Jesus died to bring flesh to death, to resurrect His life in its place and to redeem all the rewards and blessings that we missed because of our sinful reactions and behaviors.

This must be made perfectly clear: seeking deliverance without also bringing fleshly structures to the Cross for Jesus to put to death is a formula for failure. Actually, we are commanded to deal with our flesh more often than we are told to seek deliverance. Our flesh comes between us and God, excusing and encouraging us to continue in these sinful fleshly patterns, to the point that we often refuse the liberty offered by Holy Spirit. Without truly hating our fleshly patterns, we will not hate the agreements that we have with Satan's deceptions. These agreements with Satan's lies must be renounced before we can receive God's Truth and speak the Word of faith effectively. Without dying to our flesh, we cannot be Chris-controlled.

Sometimes pre-believers whose lives and priorities are out of control will request ministry. They are still on the throne of their life and have not invited Christ into their life as their Savior.

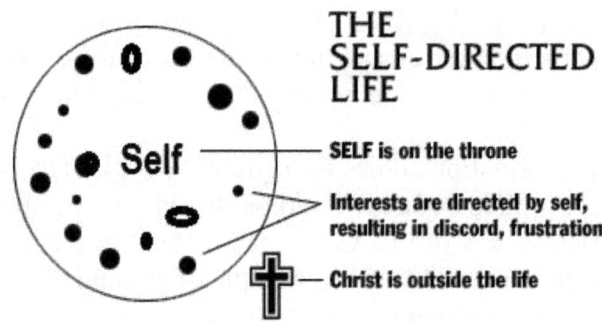

Many believers try to live a Christ-directed or assisted life. They may see Christ as inside of them, on the throne of their life, or they may picture Christ outside of them and assisting them to control "their life."

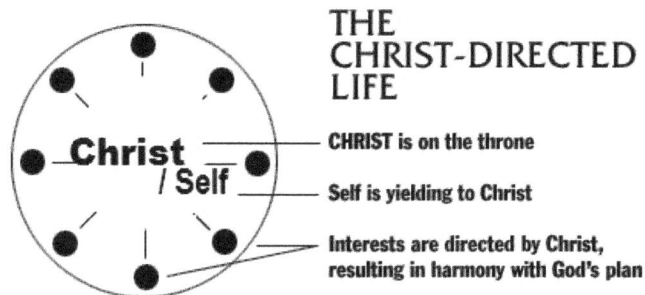

What Apostle Paul is talking about in Galatians 2:20 is actually Christ living in and through believers, in a union with us that bears much fruit according to Romans 7:4.

Here is Galatians 2:20 paraphrased in my own words:
"My old fleshly, self-centered, unredeemed nature has been crucified with Christ; but nevertheless the real me, a new creature, a partaker of the divine nature, is still living; yet not I alone but Christ is living His life in me and through me. The life I live now is not even by my own faith but with the faith OF the Son of God, who loves me and gives Himself daily for me."

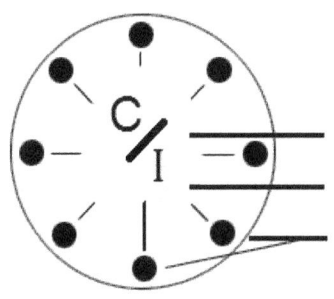

CHRIST IN YOU THROUGH YOU

One with Christ

One with His mind, will, way and timing

His fruit is born

Restoration ministers must ask Holy Spirit to lead them to ask the right questions to help the prayer receiver to recognize if they have invited in Christ to be their Savior and Lord of their life.

Being Born Again?

Thank you, Campus Crusade for Christ for teaching me with circles! But many times, although we have true compassion for others who desperately want peace with God, we don't know what else to say to them. Maybe they prayed a prayer but aren't sure they are born again in Christ. We may not know how to tell them what born again is. We are sure that God loves them, has a wonderful plan for their life and that He came in the form of Jesus Christ to tell them so. We know that Christianity is not just a religion but is being born again into the family of God. We want them to know that they will be supernaturally transformed and set free when they choose to invite Jesus Christ to come to live inside their hearts. (Revelation 3:20)

What do you believe really happens when someone is born again? Are they the same person with the same old nature but they are now going to Heaven? Do they now have the old nature and a new nature? Is the old nature now dead and they have a new divine nature? What becomes new? Their soul or spirit? If the old man dies, exactly what passes away? If you are born again, are you actually able to live the Christian life? Read Romans 6 again with these questions in mind.

If they are not sure they are born again, I encourage you to ask questions versus trying to persuade them that they have eternal salvation already. If someone wants to invite Jesus to be their Lord and Savior but asks you what happened to you when you prayed the prayer of acceptance, what would you say?

Here is a list of what happened when you were born again. Read and study these blessings and privileges God bestows freely on His children.

- I will not perish but have eternal life = a new past and a new future (John 3:16).
- I am saved by grace totally apart from my good works (Ephesians 2:8-9)
- I can be absolutely sure that I am going to heaven (1 John 5:11-13).
- I have increasing faith as I know the Word of God. (Romans 10:17).
- I am adopted by God who is my *Abba*— "Father" (Romans 8:15).
- I automatically receive righteousness as a gift (Romans 5:18, 21).
- I am totally forgiven and cleansed of all unrighteousness (1 John 1:9).
- Jesus makes me holy and without blame before Him (Ephesians 1:4).
- I am partaker of the divine nature by the Spirit of God (2 Peter 1:4).
- I am born again in Spirit = primarily a spiritual creature (John 3:5).
- I know I have eternal life; I have the Son of God inside (1 John 5:12).
- My old nature dies, is buried; I am raised to newness of life (Romans 6).
- I am a new creation in Christ; all things are made new (2 Corinthians 5:17).
- I am sealed with the Holy Spirit of God (Ephesians 1:13).
- I am hopeful and not ashamed because God loves me (Romans 5:5).
- I have no fear of condemnation because I am in Christ (Romans 8:1).
- The Holy Spirit assures me that I am a child of God (Romans 8:16).
- God gives me wisdom and healing (James 1:5; 5:16).
- I have life and life abundantly because Jesus is the Life (John 10:10).
- He is my Shepherd; I am His sheep: I hear His voice (John 10:16).
- I have the fruit of the Holy Spirit who is inside me (Galatians 5:22).
- I ask, believing God's Word, and my prayer is answered (Mark 11:24).
- If I abide in Christ and His Word, I will be fruitful (John 15:5).
- I have peace with God, beyond understanding (Philippians 4:7; Romans 8:6).
- I am transformed by the renewing of my mind (Romans 12:2).
- I can do all things through Christ who strengthens me (Philippians 4:13).
- I am loved and accepted unconditionally in God's family (Ephesians 1:6).
- I am finally complete in Christ, lacking nothing (Colossians 2:10).
- I have been given everything I need for life and godliness (2 Peter 1:3).
- I have God's perfect love that casts out all my fears (1 John 4:18).
- I have love, power and a sound mind instead of intimidation (2 Timothy 1:7).
- God's truth makes me truly free from bondage (John 8:32; Romans 8:14-15).

- I can be sure that I will be resurrected and go to heaven (Romans 6:5).
- Jesus Christ in me will live the Christian life through me (Galatians 2:20).
- I am filled with Holy Spirit and gifts (1 Corinthians. 12, 14; Ephesians 5:18).
- I am one spirit with Holy Spirit, Jesus and Father God (2 Cor. 6:17; John 17).

You Can Know God Personally! – Adapted from Campus Crusade at www.cru.org

Because of God's deep love for you, He has already made all the necessary arrangements for you to enjoy His wonderful plan for your life. We aren't born again by our own efforts to reach God. We need a whole new heart or spirit that can have fellowship with God. Through the death and resurrection of Jesus Christ, you can enjoy a personal relationship with God. Jesus made it possible to bridge the chasm which separates us from God.

John 17:3 tells us, "Now this is eternal life: that they may know you, the only true God, and Jesus Christ, whom you have sent."

How can we be born again?

1 John 5:11-13 says, "And this is the testimony: God has given us eternal life, and this life is in his Son. [12] Whoever has the Son has life; whoever does not have the Son of God does not have life."

What prevents us from knowing God personally? We are separated from God because of our sin.

Romans 8:6-8: "The mind of sinful man is death, but the mind controlled by the Spirit is life and peace; the sinful mind is hostile to God. It does not submit to God's law, nor can it do so. Those controlled by the sinful nature cannot please God."

A great gulf separates man from God. Man is continually trying to reach God and establish a personal relationship with Him through human efforts, such as living a good life, philosophy, or religious efforts. But man's efforts to bridge the gap between man and God inevitably fail.

Jesus Christ is God's Son and His ONLY provision for man's sin. Through Him alone, we can know God personally and experience God's love. Jesus broke the power of sin by His death and resurrection. By giving His perfect life in exchange for our sinful ones, He made the perfect sacrifice and paid the full price to open the way to God.

Romans 5:8: "God demonstrates His own love toward us, in that while we were yet sinners, Christ died for us."

1 Corinthians 15:3-6: "Christ died for our sins... he was buried... he was raised on the third day according to the scriptures... he appeared to Peter, then to the twelve. After that he appeared to more than five hundred..."

John 14:6: "Jesus said to him, 'I am the way, the truth and the life. No one comes to the Father except through me.'"

We must individually RECEIVE Jesus Christ as Lord and Savior; then we can know God personally and experience His love.

John 1:12: "As many as received him, to them he gave the right to become children of God, even to those who believe in his name."

Ephesians 2:8-9: "For it is by grace that you have been saved, through faith. This does not depend on anything you have achieved, it is the free gift of God; and because it is not earned no one can boast about it."

Receiving Christ involves turning from self to God (a spirit of repentance) and trusting Christ to come into our lives to forgive us of our sins and make us what He wants us to be. Just to agree intellectually that Jesus Christ is the Son of God and that He died on the Cross for our sins is not enough. Nor is it enough to have an emotional experience. We receive Jesus Christ by faith as an act of our will as we choose to receive Him as our Lord and Master.

Jesus Christ is waiting for an invitation to come into your life. In fact, He says, "Behold, I stand at the door and knock; if anyone hears my voice and opens the door, I will come in" (Revelation 3:20).

Perhaps you can sense Christ knocking at the door of your heart. You can invite Him in by faith right now. God knows your heart, so it doesn't matter exactly what words you use.

Here's a suggested prayer to receive Christ as your Lord and Savior:

***Lord Jesus**, I want to know you personally. Thank you for dying on the Cross for my sins. I open the door of my life to you and ask you to come in as my Savior and Lord. Take control of my life. Thank you for forgiving my sins and giving me eternal life. Make me the kind of person you want me to be. Amen*

If this prayer expresses the desire of your heart, pray it right now and Jesus Christ will come into your life, just as He has promised. Once you invite Christ into your life, He promises to never leave you.

Hebrews 13:5: "God has said, 'Never will I leave you; never will I forsake you.'"

What if you are praying with someone who is not a born-again believer?

Years ago, a man who had been a preacher's kid applied to receive my 18-hour whole life Restoration Prayer Ministry. He read the four articles, which clearly describe our Christian ministry and prayers, and he sent the 10-page application. I asked one of my dear RPM interns to assist me for the four days of ministry. He flew in, and she drove three hours to join us, and we all met in Florida.

Our prayer receiver began our first session by asking, "Does it matter that I am a Mormon?" I hear God very well and heard God saying to tell our receiver, "God is not surprised and He will restore you." (Never mind that I was shocked that he never happened to mention his Mormon faith before.) But God …

God is omniscient, knowing all things, and he had told me to ask Liz to be my assistant for this receiver. That day, Liz shared her testimony of being raised as a Mormon but later learning that Jesus Christ is the ONLY begotten Son of God Most High. Only Jesus Christ is God Himself come in the flesh yet perfect in every way. Only Jesus is the Way, the Truth the Life, because He is alone is God …

God knew that Liz was more familiar with the false beliefs of the Mormon Church and especially the false claims of who Christ is. She was loving and able to kindly invite him to receive Jesus, the Name above all names, who alone is able to provide salvation, by paying the price for our sins. He alone has proven that He has the keys to eternal life by rising from the dead, and He is alive today. All the former religious leaders in the world are now dead and gone. Praise God that He is always orchestrating all things for the good of those who love Him and are called according to His purposes.

Knowing the Power of Forgiveness

People requesting prayer for healing of an emotional wound of some kind may actually be seeking vindication for their feelings of pain or anger. They may want to hear words of consolation and sympathy; the thought of forgiving their offenders is the farthest thing from their mind. But forgiveness is the key that opens the door to healing and allows Jesus to take the pain and restore their soul.

Withholding forgiveness will not lead to healing; it will lock up the seekers in a cell just as formidable as the ones they envision for their offenders. Forgiveness sets both the offended and the offender free to be healed. Willingness to release the offender to Jesus is the choice that gives Jesus access to the wounds that need healing.

First of all, the true meaning of forgiveness must be understood. It doesn't mean denying that anything bad happened or pretending all is well when it isn't. It doesn't mean sweeping things under the rug, so to speak, and looking the other way in avoidance or total denial. It doesn't mean trying in our own strength to simply "forgive and forget" without coming to God for His help and healing. It doesn't mean I have to pretend that I am totally or instantly-pain free or that the offender is now innocent.

Forgiveness means acknowledging the hurt and damage done and then giving up your right to get even, pure and simple. In Ephesians 4:32, we are commanded to forgive others as God in Christ forgives us—not because we deserve it but because the price for that forgiveness has already been paid. The finished work of Christ on the Cross provides the offended one the power to give up the right to get even and then place it in God's hands to deal with in His way and in His time.

Seen this way, forgiveness doesn't mean an unrepentant offender is now off the hook. Nobody "gets away" with anything; everyone reaps what he or she sowed, more than they sowed and later than they sowed, unless they repent. For example, if we sow criticism, we will reap more criticism than we have sown (in ourselves or from others) and we will reap it much later than we sowed it. Just as a crop is not reaped at the time it is sown, when we do reap it, it is more than we have sown and later than we have sown.

We must remember there is no double jeopardy.

Either we will insist on judging and condemning them ourselves or we release them to the Judge of all the earth. Someday the offenders will stand before Almighty God to give an account. Our heavenly Father will discipline them now or later, make all things right, providing vindication and vengeance for His children. In Hebrews 10:30 we read, "Vengeance is Mine, says the Lord."

Forgiveness is also not an emotion; it is a life-changing choice. There may be an emotional reaction as the Spirit sets people free and tears of joy or pain may flow, but forgiveness is not in and of itself an emotion. We don't have to feel forgiving, but we are commanded to forgive if we want to be forgiven.

In order to receive the fullness of liberty to live the abundant life, it is not only necessary to offer full forgiveness but to receive it as well. I suggest that you ask these questions and read the scripture aloud, inviting the Holy Spirit to enlighten your mind so you can recall details of sins or sinful reactions clearly and accurately.

Did I sow it and now I am reaping it more and later? (Galatians. 6:7-8)
Did I dishonor my parents or authorities in this area? (Ephesians 6:1-3)
Did I judge someone? Do I now draw that to me? (Matthew 7:1- 2; Rom. 2:1-4)
Has a bitter root sprung up in me, affecting others? (Hebrews 12:14-15)
Have I blamed, doubted or been disappointed in God? (1 John 4:20-21)

During my restoration ministry training, I was not happy when I was exhorted to ask forgiveness for myself five ways and to forgive others one way. I was quick to notice that it seemed to imply that my sinful reactions were at least 80% of the problem. The good news is that I can control my choices to ask forgiveness and can get the healing I need.

Biblical forgiveness is not only forgiving others but also asking for forgiveness.

I repent, asking for forgiveness in five ways. Father forgive me for my sins of:

- not asking others to forgive me
- judging and not forgiving others
- my own sin and sinful reactions
- blaming or doubting you God
- not forgiving myself

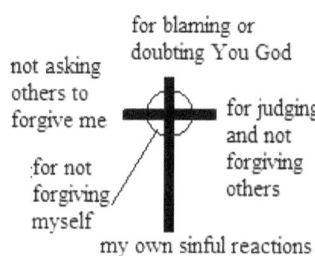

After forgiving, repenting and asking forgiveness in these five ways, believers will notice they have less of a problem in the areas they have prayed about, but further inquiry of the Holy Spirit is helpful before they may know what needs forgiving in five ways.

You will notice that these descriptions are sometimes written to you as a prayer minister who is praying for others and sometimes to you as you pray for your own healing and restoration. Either way, Holy Spirit will be faithful to hear your fervent prayer and restore any soul who cries out to Him with a humble heart. I have provided sample prayers regarding many common issues in Part II.

Nothing will be impossible for those that believe, because Jesus will do anything for radical lovers.

Years ago, my life began to change as I learned to pray the Cross Walk Prayer from Ellen Ferry in Atlanta, Georgia. Below is my version of this amazing prayer. Feel free to use it verbatim or let believers make up their own words as they become more proficient in praying this prayer, listening carefully to the Holy Spirit and confessing anything He brings to mind.

For example, if you have had a lot of critical people in your life and this has produced in you a negative pattern of having a critical attitude, try plugging the problem "critical attitude" into the blanks in the Cross Walk Prayer to see how this works.

Cross Walk Prayer

Dear Lord Jesus,

I have a negative pattern in my life, that is not Godly and I cannot get rid of it by myself. I know that a bad fruit has a bad root. I don't want this pattern of _____ any longer. I don't want to reap this in my own life or in the people around me. Please show me the spiritual root of it and how to deal with my part of this problem (even if I am only 10% of the problem.)

Did I sow this and now I am reaping it, more and later?	Galatians 6:7-10
Did I dishonor my parents or authorities in this area?	Ephesians 6:1-3
Did I judge someone and now I draw that thing to me?	Matthew 7:1, Romans 2:1-4
Did a bitter expectation spring up in me, defiling others?	Hebrews 12:14-15
Did I make an inner vow in not to be like them?	James 5:12, Matthew 5:37

1. **I RECOGNIZE** that the reason this problem of _____ is now a pattern in my own life, is because of my sinful reaction of (dishonor, judgment, sowing the sin myself, inner vows or bitter root expectation.) The fruit is that I am reaping similar problems in others and myself according to the LAW of sowing and reaping. I am reaping this crop because of my sinful reactions to their sin. I am reaping from the sinful seed that I have sown - not from what they have sown.

2. **I REPENT** and ask forgiveness in five ways. Please forgive me:

   1. for not asking others to forgive me
   2. for judging others and not forgiving others
   3. for sowing my own sin / sinful reactions
   4. for blaming or doubting you God
   5. and for not forgiving myself

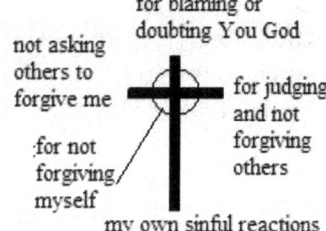

3. **I RENOUNCE** my sin of dishonor, judgment, sowing the sin myself, bitter root expectations or fleshly inner vows. I choose to forgive them, releasing them to you, the Judge of all the earth.

4. **RELEASE** me from reaping this crop that is mine to reap because of my sinful reactions to others.

5. **I RECKON** dead on the cross all flesh that identifies with this reaction and all automatic reactions that I have developed with it. I ask you Jesus to bring it to death because I cannot. Create in me a pure heart that agrees with your responses.

6. **RESURRECT** your likeness into every area that you have brought to death.

7. **RESTORE** all the years that the locusts have eaten while I was disobedient.

8. **I RECLAIM** all the spiritual blessings that my family and I have missed.

9. **REWARD** us for generations to come, as we sow true discernment, grace and mercy. Thank you Lord for the forgiveness you have provided for us on the cross and all the blessings that we are free to walk in now. We believe you for them! Amen

If you want to learn the easy way and MUCH _FASTER_ ... Simply make a list of all your parent's faults (without mercy.) Assume that as a child, you probably judged and dishonored them at some point. You can include other authorities too if you really want to get free fast!!

This prayer is an excellent maintenance prayer as the Holy Spirit brings to mind each new ungodly belief or fleshly pattern on the road to complete liberty. Being healed, delivered and baptized in the Holy Spirit is only the beginning and God's enemy is not going to be deterred from his plan to destroy believers.

We have to learn to pray, to meditate on the Word, to declare scripture daily and to stay in agreement with God in order to maintain our freedom and appropriate all God has promised us.

Want a shortcut to healing and freedom? Stop now and make a list of all the judgments you may have made against others in the past, especially family and authorities. Then pray the Cross Walk Prayer and break the sowing and reaping cycle.

The Cross Walk Prayer will be referred to as an Exhibit after this.

A Testimony of Restoration in Jesus

Since working through 18 hours of personal Restoration Prayer Ministry over a decade ago, I was really made aware of the generational sins passed down to me and how my responses to those sins were what caused the most trouble in my spiritual walk. It was life changing to recognize the freedom in asking for forgiveness 5 ways and allowing the Lord to really heal and purify my heart towards my parents (and others). Today I have a tangible way to work through strongholds, as I still apply the Cross Walk Prayer and immediately feel the presence of the Lord once I do. I am so thankful to have this prayer method in my life, as it is the only thing that has really addressed resentments, hurts and judgment in my heart.

Through working one on one with Carlotta, I've also been able to understand more fully what it means to be one with Christ and how to identify when my thoughts are not in agreement with that reality. I had no idea that separated thinking dominated my thought life until I began to press in to what she has taught me--that intimacy with Jesus as my spiritual Husband is where the excitement of life is really found!

Blessings,

Jennifer C.

Part II: Insights and Prayers

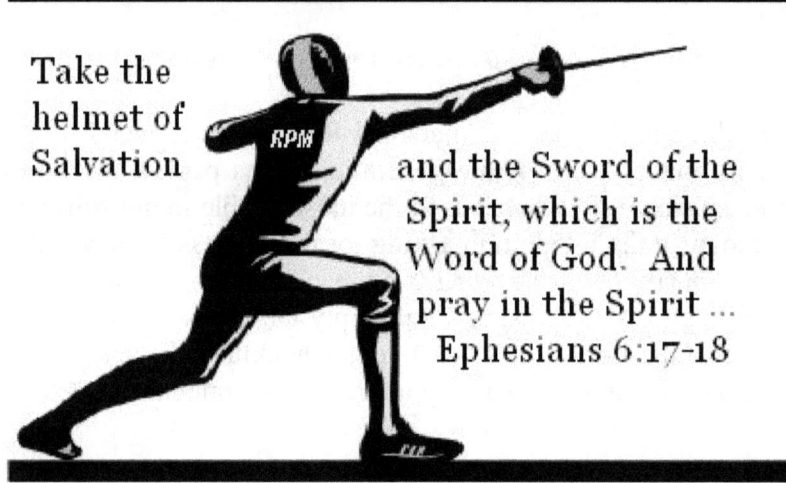

Abortion and PAS

Did you know that despite recent declines in the abortion rate, still one in four women have had an abortion? Who are they? They are your sister, relative, schoolmate, co-worker or neighbor, from every kind of group, every race, status or religion. What amazes me is that there are not more healing or support groups for women and men who are hurting after abortion. Jesus stands ready to heal them and set them free if someone would only tell them.

Often women are told they will feel better after an abortion; instead, they find themselves struggling with painful emotions. They need to know they are not alone. After an abortion, many women attempt to shut down feelings of grief, anger, guilt, regret and emptiness but cannot. Whether they had a miscarriage or chose abortion, it is not uncommon to feel as though something is missing or to continue to grieve the loss of the child. These feelings are often referred to as **Post-Abortion Stress** or PAS.

PAS results when a woman or man represses the emotions they have after an abortion. Many women isolate and carry their secret for ten, twenty or thirty years. If they had a miscarriage, they may wonder what role they might have played in their baby's death. If they chose abortion, they know beyond a shadow of a doubt what role they played in that death. The grieving that follows abortion includes most of the normal stages of grief, plus some added emotions: relief, denial, anger, depression, and acceptance.

At first, they may feel **relief** that the decision was made and they are no longer pregnant. But then the feelings of relief give way to memories of the actual facts of the abortion and **denial** begins. They may try to justify their actions by saying, "It wasn't really a baby; it was only a fetus. I just terminated a pregnancy." Moving out of denial may take years depending on the person. Denial may end when they see pictures of fetal development or become pregnant again. Now they know and recognize that it was not just a product of conception, but an actual child—their child.

Then come the **anger and blame**. They may be angry at the clinic, the father, even friends or family for what they said to them. They may blame others for not being there for them or pressuring them into an abortion. If they do not deal with this anger, they may become bitter, resentful and unforgiving of those who have not understood how they have hurt them.

If they do not forgive themselves and others, they may become overwhelmed by **depression**, guilt, self-pity or shame. Condemning or punishing themselves may push them into self-punishing behaviors such as destructive alcohol and drug use, overeating, choosing unhealthy relationships, self-deprecation or self-sabotage. If this happens, it may be from trying to suppress the feelings, the memories and the thoughts about the abortion.

You can help move hurting men and women into the stage of **acceptance**, healing and wholeness. They need to accept that they cannot change the past, but they can choose to forgive and release those who hurt them. In essence, they can change how they respond to the past. With the right support and guidance, Jesus can lead them to release those who have hurt them, to forgive themselves and accept God's forgiveness. Once they face the emotions, walls and blocks left in their lives by abortion, they can invite God's healing truth into those areas.

You will be amazed as you watch God at work in the lives of these wounded hearts. God makes their weakest places strong, and they eventually begin to encourage others to find health and freedom in Christ. God can and will redeem every experience, taking the pain out of the memories and filling them with a new vision for His plan for their lives.

When our spirits reach out to God for healing, the cobwebs in our heads get cleaned out, and the fog begins to lift as the noisy clatter of our emotions fades. We begin to see more clearly into His ways of thinking. His ways are not our ways, and He works in some mighty mysterious ways at times, but the Bible says that believers have the Holy Spirit to teach them (I Corinthians 2:11-12).

As we follow God, listening to the Spirit becomes our lifestyle. We understand that God's plan for us is one of exchange. He exchanges His righteousness for our sin, His beauty for our ashes, His comfort for our mourning, His garment of praise for our heaviness of spirit. As our minds are renewed daily by the resurrection power of Christ within us, we experience this exchange and glorify God.

How do you know if you still need more healing?

1. Are you still trying to forget the feelings?
2. Do you still react when the subject is brought up?
3. Do you avoid things that remind you of it?
4. Are you depressed at certain times of the year?
5. Are you still resentful and unforgiving?
6. Is your lifestyle one that could lead to hurt again?
7. Have your relationships become less healthy?
8. Are you using food, alcohol or drugs to cover pain?
9. Do you often have flashback memories?
10. Do you feel empty, angry, guilty or shamed?
11. Have you stopped growing emotionally since then?
12. Do you look at life as before or after the abortion?
13. Are you still keeping it a secret? Or telling too much?
14. Are you performing to prove that you are okay?
15. Has God felt distant since then?

Prayer for healing after an abortion.

Heavenly Father, please give me the courage to hold my heart open to you and to receive healing and restoration. I confess my sin of trying to solve my problems my way in my own strength. I receive your grace and forgiveness for not trusting you and for listening to worldly advice. In turn, I choose to forgive those who were not there for me or who pressured me to have an abortion. I release them from blame and turn them over to you; they are your children, Father. Forgive me for judging them and for not forgiving them sooner. I also repent of any way I may have implied that you were not there for me, Father God. I repent of doubting your plan for my life, compromising with sin and choosing a path that was outside of your will. Lastly, I forgive myself for making poor choices that led me and my unborn child into this situation.

I choose to believe that Jesus has paid the price for my redemption and He is redeeming all the experiences I have had, taking the pain out of them and leaving me with His divine wisdom. Restore my soul with your unlimited grace and help me to believe that you shed your blood and died on the Cross to make me holy, righteous and blameless again. I choose to receive your consolation for my loss and know that you will even turn my mourning into dancing. I believe that you heal the brokenhearted and comfort all who come to you with a contrite heart. You will give me a crown of beauty instead of ashes, oil of joy instead of mourning and a garment of praise instead of a spirit of despair. I trust you to help me rebuild my life, to take my shame and even to give me double portions. (Isaiah 61:1-7)

Thank you, for surrounding my innocent child with your perfect love and acceptance. Thank you, for instructing him/her with your Truth and your Word. Thank you, for teaching him/her to forgive me and I look forward to being together in Heaven one day. Thank you, for your ministry to my family and friends and all who were hurt by the abortion. Thank you, for working all things out for good for those who are called according to your purpose, to be conformed to your image.

Addictions and Sexuality

There is such a great need to provide healing for the effects of sexual trauma like incest, abuse, fornication, adultery, abortion and sexual addictions. It's not enough to say, "The church steeple is up; people know where to go to find forgiveness." We need assistant group leaders who can identify with people who have been struggling alone but need supportive healing prayer that will restore their souls.

Would you like to be trained to pray for people through the use of healing groups? Part of our vision is to provide training to teach people how to care for the wounded in safe healing groups. Prayer ministers will be sharing and praying with other people who have similar issues and understand the torment they feel. They feel hopeless because their identity today is damaged because of someone's sexual sin yesterday.

God wants to give gifts of restoration where the joy of sex was lost due to violations of covenant relationships. God wants us to give gifts of healing to those who were imprinted with traumatic understandings of sexuality because their first sexual experience was incest, molestation or a violent rape. Many women have never told anyone, but they want to be released from the shame and fear that has isolated them for years.

God wants us to give gifts of deliverance to people who are tormented by impulses to escape through sexual addictions. When we confess to one another, take responsibility and become accountable to others, we gain freedom from bondages that interfere with the deep satisfaction that only real intimate relationships can provide.

God wants us to give gifts of forgiveness and to those who have hidden guilt from sexual sin or unspeakable regrets from abortion. Many are tormented by memories, dreams, reactions, depression or flashbacks. He wants to cleanse the past, replacing the guilt and shame with honor and His gift of righteousness.

God wants to heal relationships where the woman has traded sex for being taken care of. Men need healing of resentment because "she sold herself to me." Women need forgiveness and hope that when they confess, God will bless with a covenant relationship of true love and appreciation.

When we are wounded by relationships, we will also be healed in relationships. God wants us to demonstrate faith that will give others hope that their slate can be wiped clean, thoughts can be untwisted, defilement can be cleansed and marriage beds can be infused with holy passion and purity. He wants to visit homes and give each one a new identity of wholeness as He makes the weak places strong.

The very areas where God heals us, become testimonies of the supernatural power of God to bring hope and healing. God will take the shame and impart an ability to comfort others as He comforted us. I believe that the enemy attacks us in the very area that he knows we will be called to minister.

What we give God, He will take. What He takes, He will cleanse. What He cleanses, He will use. I would like to share this testimony written by an intern of ours regarding the benefits of Restoration Prayer Ministry training.

TESTIMONY: NOW GOD IS HEALING OTHERS THROUGH ME!

I had the excellent opportunity to enroll in a two-semester class on Restoration Prayer Ministry. Initially, I thought it was a good idea because of my involvement as a volunteer at a juvenile correctional facility.

As I took the class, it became more and more clear that I wasn't there for the knowledge I would gain for use at the correctional facility but for what I would learn about myself. Over and over again I was struck by the simplicity of concepts that could radically change my life. In July, I was able to go through the Ministry process for myself. While I had already experienced some transformation, I was excited about the possibility of a renewed relationship with my father from whom I'd been estranged for nearly ten years. Long story short; ten years ago, I had confronted him with the immediate family present, about his sexual abuse of me as a child and he couldn't handle it.

Then, I had the chance this month to assist in the healing process of another individual. As we went through, I essentially got a refresher course in my personal situation. I found myself excited all over again, because I was planning a trip "back home" and knew I was finally going to see the fruit of my labor.

Well, there I was, back home where I grew up and it was better than I ever expected. First, my father was at the airport to greet me upon arrival. Then, he spent the entire afternoon visiting with me at my sister's. Then, he called me to ask me to dinner so we could talk one on one. At dinner, he eventually brought up our "issue" and it was immediately clear to me that he didn't remember things the way I did and yet I was totally able to accept him where he was without any need to "set him straight." I was finally and truly past the hurt! How awesome is that?

We talked for two hours at dinner and three more hours after that about anything and everything. In the end, he told me he was glad that we'd gotten together. He felt like he understood me better and he knows that I do love him. Praise be to God, it is only because of His love for me that we could come to this point. I thank God for all that he has done for me through Carlotta and I look forward to being able to share the same wonderful blessings with others.

For more information on receiving Restoration Prayer Ministry or training to minister to others, see www.pprpm.com/restoration.html

Anger Management or a Spirit of Anger?

How do I know if I have normal angry responses or a spirit of anger? Can anger management solve my anger problem? Do I need a spiritual healing? Deliverance? Do I have sinful reactions and sinful behaviors with anger or just righteous indignation?

How do I know if my anger is a healthy signal that an adjustment needs to be made or if it is sin? When do I need anger management and when do I need deliverance? The Bible says, "Be ye angry, and sin not; Let not the sun go down upon your wrath; Neither give place to the devil" (Eph. 4:26-27). Where is this room for the devil? Does this spirit of anger come out in the dark of night?

Anger + ? = sin?

Here's the proper equation. Anger plus sinful reactions and sinful behaviors plus time make room for the devil.

Anger + sin + time = room for the devil.

Having a spirit of anger is not just appropriate anger about a current violation that can be re-directed with anger management. It began with a buildup of tension from unresolved conflicts over time. Colossians 3:8 describes the growing buildup from normal anger to toxic anger when it says, "Put off all these; anger - wrath - malice - blasphemy - filthy communication out of your mouth."

A spirit of anger is a demonic power that has entered a person's life to influence their relationships, change their whole disposition and control their reactions. Jesus died to provide not only forgiveness but also spiritual healing and deliverance from a spirit of anger.

Would you like to privately test yourself for a spirit of anger?

1. Do you still justify letting the sun go down on your anger?
2. Do people tell you that you were louder and more intense than you recall?
3. Do they say your anger is not appropriate but is more like wrath or malice?
4. Do you still believe your buildup of anger can be managed?
5. Do you try to dominate and control conversations with loud, angry tones?

6. Does it relieve your pent-up tensions and frustrations to "go off" on others?
7. Are you quick to take offense or to take up the offense of others?
8. Is your angry temper a generational thing that you "came by honestly?"
9. Do you argue just for the fun of overpowering your opponent?
10. Does it seem impossible to truly forgive those who have hurt you?
11. Are you still surprised when you overreact with anger or rage?
12. Did your anger lead to bad habits or addictions that you now justify?
13. Do you usually blame someone else for "making you angry" or frustrating you?
14. Just how many hours do you stay angry at them before suppressing your anger?
15. Is God not favoring, not answering prayer, not healing or not prospering you?
16. Do people say that you jump to judgmental or condemning conclusions?
17. Do you react rashly without checking out your conclusions with others?
18. Have you noticed a pattern of anger regarding authority issues?
19. Do you presume to know the unspoken thoughts and motives of others?
20. Do others accuse you of believing the worst of them?

There are many ways we can manifest our wrath (and the spirit of anger) when we indulge in anger + sin. So let's measure to what level of sin we actually descend, by listing them in increasing intensity and potential harm to others. What do others say about your present anger management? Are you overreacting out of guilt, grief, frustration, shame or fear of failure? Are you demonstrating anger in constructive ways or do you indulge in some of the ways below?

When I was 30, I heard Dr. Ross Campbell teach about his anger ladder on the radio. While I was not able to take notes, the main points were burned into my angry mind. This list is my amplification of that list, from least sinful to the most sinful.

- Mean, proud, rejecting looks
- Condescending, judgmental, sarcastic remarks
- Bringing up peripheral issues besides the primary complaint
- Irritating, controlling or dominating with loud volume
- Shut down tones that say "Don't talk!" or "Don't feel that way!"
- Negative or aggressive body language
- Walking out with no plan to resume talking
- Overpowering them with threats or separating comments
- Monopolizing or repeatedly interrupting, to avoid listening
- Dredging up their past failures or those of their family
- Yelling, attacking, cursing or verbal abuse
- Public putdowns, humiliation, gossip or slander
- Physical abuse, threats of it, or abusing property as if it were them
- Passive aggression (acting out anger on purpose and then denying it)
- Punishing behavior or fantasies, with intent to make them sorry
- Suicidal thoughts or attempts, because you hate yourself
- Homicidal thoughts or attempts

On which rung of this "anger ladder" does your anger finally stop? The top rung of *mean looks* is "less sinful" and, of course, the low *homicide* rung is the most sinful. When you are angry and have a sinful reaction, check yourself out on the "anger ladder" and see where you fall.

Usually, when we overreact to our current irritations, it is a result of unhealed hurts and wounds from the past. While we are down, so to speak, the devil comes in and tells us lies about ourselves and we believe them. Then when other people "tick us off," they get their share of our present anger and some from the past as well.

Are you willing to take a fearless, honest inventory of your history of anger, hurt and sinful reactions? Take a piece of paper and place on it these two headings:

Present causes of anger   *Past causes of anger*

Beneath these two headings, list everything and everyone you feel has had a hand in contributing to your anger. If you are willing to accept responsibility for your unresolved anger and to admit that unresolved anger is a sin, there is hope. When you are ready, you need to pray through this list, using the Cross Walk Prayer and asking for forgiveness in five ways.

Are you willing to be accountable for your behavior? Ask your family how they know when you are angry. Ask them how often you get angry and if your anger management is working. Do they say you need spiritual healing or deliverance?

If you are willing to hear them tell you how badly you have hurt them and are ready to ask for their forgiveness, there is indeed hope. Ask them to pray for you as you attempt to get healing for your hurts, to get delivered of a spirit of anger and to allow Jesus to crucify your fleshly indulgences.

Then seek help from a qualified counselor or prayer minister. You can have appropriate anger, fleshly anger or a spirit of anger that is taking over your responses. Sometimes you may feel guilty for expressing appropriate anger when anger is a normal emotion in certain circumstances, i.e. someone's intentional violations of your child's boundaries. The Bible recorded many instances when God became angry when His law was broken year after year. So there is anger that is without sin, but you may need help in discerning it.

If you have 1.) tolerated sinful thoughts and sinful behaviors over a period of time, 2.) denied it even when people who love you try to make you aware of their hurt and 3.) even justified your right to feel and act that way—you have a stronghold of anger or bitterness in your life.

Would you like help with tearing down this stronghold? The Holy Spirit of God is ready to gently reveal not only the surface causes and evidence but also the root causes and evidence that allowed the spirit of anger in. When we invite Jesus, the Spirit of Truth, to lead our ministry sessions, He is able to take the pain out of every hurt, forgive every sin, remove the shame and guilt and even to take our blame upon Himself on the Cross. He died to take our every sin upon Himself and to set us free with His truth. He is the Way, the Truth and the Life!

Prayer for freedom from a spirit of anger

Lord, I stand devastated before you, undone not only by the damage I have caused another but by how I have grieved you as well. Help me to discern appropriate anger from a spirit of anger that needs to be cast out. My anger with sin has resulted in broken trust and shattered relationships. Father, I am so very sorry for the pain and sorrow I have caused.

Although it hurts to see and feel the pain I brought to someone else, impress the cost of my sin deeply into my heart so that I won't forget. I never want another person to be injured like this again because of my sin of anger. Guard me against repeating this in anyone else's life and keep me keep me dependent on you to live your life of love through me.

Forgive me for my cruel actions and words. Wash me clean in the blood of Christ, who loved me and gave His life to provide for my forgiveness. Transform me into the image of Jesus, who died and rose again to supply me with the strength to live a changed life. I choose to bring to you all my angry baggage from the past that causes me to overreact to issues in the present. I ask you to forgive me for sinful reactions and behaviors and I forgive others for their sinful reactions also. Forgive me Lord when I doubted you or implied that you were not faithful to me. I forgive myself for not keeping short accounts with you Father and letting the sun go down on my anger.

Lord, bless the person(s) I have sinned against and pour the oil of comfort into those wounds. Don't let anger or bitterness get a foothold in their life. Create a fresh understanding of the presence of your Holy Spirit. Prepare our hearts to extend and receive forgiveness as you bring healing to us both. The bad fruit on my tree is a result of bad roots on my tree. I repent of judging others for the splinter in their eye and I repent of not asking them to forgive me sooner.

In Jesus' Name, I take authority over the demons of anger with sin and command you demons of anger with sin to leave me/us now based on the finished work of Christ on the Cross and His shed Blood. In the Name of Jesus Christ of Nazareth, the Anointed One, Who has given me spiritual authority, I command the demons of anger with sin to go to the dry uninhabited places and never come back. I receive my freedom and the ability to discern rightly.

Lord, as I repent, I trust you to also heal the losses that I have suffered. I lost my inner circle, some church friends, family and business relationships. My pride has turned to shame and depression. I lost my definition of myself - my identity. I still grieve over material losses that I never anticipated when I chose to sin. Most of all my family relationships have to be rebuilt one day at a time, one memory at a time.

I choose to give you time to transform me from the inside out. When I have fully met your requirements for restoration and have brought healing to others with restitution, help me to rest in you as my source forever. Cause my eyes to see you in my leaders who guide me back to the ministry you want to do through me. Give me a new vision of restoration, to walk in your gifts and to fulfill your call. Let the memory of this experience empower me to discover what restitution is needed to rebuild trust and friendship. By your resurrection power within me, help me walk worthy as a child of the Light, for that will bring honor and glory to your name.

Breaking the Power of Word Curses or Negativity

Probably the greatest task of prayer counseling ministry is to break the spiritual power of negative words that have been spoken. We can all remember words we have spoken that we immediately wish we could have taken back. We surely remember negative words spoken to us that actually damaged our self-esteem and hindered our progress.

Even though they were spoken many years ago, certain discouraging words from a teacher, sibling, minister or parent come to mind immediately. Words have more than psychological power: they have spiritual power too. When we agree with those lies, our enemy, the devil, works hard to make those negative words come true.

God created the whole universe using words and we are created in His image. He has delegated to us the power to build or tear down our own house with our words. How? We tend to blame others we believe have blocked our success, but the Bible says that we reap what we sow, not what they sow. You may believe that they caused the repetitive negative cycles in your life, but God says that **a curse without a cause cannot light (Proverbs. 26:2).**

That's good news! It means that no matter how much someone cursed you, their words don't necessarily have a lasting effect. You may believe the lie and empower it—or react sinfully and empower it even more. (Silent unspoken reactions count.) If you judge them with condemnation, hold resentment and unforgiveness or curse them back, you will begin to reap the curse in your life. If you bless them back, their words cannot harm you. The law of sowing and reaping says YOU WILL REAP WHAT YOU SOW, MORE THAN YOU SOW AND LATER THAN YOU SOW.

Don't repay evil for evil. "Don't be overcome with evil, but overcome evil with good" (Romans. 12:21). Spiritual laws are just as sure as physical laws, whether you believe them or not. Gravity works whether you are a believer or not and you reap what you sow regardless. If you sow blessing, you will reap blessing. If you sow cursing—even to those who cursed you—that is what you are going to reap. Sowing negative words is like planting a time bomb that will surely go off sooner or later.

How can you break the power of word curses spoken over you? The answer is in the Cross Walk Prayer, forgiving and asking for forgiveness in five ways. First, you know you have to 1.) Forgive them for saying the curse, like, "You will never be able to … " But that is only part of the solution. You also have to ask for forgiveness for your sinful reactions. 2.) If you judged them with condemnation, you must ask God to forgive you too. 3.) If you blamed God for their behavior, you must ask God's forgiveness. 4.) If you returned evil for evil, you must ask for forgiveness for your own sin. 5.) If you believed the lie, you must forgive yourself for believing the lie as well.

How can these curses be broken? Ask someone in spiritual authority over you to pray with you. First, make a list of all the word curses that have been spoken over you. Then pray The Cross Walk Prayer and ask for forgiveness in five ways. Jesus will release you from having to reap what you have sown in reaction to their sin. Jesus is not a time-limited creature. He will go back in time and break the power of the words spoken. He died on the Cross to provide for your healing—body, soul and spirit. When you invited Christ to live inside you, you received the power to bless others.

Curses from a demonic source will bring mental torment, afflictions, disasters, misfortune and patterns of loss or they can weaken your business, income, ministry, effectiveness or reproduction. The intention of demonic curses is to cause you to be so discouraged, disillusioned, defeated or depressed that you will be intimidated and give up. If you give in to helplessness or hopelessness, you will not possess, occupy and multiply what God has promised to you.

Luke 11:21-22 says, "When a strong man, fully armed, guards his own palace, his goods are in peace. But when a man stronger than he comes upon him and overcomes him, he takes from him all his armor in which he trusted, and divides his spoils." This scripture teaches us that in order to break the power of demonic assignments and resulting curses, we must bind the strongman that is assigned to devastate our family, finances, businesses or ministries. When a demonic strongman takes over our house, he is in peace and we are not. When a power stronger than he—Christ in us—overcomes, we take it back.

The following scripture makes it clear that we come against principalities, powers, rulers and master spirits. The way to take a stand is to take out the ruler and all the rest will surrender. "For we do not wrestle against flesh and blood, but against principalities, against powers, against the rulers of the darkness of this age, against spiritual hosts of wickedness in the heavenly places. Therefore take up the whole armor of God, that you may be able to withstand in the evil day, and having done all, to stand." (Ephesians 6:12-13)

Even if you are in agreement with God now, curses may still be limiting your prosperity if you have never repented of and renounced your previous agreements with principalities, power, rulers and master spirits. Ask the Holy Spirit to reveal the times when you have sown disobedience and reaped poverty and ineffectiveness.

Satan wants to cause you to lose faith and to violate God's principles by causing you to disobey God. When you agree with spirits of fear, doubt and worry you have opened doors to demonic curses. The enemy's goal is to cause you to doubt God's faithfulness to you. He wants to convince you that you do not have the spiritual power and authority to defeat the principalities and demonic agents hindering your prosperity and effectiveness today. He knows that if you defeat the strongmen (agents or principalities) then every demon under them can be cast out as well. If he can cause you to sin and prevent you from repenting, he has the power to maintain curses over you.

Jesus is ready to forgive you, to bring the crop that you have sown to death and to resurrect a whole new crop of blessing in its place. He will take the pain out of the lies spoken over you as He heals each wound. His desire is to leave the wisdom you gained from the memory. II Timothy 2:25 says that with humility we can gently instruct others who are opposing themselves and the Lord, hoping that they will repent and know the truth, escaping a snare.

I am preaching to myself here. Please pray that we can all understand the power of sowing blessing into the lives of others. We have a choice. When we criticize and condemn, we put more prison bars around them and their weakness. We actually assist the devil to imprison them with the fault. Our other option is to choose to speak God's truth into their lives, thereby assisting the angels to empower them to overcome their weaknesses. We help them to believe God's truth about themselves as we speak new strength, hope and supernatural ability into their hearts. Praise God for His inexhaustible grace!

Prayer to break the power of negativity or word curses
(best prayed in the power of agreement with someone with spiritual authority)

Father, thank you for your resurrection life *in us that grants us the authority to break the power of any word curses or negativity spoken over us. Thank you for dying on the Cross to provide forgiveness for our sins and for the sins of those who speak against us. Because you have forgiven us, we choose to forgive others. Live your life through us and share your love for the world through us.*

Thank you that we have been born again *as new creations with new spirits. As we pray the Cross Walk Prayer, we ask that you purify all our fleshly desires and heal any wounds that block our ability to trust you without reservation. Tear down every idol in our lives that prevent us from making you Lord of our lives in every way.*

Show us how to forgive as you forgive, *to set others free as you have given us liberty. We long to follow your purposes and plans for our lives. In humility, we bow to your authority and receive your spiritual authority as negativity and curses fall away empty and powerless before your majesty.*

In the name of the Lord Jesus Christ, we say, "The Lord rebuke you" *to all the principalities, powers and rulers of darkness in high places! In the mighty name of Jesus, Son of God Most High, we cancel every assignment of the enemy against us, our pets, possessions, property, everything and everybody we care about. We ask you to release your blessings as you remove all curses for your glory.*

We yield ourselves as totally surrendered *to whatever you reveal to us. Teach us how to be good sons and daughters to you because you are an awesome Father. Speak through our mouths, serve with our hands, pour out our lives as a sweet sacrifice to all who will listen, that all may know the fragrance of your presence. In the mighty name of the Lord Jesus, amen.*

Burnout for Burden Bearers

"Bear one another's burdens and thus fulfill the law of Christ" (Galatians 6:2).

Are you at risk? Do you know how to prevent burnout?

Today, ministers are burning out at a faster rate than ever before. Statistics on this vary but almost half of pastors of their spouses report that they are suffering from burnout, frantic schedules and unrealistic expectations. There are many causes like the negative impact of their family, financial burdens, marital conflict, family dysfunction and their own need for counseling for moral failure or some other sin. There are other contributing factors like working too many hours, feeling inadequate for the role, loss of self-esteem, conflicts in the church or lack of a close friend.

Ready to let the Holy Spirit bear burdens through you and in so doing truly make the yoke easy and the burden light? Every minister needs to know how to bear another's burdens, without bearing them in their own body, soul and spirit at the same time.

If you have a burden-bearing personality, you may have been born with more sensitivity to what is happening in environments, buildings and people. You may be able to sense what people are feeling even if they are many miles away. You may have had spiritual discernment that caused you to be weighed down with intercession for burdens that others may only barely notice. It can be wonderful to have these abilities, but it can also lead to wounding because you are perceived as different from other people since they do not sense or understand what you are so concerned about.

If you don't know how to partner with Jesus to make the burden light, you may find that you are tempted to take up their offense which could cause you to have more angry reactions, mood swings, depression, chest pressure, ulcers or more frequent illnesses. You may get more involved than you should and become the enabler, rescuer or fixer, neglecting your own needs and finding that your own life is becoming chaotic. Or you may finally swing to the other extreme and withdraw, isolating yourself from people's problems or people who do not understand you.

How many of these preventive measures do you take regularly?

- Receive inner healing or restoration prayer ministry when stressed.
- Have a listening friend who allows you to vent and pour it out regularly.
- Have a "watchdog" friend who sees your fatigue and asks you out to play.
- Take a day off once a week (not to minister) without fail.
- Someone to intercept stressful phone calls or to do delegated tasks.
- Took a real vacation annually (not to visit family or to minister.)
- Communicate needs to a group of intercessors who pray daily.
- Proactive plan to eat healthily, take supplements and sleep well.
- Periods of fasting to build immunity or fasted when God called.
- Go out to nature - earthiness - to be refreshed versus religious trips.
- Inviolate observation of the Sabbath to worship and rest.
- Frequent fun with a hobby to take your mind off work or stress.
- Regular vigorous physical discipline, sports or exercise.
- Regular humor, laughter, play, movies, theater or music.
- Very frequent devotional life with a spouse or a good friend.
- Balanced equal partner relationship with your spouse.
- Mutual submission to your pastor or board or equivalent.
- Have boundaries you enforce or ways you protect your alone times.
- Allowed yourself to stop, let go and move away from stress.
- Said "NO" when necessary without guilt or self-condemnation.
- Consciously limit your ministry to what Father God said to do

Using the above list, test yourself to see how many of the preventives against burnout you already practice.

Another important way to avoid burnout in ministry or other walks of life is to learn how to avoid taking offense with a sovereign God who allows so much suffering in the world by coming to accept that He is in charge, not us. In building up our faith in a loving God, we can seek His wisdom to find out how to keep our ministry life and personal life in balance, to get the support we need, to "depressurize," and finally to release burdens to Jesus and partner with Him in burden-bearing as we enter into His rest and let Him do the work through us instead of striving in our own strength.

Symptoms of burnout stage one
- Depleted resources and too little care for self
- Despair, anger, depression and lack of energy to deal with stress
- Wounding and hurts come too often and less ability to recover
- Chronic fatigue, lack of refreshing sleep, headaches, fear and anxiety

Symptoms of burnout stage two
- Adrenal burnout and associated physical symptoms

- Lack of confidence, constant fears, withdrawal
- Anger at needy people and rage at God
- Prayer life losing power, despair, loss of creativity
- Sex life suffering, marriage issues increasing

Symptoms of burnout stage three
- Stage two intensified but without a plan to recover
- Adrenal burnout, stress addictions, body aches and pains
- Digestive symptoms, nausea, food addictions, cravings
- Possible heart problems, angina, high blood pressure, etc.
- Feel betrayed, defenseless, cornered, fearful, explosive anger
- Irritated, raw nerves, ministering is painful, continuous withdrawal
- Tempted with moral failure, worldly escapes, destructive behavior
- Loss of confidence in self and a distant God

Prayer for someone who is burned out

Lord Jesus, I stand in the gap for this one who has burned out. *I do not pray for more strength for him to go on, to try harder or for Job's counselors to tell him what he should do. I pray that you will bring wise burden bearers who will only listen, pray at a distance, make no demands and refrain from offering unsolicited advice. I pray that he will find a safe place to share when he is ready and without pressure for fear of condemnation.*

I pray that he will take time to feed and nurture his spirit, soul and body, *without guilt and in ways that do not further exhaust his energy. I pray for friends who are committed to discreetly shield him from phone calls, needy people, demanding appointments or even family when necessary. I pray that wise counselors will help him choose a plan for a sabbatical rest that is long enough to enable him to rebuild his health. Please shield him from legalistic demands and false guilt when he cannot pray like he used to.*

Holy Spirit, I pray you will deliver him from self-destructive thinking patterns:
- *I have to work until I am totally exhausted and cannot continue*
- *I don't have time for rest, relaxation, restoration or exercise*
- *No one can meet the needs of my people but me; I cannot delegate this*
- *If it needs to be done, I will have to do it; it is my job*
- *Release him from the demands of controlling or manipulative people*
- *Enable him to trust those who will shield him from demands*
- *I must be a failure, inadequate, inferior or letting God down*
- *I cannot take time to keep the Sabbath or for healthy eating*
- *I must drive myself to perform to earn acceptance and approval*

Father, as he comes to the end of his own strength to do things in self-effort, *I pray that he will be able to bring his wounds, fears, doubt, worries insecurities and drivenness to you. As he confesses his sin to others, I pray that all involved will forgive him and show him godly mercy and grace. Help him, Lord, to accept their forgiveness and permission to* *take care of himself in new ways. As he asks for forgiveness for judging others, holding resentment, abusing himself and even blaming God, I pray that he will receive a clean slate and a fresh start.*

Thank you, Lord, for new direction, *strong boundaries, wisdom and freedom to be led by Holy Spirit. Thank you, for healthy friends who nourish his spirit and invite him out to play. I pray that he will learn how to enter into your rest daily and carry your presence everywhere he goes. Surround him with friends who not only believe in him and his vision but consider it an honor to invest in him. Thank you, for never giving up on Him.*

This space can be used to jot down some ideas for a plan for recovery.

Captive Spirit

Christians sometimes make the choice at some point very early in life to withdraw from the unbearable pain of living. Little do they know that a demonic spirit could take advantage of that choice to disconnect or dissociate and place prison bars around their personal spirits. In later life, they may feel unable to take their spirits back by themselves.

Unlike the person with a slumbering spirit, these Christians are not "sleeping through life." They are painfully aware that something has captivated them. At times, they are unable to function, cannot respond or connect. They may notice that when they are faced with conflict, pressure or are in an unusually anointed service, they feel that a spirit has shut them down. They may want to respond to ministry but cannot. What they thought was originally their own choice to control their environment, now automatically controls them.

I clearly remember trying to minister restoration to a university professor who was normally very articulate and receptive. Suddenly, she shut her eyes and her spirit, disconnecting from any communication or ministry from us. My assistant and I prayed scriptures for 25 minutes in order to break the power of this captivity. She reported how odd it feels to "know what you know" and to be "very articulate" but unable to speak or respond to ministry. Praise God for setting her spirit free.

The trauma or agony of an imprisoned spirit is evidenced in many ways.

They feel hollow, vacant or empty inside when they allow their inner vows to withdraw to isolate them, causing loneliness. They feel tormented even if no one is around. Those with captive spirits can't unlock their talents and gifts for God's use or for their own use. Marital sex may seem flat or mechanical. Although they may rage at their prison bars or feel despair, they don't know how to set themselves free.

Physical ailments may appear, as captive spirits sometimes feel "pinned" or feel vertigo. They may have dyslexia or fail to function in an effective and efficient manner. Captive spirits know something is amiss, that they are not living up to their capacity or fulfilling their destiny, but they are in a rut without proper guidance to help them choose life again.

People with captive spirits need godly authorities or counselors who know how to discern their struggle to connect again and how to release their spirits from captivity. Anointed prayer ministers know when to empathize or offer comfort or when to insist on obedience to God. They can teach them how to have boundaries without the tendency for dissociating and impart the ability to trust God again.

Using the Cross Walk Prayer, captive people can be taught what to repent of and what to renounce, so that their imprisoned spirits, gifts and talents can be resurrected and they are set free to trust God's love and protection again.

Prayer to free a captive spirit

Lord, I sense my spirit is held in prison, a cell of my own making. In the past, when I chose to withdraw from the pain in my life, I didn't realize that demonic powers would come to place prison bars around me. Now my spirit has been taken captive and I am powerless to take it back by myself.

Because of an event in my past (hurt, trauma, physical abuse, ritual abuse, verbal abuse, emotional or psychological abuse, rejection), I vowed never to be hurt again, not to feel or to love and vowed not to share, talk, tell or ask. Isolating my heart for protection, I disconnected myself from you and other people, determined to retreat from life. I fell for Satan's plan to separate me from God, from others and even from myself.

Lord Jesus, I ask you to lead me to my captive spirit, to melt my walls and to set me free. Breathe life into my spirit again. Make me whole in you; revive my wounded body, soul and spirit. I choose to receive your truth about myself and my life. I choose to renounce the ungodly beliefs, lies and deception that I believed. (List them.) They have been the prison bars that have held my spirit captive.

Forgive me for withdrawing from my own life, for burying my talents, refusing to serve you or avoiding opportunities to help others. Forgive me for my sinful reactions to the sinful behaviors of others. Forgive me for believing that you didn't care to intervene for me. I was too bound up to see how I could have ministered to your people. I lost many opportunities by shielding my heart with indifference.

Since then, many times I have disconnected automatically and didn't know how to take my spirit back again. I feel withered inside, dry and dusty. I need your living water to flood my prison cell and burst open the door, freeing me to trust, to love, to feel, to live the life you've given me.

I forgive my parents/family for any neglect in my childhood, for being cold or unloving, for not nurturing my spirit to trust, and especially for not modeling godly behavior. Lord, I didn't see you in their lives, and I judged them for their shortcomings. I'm so sorry.

Father, I repent for my spiritual rebellion against you. I blamed you for Satan's work, for not protecting me or answering my prayers the way I wanted. Teach me to rest in your decisions for me, to know that you have always had my best interests at heart and anything you allow to happen to me is ultimately for my good, to make me a stronger Christian.

Lord, I forgive anyone who may have contributed to my fleshly vow of isolation by using harsh words that hurt me, abusing me or playing mind games that led me to mistrust people. As you forgive me, so I forgive them—because the price for that forgiveness has been paid for by the death of Jesus Christ on the Cross.

By His resurrection power within me, I forgive myself *for thinking I could do a better job of handling life without your help or the support of other people. So many times I kicked away comfort, thinking I was standing alone when my blindness wouldn't let me see all the angels you had sent to my aid. Shine your righteousness onto my path and lead me into your righteousness.*

Lord, take my armor of flesh *and throw it as far as the east is from the west. I no longer need it or want it to shield my heart from life. Through your strength in me, I choose to trust you to protect me as I serve you. I choose to take refuge in your constant care. Release all the gifts, talents, and creativity you have given me that I so selfishly locked away from view. I choose to live a full life in your power and in your blessing. Dismantle my defensiveness, Lord. I renounce my vow of isolation.*

Lord Jesus, bring people into my life *who can help show me the way to complete freedom. I want to feel, to have the courage to give and to receive love. I choose to believe that you will bring people into my life who will not only love and accept me but who will also believe in me and my calling. I believe they will consider it an honor and joy to invest in me. I choose to live out of my personal spirit and to be one spirit with your Spirit. Amen.*

Notes to self: How to avoid becoming captive again

Deliverance after Integrated Ministry

We have seen the most lasting success when we do deliverance after we have broken the power of the underlying patterns described in Part I of this book. Resisting the devil can be done on an individual basis with the power and authority of Christ. Believers are called to cast out demons but we say, "The Lord rebuke you!" to principalities, powers and rulers of darkness in high places. Both ministries must be done as a team effort with prayer ministers who are trained and gifted by God for this specific work.

Below is a list you can follow if you have been anointed for this work.

- Be sure you yourself are leading a holy life, with no hidden or unconfessed sin or fleshly structure you have not taken to the Cross to be crucified. Having a special anointing is not a substitute for the diligent work of progressive sanctification.
- Discern what demonic kings, principalities, powers, rulers, etc. are oppressing your prayer receiver.
- **See resources in Restoration Prayer Ministry Manual One if you are led to do a complete deliverance in every area of their life.**
- Discern what your assignment is and what spiritual power and authority you have.
- Lead to them to confession and repentance of all known and hidden sin, inner vows, and generational sin, using the Cross Walk Prayer.
- Understand how to come against principalities from the top to the bottom (Ephesians 6).
- Say, "The Lord rebuked you!" and command demonic rulers to fall like lightning under the anointing power and authority of Jesus Christ.
- Free your prayer receiver, yourself and your families from infirmities and all associated demonic spirits.
- Loose people under your authority from addictions to prescription or recreational drugs, alcohol, sex, pornography, etc.
- Break the power of biological, bacterial, viral, pestilence, etc. over your prayer receiver. (Psalm 91).
- Release creative miracles to restore any diseased body parts to better than new.
- Discern whether a forty-day fast or partial fast is part of the deliverance strategy or follow up maintenance.

Staying vigilant after deliverance is often a skill that must be learned. The Kylstra's taught me how Holy Spirit usually leads them to minister to the most common problem areas. This chapter is my version and adaptation of points from their "Issued-Focused Ministry" used with their permission. (Chester and Betsy Kylstra, Founders of Restoring the Foundations International, Hendersonville, NC. www.RestoringtheFoundations.org) See also my bibliography.

Freedom from Demonic Oppression, Bondages and Addictions

Who can cast out devils? Jesus Said He Came To Destroy the Works of the Devil!
Jesus said, "Believers shall cast out demons." You don't have to be "Super Christian" to cast out demons. Just be a believer! Mark 16:17

Jesus commanded you to -- in spiritual power and authority -- in His name.

The "Don'ts" of casting out demons:

- Don't be shy or beg them
- Don't get scared of evil
- Don't expect to throw up
- Don't yell at the demons
- Don't be weird or spooky
- Don't close your eyes
- Don't yell or to be dramatic
- Don't beg demons
- Don't hope for a manifestation
- Don't ignore a manifestation
- Don't overlook unhealed hurts

Every demon knows it has to bow when we command them in the Name of Jesus Christ, owning our spiritual power and authority and the resurrection power we have in Christ.

The "Do's" of casting out demons:

- Do have a partner or team
- Do have intercessors praying
- Do ask forgiveness in five ways first
- Do get into agreement with God
- Do confess the sins of the fathers
- Do break the resulting curses
- Do set your will to choose freedom
- Do remember all demons are liars
- Do insist that each demon leave
- Do keep insisting until they leave
- Do command demons never to return
- Do replace them with good
- Do discern their open eyes
- Do have tissues handy
- Do address pains or tightness
- Do use scriptures and praises
- Do pray again when necessary

Demonic Oppression not Possession
1 John 3:8 …**For this PURPOSE** the Son of God was manifested, that he might destroy the works of the devil.

Acts 10:38 How God anointed Jesus of Nazareth with the Holy Ghost and with power: who went about doing good, and **healing all that were OPPRESSED** of the devil; for God was with him

Mark 16:17 And the signs shall follow them that believe**; In my name they shall cast out DEVILS; …**

God's plan: "Little by Little"
In Exodus 23: 29-30, God gives a picture of the process of taking back all God has promised you. He says that the **giants would be driven out** little by little. As we gain spiritual strength, we overcome and take back our land. So whether you want to win the world to Christ or to get rid of your own baggage, Truth will make you FREE!

How to Keep Your Deliverance

1. Read God's Word daily.
2. Find a group of Bible-believing people, preferably a church, and regularly meet with them for worship, study and ministry.
3. Determine to follow God's instructions on godly living as found in His Word and let Christ in you live the Christian life through you, in His power.
4. Pray the blood of Jesus over yourself and your family.
5. Determine as nearly as you can which spirits have been cast out of you and make a list of areas Satan will try to recapture.
6. The way demons gain re-entry is through an undisciplined thought life that leaves itself open to sin. The mind is the battlefield. You must cast down imaginations and bring every thought into the obedience of Christ (II Corinthians 10:5).

Know what the Bible says about staying away from the occult

Satanism, witchcraft and Wicca are some of the fastest-growing religions, recruiting new members in record numbers. There is a reason that there are so many missing children (and adults) in the last couple of decades.

Cults and covens prey on children and emotionally exhausted adults who are helpless to discern their demonic motivations to control, abuse, and program or even to sacrifice them in their rituals. All satanic covens around the world look for victims to use as their human sacrifices during October.

I am horrified by Christian parents who are allowing their children to attend Halloween parties, to be involved in satanic and witchcraft activities and to own satanic and witchcraft books, objects, games, jewelry and movies. Parents should become familiar with the signs of danger that are proudly displayed by gangs, clubs, businesses, secret societies, schools, etc.

Satan has a plan to steal, kill and destroy those who are uninformed or foolish enough to expose themselves and their children to occult powers. Jesus Christ died to provide healing, freedom and deliverance from the devil's power. An effective prayer minister can guide people to break the power of open doors to the devil's influence through the power and name of Jesus Christ.

For example: Occult dealings can open doors to some mental illnesses or physical ailments like epilepsy. Jesus often did healing and deliverance together. Demonic influences can invite attitudes of rebellion or stubbornness and can cause some extreme behavior changes.

Even though King Saul had cleansed the land of witchcraft (I Samuel 28:7), we see a major change in King Saul after he sent for the medium in Endor. Afterward, King Saul was different; he had unpredictable and violent mood swings. He would ask David to play worship music one hour, throw a spear at him the next and was loving

David as a son at other times. I Samuel 18:10 says an evil spirit came upon Saul and he "raved madly" in his house.

If those seeking deliverance have left doors of opportunity open through unconfessed sin, it is possible that even though certain cultic spirits that are used to advance the devil's kingdom of darkness are vanquished, there remain behind other spirits of lust, anger, bitterness, etc. that attack the personal spirits of Christians. In this way, defeated satanic agents are still able to do damage to God's kingdom by making His servants ineffective.

Open doors may come through hidden spiritual rebellion against God or His chosen authorities (godly parents or church leaders, for example) and objects or books of occult influence that are retained (spells, Ouija boards, clothing with words or pictures pertaining to the occult, horoscopes, etc.).

Whenever we try to substitute anything else for God in our lives, this constitutes idolatry and is in direct violation of the First Commandment to keep God uppermost in our lives and to worship and love Him above all else.

If people are looking for answers in psychics, love potions, occult arts or Harry Potter, their astrology charts may convince them there is no hope of ever being free. But the truth is that Jesus came to set us free so that we could know Him and enter into an eternal personal relationship with Him. He can go back in time and heal every wound and restore us to our true identity, replace everything we lost to the enemy and give us the wisdom and strength to fulfill our God-given destiny in life.

This book will not make you a prayer ministry counselor and these teachings alone are not adequate to fully equip you to minister to those who are blinded and deceived by the devil to one degree or another. But it may help you discern the signs that your children, prayer receivers or church members have left some doors wide open to occult influence and need advanced prayer counseling ministry.

If you sense God's call to be trained to offer whole life Restoration Prayer Ministry (RPM), integrating all the areas of ministry mentioned in this book, please order *Restoration Prayer Ministry Manual* **One** from Amazon or from my condensed site at www. Restoration Prayer Ministry.com/manual.html

I advise you to study the issue focused prayer ministry as outlined in Manual One and then to contact me if you would like to apply to be trained to do whole life RPM. See more about mentoring and internships on the same site. You can also request training at your location or by coming to Cross Walk Life in person.

Also see an even more detailed manual by Kylstra, Chester and Betsy. *Biblical Healing and Deliverance A Guide to Experiencing Freedom from Sins of the Past, Destructive Beliefs, Emotional and Spiritual Pain, Curses and Oppression.* Chosen Books Pub Co, 2014. See my adaptation of their prayer card under resources.

Prayers of deliverance for one issue

Warning: (Keep in mind that it can be very dangerous to minister to anyone under an occult influence if God has not called you to do it.) *

Heavenly Father, thank you for the work *being done here today. We acknowledge our position in Christ, anointed through His name and with His delegated authority. We ask that you cut any ungodly soul ties that may have been formed because of this deliverance. Let no transference take place between our spirits or bodies. We pray a hedge of protection around ourselves, our families, our pets, possessions and property and everything or everyone we care about. Because we stand in your name with your authority, there can be no backlash from the enemy.*

Prayer of deliverance and freedom from bondage
I confess my sin of agreeing with demonic spirits of _____ and forgive all who may have influenced me to sin. I repent for giving place to the demons of _____ . I forgive myself for the pain and limitations I have allowed all these demons (or stronghold) to inflict me. In the Name of Jesus, I renounce and break all agreement with the demons or stronghold of _____ , including all associated demons of _____ , _____ , _____ , or _____ , etc. I take authority and command all of you to leave me now based on the finished work of Christ on the Cross and His shed blood. I command the demons of _____ to go to the dry uninhabited places (or to the feet of Jesus) and to never come back. In their place, I choose to receive _____ .

* Contact me for help doing more complex deliverance

Prayer of the one who was delivered

Jesus, my Lord, your blood was shed to break all bondage *and I thank you for breaking off my bondage to evil through my sin and/or foolish dealings with the occult. You became a curse for me in order to break all curses and I thank you for setting me free from all curses and evil influences assigned to me or my family. Through the resurrection power of the Son of God, I now declare every curse broken, nailed to the Cross and reversed into a blessing. Thank you, Jesus!*

I declare myself a citizen of the Kingdom of God *and I choose to serve Him forever. Therefore, I declare a divorce from the kingdom of Satan and any and all connections I may have made through intention or ignorance. Because of what my Lord did for me on the Cross, I am no longer a slave to the enemy to do his bidding but have been transformed by God's power from darkness into light.*

Through the power of the Holy Spirit within me, *I choose to refuse any further dealings with the occult and will no longer use my sinful intents as a substitute for knowing God. Teach me, Father, to know you and keep me close to your heart. Fulfill your plan for my life. In Jesus' name, amen.*

Depression, Discouragement and Hopelessness

A broken heart is usually an open door for ungodly beliefs and reactions. People who are depressed or discouraged feel hopeless and helpless to change, despite knowing God's truth. Often they hold ungodly beliefs about God's love or willingness to break the power of their depression cycles.

Would you know how to minister to someone who came to you asking for prayer and complaining of most of these symptoms of depression? Are you "stressing out" and heading for depression yourself?

1. Do you have low energy or motivation?
2. Do you have more trouble sleeping or getting up?
3. Do you have more difficulty remembering things?
4. Have you lost your self-confidence?
5. Are you pushing yourself with sugar and caffeine?
6. Is it harder to find a reason to get up in the morning?
7. Do you feel lonely or withdrawn from the world?
8. Do you sometimes feel like crying for no particular reason?
9. Do you have guilt, shame or regret that won't go away?
10. Have you been feeling tense or agitated?
11. Have you been argumentative or defensive?
12. Do you feel your life is without purpose or worthless?
13. Do you have less "bounce back" or patience?
14. Has your appetite changed—increased or decreased?
15. Has your sexual appetite decreased?
16. Are you withdrawing or isolating yourself?
17. Are you burned out from people pleasing?
18. Do you feel that your life is empty and meaningless?
19. Do you sometimes feel helpless and hopeless?
20. Are you procrastinating or avoiding doing things?
21. Have you been thinking you have no future?
22. Have you considered committing suicide?
23. Have you been having mood swings?
24. Do you feel like you are trapped or stuck?
25. Do you have physical symptoms like grinding your teeth?
26. Do you drink or medicate to numb out?
27. Have you had a severe loss or higher stress lately?
28. Do you think your situation is hopeless?
29. Do you feel tired for no apparent reason?
30. Do you have resentment or deep emotional wounds?
31. Is it harder to concentrate or make decisions?
32. Have you lost interest in your interests?
33. Do you sense you can't cope as well?

Give yourself three points for each "yes." How did you do? Do you need Restoration Prayer Ministry for yourself before trying to help someone else?

It's different to minister to someone who is depressed; the dos and don'ts are not what you might think. It is very important to know how to partner with the Holy Spirit, to minister to those who are suffering from depression.

Offering tired platitudes about "tying a knot and hanging on when you get to the end of your rope" or "keeping the faith" is the last thing these people need to hear. They need truth. Those in the throes of depression usually have lost faith in God or in His ability to do something for them. Or they know He can but aren't sure He will. They don't see their value or worth from God's point of view.

Depressed people need to be comforted and assured of God's unending love.

When they are through with self-pity and are ready to climb out of their mental dungeon, they need a prayer minister who can help them see the negative belief patterns and behaviors they've been demonstrating. They may need someone to hold a mirror up to their souls to help them decipher the lies they bought into before looking to God for truth and light.

Depression can immobilize the spirit, soul and body to the point that it may take several sessions for progress to be seen. They see God through their circumstances and they aren't wearing rose-colored glasses. Gently but firmly, guide these tender, hurting souls to see their circumstances through God's eyes and to understand and accept their true identity in Christ.

At first, the most important thing is active listening with an intent to empathize with their pain. While we cannot take up their offense or join a pity party, we can acknowledge difficult losses or circumstances by saying, "That would have been difficult for me too." Do not say, "I know exactly how you feel" or begin to trump their story with stories of your own.

Discern if it is the right time to ask them to share a timeline of blessings in their life. Counting your blessings may sound trite but can be helpful <u>if the timing is right</u>. That's at least a place to start in exchanging the clouds of despair for a thankful attitude. It's the times we don't feel like thanking God at all that we most need to thank Him. Teach them to take baby steps. Being grateful for little blessings will eventually blossom into a greater vision to be able to see bigger ones.

God's principle of exchange works on negative tendencies as well. Every time a negative thought or behavior pattern emerges, re-direct them to replace it with a positive thought about God, their relationship to Him or something to thank Him for, even if it's just that the electric bill was lower this month.

As we begin to follow the scriptural advice to think on things that are good, honest, pleasant and praiseworthy (Philippians 4:8), we develop the habit of a Godly mindset that has the power to push out negativity and invite in joy. With our God-given free will, we can choose what we want to think about. With our God-provided freedom because of the Cross, we can choose how we want to live our lives.

Feeling – thinking – believing – depression and discouragement?

Identify the negative beliefs or behaviors and take them to the Cross to be crucified. Then ask Holy Spirit for godly beliefs to replace them. We will have the fruit of our own lips as we declare these godly beliefs daily and we can work this for good.

Below are sample negative beliefs, behaviors and expectations to be renounced, forgiven and brought to Jesus Who will bring them to death on the Cross as we repent.

- I dwell on what might go wrong.
- I can't speak to people or groups.
- My interests and motivation are low.
- I am not able to concentrate anymore.
- I can't forgive offenses of the past.
- If others know me, they will reject me.
- No one will ever love and accept me.
- I failed; I deserve to be punished.
- It is not OK for me to express anger.
- This is the way I am; there's no hope.
- ?

Godly beliefs and behaviors to be raised to life instead
- God works all things for good for His purposes.
- If God says to open my mouth, He will fill it.
- I receive God's vision, purposes and power.
- Meditating on Bible verses is renewing my mind.
- As I forgive others, I am set free of unforgiveness.
- I choose to accept my uniqueness, talents and gifts.
- I am loving and lovable as I receive God's love.
- Jesus took my punishment and totally forgave me
- Anger is a sign that an adjustment needs to be made.
- God is renewing my mind and restoring my soul.

Jesus *does* bind up the brokenhearted and proclaim freedom for the captives. He *does* restore all that's been lost, making us joyful people who are equipped to usher in His Kingdom. You can become a vibrant, living demonstration of the power of Jesus Christ's never-ending love. Let Him transform your depression and despair into a dance of rejoicing in His arms of love.

Prayer before ministry to one who is in depression
Prayer minister (prays to God alone before the session)

Father, I bring _____ to you, your child who is hurting, *who has called out to you in the past but cannot hear your voice now and desperately needs to hear your loving reply. They have lost their joy, their peace, their strength, purpose and self-confidence. They feel stuck, hopeless, helpless and are too tired to find the will to try. I pray that you, the light of the world, will come into the darkness of this one's life. You are the light they can walk toward and walk out of this black tunnel of despair.*

Lord, you are the light. you are the way out. *Come and light their pilot light again; rekindle their spiritual flame. In your own way and in your own time, let the warmth of your caring presence and anointing flow through their starving spirit, bringing hope, faith, confidence and new purpose for living.*

Before we begin, Lord, I lay down on the altar *all my training, experience, successes and failures and choose to believe you for every step of this ministry. I believe for living water and fresh bread with utmost discernment and sensitivity. I rely on your power, presence and anointing, not eloquent words or methods that have worked in the past. I believe for your gift of healing and faith.*

Lord, you are leading me to listen quietly, *not overwhelming them with words, teachings or answers. With the same power that raised Jesus Christ from the dead, I ask you to raise up _____'s spirit as we come before you in prayer, believing for your love that casts out every fear. Feed their starving spirit and breathe new life into them as only you can do. Impart new vision in dreams, visions and divine appointments. Bring heavenly connections that will affirm their worth and value.*

Grant rest and sleep that reaches beyond their exhaustion *and brings refreshing peace. Bring healing to their physical symptoms and creative miracles to rebuild damaged areas of their tired body. Help me to discern my assignments in their life and my commitments to stand by them, believing in them and believing that you will complete that which you have begun in them.*

Show us where we need to start and what baby steps to take. *Make it clear what we need to do to start the healing process. Let their anger and bitterness surface so they can be exchanged for freedom and new direction. Give me patience as you gently reveal the spiritual roots of depression, the fears, wounds, losses, stresses, trauma, fleshly inner vows, resentments, wrong attitudes or unforgiveness. Help us both to believe your promise to give beauty in exchange for ashes, the oil of joy instead of sadness.*

Tune my ears to hear when YOU say I am needed *and guard me from pat answers, trite platitudes and ineffective clichés. Help me to discern how to "pace" them—not rush them. I receive your mind, your heart, your wisdom and insight as I lead in your* *name and in your authority. I enter into your rest myself, believing that you are committed to redeeming every experience, heal every wound and restore their souls. I receive your forgiveness when I miss it.*

Speak through me to uncover the lies of the enemy *without any condemnation. Speak truth through me that will set them free without being insensitive to them. Be your unconditional love and acceptance through me, if they quit "performing" and transfer their anger to me. Help me to be that safe place where they can finally let their anger, disappointment, hurt or resentment out. May I be an expression of your grace and mercy, no matter what.*

When they confess their worst sins that have been hidden *in the back rooms of their heart all of their life, may I impart total forgiveness. When the time comes, show me how to use our inherited spiritual power and authority to break the power of the "anniversary dates" and oppression that torments them. As they receive your truth, deliver them from every lie, word curse and deception that chains them to their past. Impart new vision that their weak places will be made strong because your blood has not lost its power and you died to restore every area of their life.*

Just as they were wounded in hurtful relationships, *bring other healing relationships into their lives—people who will truly love them, believe in them, invest in them and consider it a pleasure to sow into them. Bring those who have eyes to affirm their value and worth as contributing members in the Body of Christ. Bring a Priscilla or Aquilla who will mentor them to fulfill their destiny and calling. Prepare those who will teach, train and activate them to comfort others with the comfort they received from you. Fill them with a new ability to trust you to transform every area of their life.*

While I stand with them in your authority, *may they actually become dependent on you, not on me. May they finally know your love like never before. May they "know that they know" that you are more than enough, far above everything they ask or think and that they are truly complete in YOU. Lord, may they one day testify that it was in this depression that they discovered an intimate relationship with you, that you were all they needed, their all in all. Amen*

Prayer offered by the one seeking release from depression

Lord Jesus, I come asking you for the courage to hold my heart open for healing. Help me to choose to allow your light into my darkness. All my energy is used up but I come relying on you to work through your prayer minister with your love and wisdom. Where my hope is gone, bring me new hope. When I cannot see the point in trying, open my eyes. My pilot light has gone out and I need you to ignite a fire in me again. Where I feel dead and cold, bring your warmth and bring me back to life. Where I have nothing but doubts, I ask you to give me a new spark of faith. I bring you my exhaustion and ask you for restful sleep. I cannot strive any longer and need to know what it is to enter into your rest. Thank you.

Destiny Blockages: God's Unfulfilled Life Plan for You

Are destiny codes or predispositions already built into our DNA? The Bible says that we were predestined before we were born, from the foundations of the earth, to have a God-given destiny. God loves us and has a wonderful plan for our lives. He has been busy building faith-growing incidents into our lives and stretching our faith so that we will embrace our destiny. Father God orchestrates opportunities that will increase our trust in Him and equip us for His purposes and plans.

In spite of all the ways that God makes rich deposits in our lives, many times we simply choose not to take the next step into our God-given destiny. When I was in Pennsylvania, I heard Dr. Mark Chirona teach about destiny and after doing more study, I decided to identify my top destiny blockages.

What would you say are the biggest blocks to fulfilling your destiny?

- Guilt or shame over past failures
- Lack of confidence in our ability
- Fear that we don't have what it takes
- Believing we don't have the time
- Lack of ability to handle the added stress
- Lack of focus
- Fear of shame or humiliation
- Fear of rejection
- Lack of initiative
- Lack of ability to connect with others
- Lack of self-control
- Lack of ambition
- Low self-esteem or self-worth
- Lack of discipline or self-control
- Death of our vision
- Disillusionment or discouragement

The Bible says that when we delight ourselves in God, He gives us the desires of our hearts (Psalm 37:4). That doesn't mean He gives us everything we desire as in want, but that He gives the desire or vision to accomplish the destiny that He Himself placed in our DNA. Just as plants put a demand to draw certain chemicals from the soil, we are designed to desire all that we need to fulfill our destiny. Similarly, the chemical balance or imbalance in a nursing baby's saliva will place a demand on the mother for just the right nutrition.

Has God given you a vision that is bigger than you can do in your natural ability? Vision from God is always possible because He will not ask us to do something that we cannot do *in His strength*. The key is that the vision presses into a greater trust in God to fulfill the vision through us.

If you have invited Jesus Christ to live in your heart as Lord and Savior, He is resident in you to fulfill your vision with His strength, His gifts and His power. Even the prayer that we pray to fulfill our vision can be God talking to Himself through us.

The biggest destiny blocker of all is our inability to trust God.

We picture ourselves separated from God and having to fulfill our vision in our own strength. The delusions that 1.) we are alone and 2.) that we lack something, will hold us back. If our prayer is begging God to show up or begging Him to fund a vision that we believe originates from us, we are operating in doubt and unbelief. If we realize that He placed the desires and vision in our hearts, we can go forth in confidence knowing that our prayer is hearing God talking to Himself through us.

If our vision is from God, it is God placing His purpose and plan in our hearts. If we respond with a focus on our own ability, our doubts, our fear of failure or our perceived lack of self-worth, we are missing the point that Christ in us makes us complete in Him (Colossians 1:27). Christ in us has all the gifts, fruit and power that we need. If we see ourselves as one with Jesus, as He prays in John 17, we know that we have everything we need in Christ inside us.

We need to identify our scripts that keep us from trusting God to fulfill our destiny through us. Many times these scripts were formed when we were children and we have doubted ourselves ever since. These scripts have played themselves over and over in our minds, to the point where some of us have them memorized.

It's not enough to simply identify our self-destructive scripts or to analyze when and how they began. We need to write down our ungodly beliefs and ask for forgiveness in five ways to break the power of them.

I repent by asking forgiveness in five ways. Father forgive me for my own sins of believing the ungodly belief _____ and for:

- not asking others to forgive me
- judging and not forgiving others
- my own sin and sinful reactions
- blaming or doubting you God
- not forgiving myself

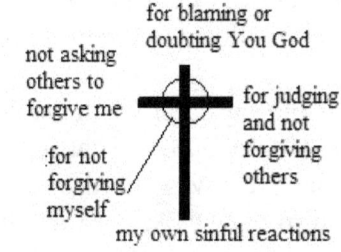

Asking for forgiveness in five ways will break the power of our ungodly beliefs and success/failure cycles. We can choose to trust God to fulfill His vision, purposes and plans through us. We come against our ungodly beliefs that we lack the ability, power, gifting, knowledge, time and energy to do all that God wants us to do. We choose to focus on *Christ in us* (John 14:20), who is conforming us to His image and transforming us into the overcomer who will succeed.

Let's also agree with the prayer of Jabez (I Chronicles 4:10) in asking God to increase our territory or our sphere of influence. Isn't it good to ask God to bless us so that we overflow in blessing to others? Let's renounce our fear of wealth and receive His funding to do His work! Let's choose to believe that it is God's pleasure to use imperfect people to bring about radical change in the world today. Success is always about God's ability more than ours. We are simply available, in the right place at the right time, and He does the supernatural work.

If our vision is from God, we can believe that there are no limits or boundaries on our ability to fulfill our vision. He has given us the desires of our hearts and will sponsor us or fund us as we obey Him. We will have divine connections and protection as we step out in faith as long as it is His will, His way and His timing.

Prayer to fulfill our God-given destiny or vision

Forgive me for falling for the lies of the enemy, *for burying my talents, refusing to serve you or avoiding new opportunities. Forgive me for doubting your Truth and promises when I should have doubted my doubts. Forgive me being content to settle for less than your best for me. Since then, many times, I have wondered if there is any hope for getting back on track with your plan A for me, for fulfilling my destiny in full power. I ask you to restore the years, rewards and blessings I have lost.*

I forgive my family and friends for *speaking shame, guilt, doubts, fears, rejection, discouragement or disillusionment over me. I renounce my agreements with family lies like lack of confidence, feeling inadequate, being too stressed out, unable to focus, lack of ambition, inability to connect or death of my vision. I forgive others for modeling lack of discipline, poor time management or lack of self-control.*

Father, I repent for my lack of faith in you and your plans for me... *Forgive me for times when I blamed you for Satan's work, for not showing me favor or answering my prayers the way I wanted. Teach me to rest in your decisions for me, to know that you have always had my best interests at heart and anything you allow to happen to me is ultimately for my good, to make me a stronger Christian. I receive your unlimited wisdom, power and promise that you have provided everything I need for life, destiny and godliness.*

Lord, please forgive me for judging or resenting anyone *who did not believe in me, my destiny and your anointing operating through me. I choose to operate in the mind of Christ and His discernment regardless of what people say. As you forgive me, so I forgive them—because the price for that forgiveness has been paid for by the death of Jesus Christ on the Cross. I forgive myself for taking the "bait of Satan" to take offense or to base my significance on what I think people think.*

Lord Jesus, by your resurrection power within me, *I choose to believe I can do anything that you want to do through me. In you, I have all the power, wisdom, gifts and favor that I need. I choose to trust you and release you to be all that you are, full strength, through me. Teach me how to hear you with certainty, clarity, confidence and courage. I am wholly given to you and your service. Amen*

You can use this space to write some godly beliefs about your:

Vision:

Mission:

Future:

Goals:

Purpose:

Identity:

Eating Disorders

Eating disorders are a serious health issue that affects as many as one out of ten women at some time in their lives, many teens and even millions of men. Eating disorders like anorexia and bulimia are more than a diet choice; they are very unhealthy and even life-threatening. They are often rooted in life-long issues, strong emotions, fear, shame, control, poor self-image, excessive perfectionism, faulty reasoning, and unresolved spiritual issues. Many times life-threatening medical issues result and professional help is needed.

There are three major types of eating disorders: *anorexia nervosa*, *bulimia nervosa* and *binge eating*. In each case, the person is attempting to meet legitimate needs in their own strength and using something other than God as their source.

Here are some signs to look for in persons who have anorexia:

- weight loss of at least 15% below normal body weight
- preoccupation with body size
- dissatisfied with specific features
- loss of menstrual period for three consecutive months
- tremendous fear of gaining weight after being healed of anorexia
- distorted body image (say they still feel fat)
- obsessive preoccupation with food and exercise
- dry skin, brittle nails, and constipation may occur
- possibly new fine, downy hair growing on the body or face
- hair may thin and fall out with long-term anorexia
- may have increased sensitivity to cold
- deny hunger or that they have an eating disorder
- refusal to eat

Bulimia is different from anorexia and involves these symptoms:

- food binges two or more times every week for at least three months
- may eventually alternate binges and fasts with no periods of normal eating
- food may be eaten inconspicuously with secret self-induced vomiting later
- food binges are followed by self-induced vomiting or purging
- inordinate use of laxatives or diuretics to force weight loss
- obsessive about exercise and fasting
- may or may not look thin but are persistently overly concerned with appearance
- may have a sore throat from vomiting
- can begin with anorexia and move to bulimia or may have both

People who display binge eating without vomiting are still emotionally sick and this can lead to anorexia or bulimia, which can be deadly. Sufferers may develop hypothermia (a low body temperature,) low heart rate, low blood pressure, a depressive disorder, turn to substance abuse, dental enamel may erode (a result of stomach acid due to vomiting or purging), electrolyte imbalance, dehydration, irregular heartbeats and occasionally sudden death.

Until I was twenty-eight years old, I was a "sugar-holic."

I started each day with dessert! I didn't realize the damage that was being done to my body until doctors told me that my lab work was like that of an alcoholic and my bones had only 66% of normal bone density. In fact, I had been proud that my addiction was not overeating, alcohol, smoking or drugs. On the outside, I was slim, trim and looked healthy. I learned that the enemy was using sugar to destroy me.

A sugar demon was the first demon that I ever heard talk out loud through a human being. He bragged unashamedly about how he was destroying someone, organ by organ. It became real to me that the root problem was in the heart, not in the mouth.

In our efforts to find comfort outside of Jesus, we may enter into the idolatry of sugar, food, alcohol or drugs. Satan suggests addictive solutions to our problems and they are meant to lead to the "desolation of the temple" of our physical bodies. Paul warned against bodily self-abuse in I Corinthians 3:16: "Do you not know that you are God's temple and that God's Spirit dwells in you? If anyone destroys God's temple, God will destroy him. For God's temple is holy and you are that temple."

Is overeating a sin, too? Jesus made it clear that external problems start from an internal source when He said, "It is not what goes into the mouth that defiles us, but what proceeds out of the heart." So it is not what is going into the mouth that is the root problem, but what is in our hearts. Perhaps the root problem is an ungodly belief, a pattern of behavior that stems from bitterness or an inability to accept our true identity in Christ.

When we abuse and deface the house of God by eating too much or too little, we sin. We are not loving God with our whole heart or even loving ourselves. Anyone who comforts themselves with eating compulsions is walking after the flesh, instead of walking in the Spirit (Romans 8:4). If we are choosing to be controlled by an eating disorder, we are worshipping our addiction as our source of comfort, instead of the Holy Comforter.

You cannot overcome the sin in your heart and your stronghold by trying harder to keep the law in your own strength. Diets can be a form of law and 1 Corinthians 15:56 says that the power of sin is the law. That is, the more you say "Thou shalt not" the more you think about doing it. Jesus overcame temptation by swinging the Sword of the Spirit by saying, "It is written" and we win over strongholds the same way.

Romans 5:20 says that when we sin, God's grace abounds more than our sin. This is great when we see our need for grace, but can we see our need for God's grace to overcome *this* sin? It can be hard to grasp the bigness of the grace of God that abounds even more. It only seems fair to us that our self-effort in trying to be good should merit more grace. Shouldn't TRYING to be good earn us more grace and righteousness?

But this is against scripture and against God's plan for us. Ephesians 2:8-10 makes it plain that God intends to work through us; it's not that we're doing Him any favors or meriting His grace because of how good we are. God asks that we PRESENT OUR BODIES, already made acceptable by Him and He will prove what is His perfect will as we let Him live His life through us (Romans 12:1-2).

Furthermore, Romans 7:1- 4 says that as we die to our own separated strength (keeping the law and trying to be good on our own) and believe that He has joined us to Jesus, we will BEAR GOOD FRUIT IN CHRIST. In essence, we will be brides, impregnated with His life and a new birth with come forth. In fact, it always takes a union to produce fruit. It is out of oneness that fruit is born.

I believe Romans 7 makes it clear that the battle is between the flesh and the spirit. In the past, the NIV (New International Version) erroneously translated "*flesh*" as "*old nature*." But a more recent translation agrees that our battle is between our new creature nature and our flesh. Our old nature has been crucified with Jesus and He has given us a new identity. We are new creations and WE CHOOSE TO BE AN EXPRESSION OF HIS SPIRIT, A TEMPLE OF THE HOLY GHOST. When you say grace at meals, say "GRACE!" and rejoice that God's grace gives you the strength to eat good food in proper portions and become healthy.

There are many causes of eating disorders. Some may be medical, such as a hormone imbalance, but most often these disorders come about as a side effect of emotional problems such as the ones listed below.

1. Perfectionism and overachieving: unreasonably high standards for one's appearance; possibly an inherited compulsion to succeed
2. Deception: hiding one's failures and addictions, obsession with needing to be in control
3. Poor self-image and low self-esteem: feels worthless, unlovable, unattractive and "fat," may withdraw socially, avoids eating with others where bulimia will be observed
4. Sexual identity ambivalence: confusion about becoming mature physically
5. Control issues: friends or family discover the addiction and try to force change
6. Performance-based acceptance: exceptionally dependent on parents for acceptance or meeting unreasonable standards of peers
7. Depression: because unrealistic goals cannot be reached, criticisms or major stresses may cause one to choose anorexia, binging and purging, overeating or bulimia. The successful and talented musician, Karen Carpenter, died of an eating disorder and it all started with depression over feeling that her life was hopelessly out of her control.

What can friends and family members do for one who suffers from anorexia, bulimia, overeating or binge eating?

We can consistently offer unconditional love and acceptance apart from their performance or appearance. As we impart value to them as a person, they will recognize the importance of their contributions, preferences and opinions and begin to make healthier choices. Stay with them during and after meals, offering strength. Avoid placing blame, power struggles, and messages of being a failure or being unacceptable. Help them to begin to like themselves.

If possible, introduce them to a healing group, as it may help them to determine the root issues and give them hope to overcome it. Listen attentively, without minimizing their pain, as they begin to share their wounds and hurts. Model other ways of handling stress. Support them in receiving God's truth about themselves as they begin to base their self-esteem on His truth, instead of the opinions of others. Rejoice with them as they begin to crave the truth of God and refuse the lies of the enemy. Take them to see a nutritionist, therapist or medical physician, if necessary.

Prayer to Heal Eating Disorders

Dear Jesus, I have come to the end of my own energy to heal myself and I am turning to you, Jehovah Rapha, my healer. I am willing to receive help and support from others who will help you care for me. Please give me the motivation to change my mind about myself and my body and to align with your Truth about me. I bring to you my fears about weight gain and all my underlying issues. I'm asking you to transform me as I allow you to renew my mind as in Romans 12:1-2.

I give you my control issues and ask you help me to depend on you with new faith. Open my eyes to see the lies I have believed about my identity and to define myself by your Truth. I renounce my fleshly inner vows that "I will" or "I will never" and ask you to teach me how to be led by your Holy Spirit every step of the way to healing. I ask you to tear down the stronghold in my mind that says, "If I can be thinner, then I will be (accepted, loved, valued, attractive, ...)

I ask you to supernaturally heal my brain functions, my beliefs, my metabolism, digestive system, bone density, organs and all the damages caused by my eating disorders. As I renounce the lies and agree with your Truth, I ask you to deliver me from spirits of fear, addiction, self-destruction, death and slow suicide.

I forgive those who influenced me to develop these disorders and ask them to forgive me for judging or blaming them. Forgive me for my sinful choices and for damaging myself rather than trusting you, Lord. I choose life. Help my unbelief! Amen

Emotions: Destructive or Negative

Jesus demonstrated how to handle very troublesome feelings when He went to the Garden of Gethsemane. He went to select friends, shared in a private place, poured out His heart with honesty and kept sharing even though His best friends didn't understand. He chose to obey and to do what the Father said to do—even though His feelings were desperately searching for a way out because obedience would hurt.

The truth is that we cannot control spontaneous feelings, but we can choose what we allow to become an emotion. A feeling becomes an emotion when we attach a belief and/or behavior to it. Feelings are valuable indicators when an adjustment needs to be made. We can also pray with people and help them identify their feelings and then make good choices about what they will believe and what they will do.

Destructive or negative emotions are feelings that have ungodly or false beliefs or behaviors attached to them. We all know people who feel inadequate and inferior in spite of having talent or ability. They may have a cycle of destructive or negative thoughts they rehearse. The struggle will be too hard for me. I will disappoint or hurt people. I am not trained and equipped. If I fail, I will lose God's approval. I don't have the gifts that I will need. Destructive or negative beliefs can make people hesitant to step out and try for fear of failing. They assume their family or friends will discourage them or that their efforts will be rejected.

People trapped by negative emotions feel like nothing they do is ever enough.

There is never enough money to succeed. They can never meet other people's expectations even though they feel they have to do as they are told in order to make everyone else happy. They feel controlled or dominated by others and their demands upon them, so they are easily swayed and hurt by criticism. They may even think that they have no option but to go along with what others want them to do because they don't value their own opinions and are fearful of the conflict that may arise if they disagree with someone else.

Negative thinking goes hand in hand with people who "enable" others because they are always trying to smooth the path for everyone else without giving much thought to how it affects their own lives. They have to "fix" everyone's problems, even if this means being taken advantage of and devalued. They try to rescue others from the consequences of their own actions, knowing they themselves will most likely be unappreciated and criticized for trying to help.

Ensnared by a sense of duty, they may spiral downward into a martyr complex, feeling like they are worthless to God and anyone else, only capable of the most menial of tasks. They deny their own needs while they burn out serving others with no intention of asking for aid because they feel they don't deserve it.

When people are set free from negativity, there is a radical transformation. These people choose godly beliefs and behaviors, understanding that true success means stepping out in faith to obey God. Rather than seeing only a gloomy future, they see themselves as valuable contributing members of the body of Christ, believing Father God will provide for what He wants to be done through them. They trust that the indwelling Holy Spirit makes every necessary gift and fruit available to them.

True self-worth is not based on the opinions of others. We can choose to operate in God's power instead of our own, to obey God and leave the results to Him. God provides the training and the abilities we need to do His will. God always loves us perfectly apart from our performance. This is a total turnaround for some people.

Freedom from the downward pull of negative emotions allows believers the liberty to choose to be free of the fear of confrontation. Instead of caving in to what others demand, they can choose to say 'yes' to God and 'no' to distractions. No longer are they shackled by the burden of duty or false responsibility to "make it all better" for others, but they allow others to be responsible and accountable for their own actions and the consequences of those actions. Other people's choices do not dictate who they are. They know whom they are in Christ—called to be servants but not doormats.

They understand that their primary responsibility is to obey God's Holy Spirit and believe in the truth about what God says about them: that He loves and accepts them unconditionally, that their feelings are valid and important, that they are His beloved and valued children, and that they have His grace and power to do whatever He asks of them. They do God's work in God's way rather than relying on their own strength.

Prayer for Dispelling Negative Emotions

Father, I thank you for the gift of emotions. *They are a part of being made in your image. Emotions form a portion of my personality and they help me know what it means to be human. I want to know the desires of your heart, Lord.*

Forgive me for the times I have allowed myself to be led *more by my emotions than by your truth. Please forgive me for the times when I have dumped intense emotions on others when I should have gotten wise counsel before sharing. Forgive me for times when I added ungodly beliefs and behaviors to legitimate feelings, making them into ungodly emotions.*

Through your grace alone, Lord, I choose to allow you *to transform my mind, my will and emotions to be a reflection of yours. I thank you for sending your Son Jesus to experience the full measure of humanity. you know not only what I think but what I feel as well. As Jesus was dying on the cross, He cried out in anguish and suffering, feeling the agony and devastating loss of fellowship with you, His Father. All this He did for me, to pay for my forgiveness and grant me a new life, empowered by the Holy Spirit within me.*

I forgive myself for building walls *that locked me away from loved ones and friends. I thought the barriers would protect me from getting hurt, but they actually kept me from your truth and intimacy. I guarded myself from others and from you as well. I called them boundaries but they were walls. I'm so sorry.*

I forgive those who may have taught me *to close my heart because of their hurtful actions and words. I ask your forgiveness for judging them for their negative bitter expectations. Help me to see how my judgmental attitudes energize my negative emotions and expectations and only make things worse. Teach me how to be fully human, to understand and accept my feelings, without being controlled by them. Give me the courage to open my heart and listen to the messages inside. I give over to you the control of my emotions, the control of my life. I choose to trust you for wisdom in handling emotional situations in the future.*

Holy Spirit of God, tutor me to be that active listener *who can be trusted to pray when others are ready to share intense feelings. I choose to be an expression of your heart, to validate other people and to give them permission to be real. May I be one who will help others to feel free to be honest, to start from where they are and yet to remain open to receive honest responses to their emotions. I choose to be empathetic with their pain but not sympathetic to sinful reactions. Help me to be an expression of your heart to others and to be led by your true discernment. Thank you, Lord, for renewing our hearts and minds. Amen.*

You can use this space to list specific negative emotions that tempt you.

Faith or Fear Faith?

Have you wondered how some Christians can just pick up and move to parts unknown with the assurance that God has led them? How can we be sure that God will provide when we take what appear to be huge risks? How can we have the confidence to risk it all when the Holy Spirit leads us to leave perfectly good jobs, friends or family and reach out to people we don't even know? Are we praying with real faith that pleases God or with fear faith that is double-minded?

"But let him ask in faith, with no doubting, for he who doubts is like a wave of the sea driven and tossed by the wind. For let not that man suppose that he will receive anything from the Lord; he is a double-minded man, unstable in all his ways." James 1:5-8

Many Spirit-filled believers are speaking fear-faith instead of faith. They want to be mighty men and women of faith but constantly sabotage their own success by agreeing with the enemy instead of praying God's Truth. In the spiritual realm, either angelic power or demonic power is released according to words we speak with our own mouths. The greatest hindrance to our progress is not what others may speak over us; it is what we speak ourselves.

As I was reading Psalms today, I was impressed that praying Psalms will help us to pray in faith rather than fear-faith. Real faith takes every apparent negative and turns it into a faith statement. David was a man after God's own heart. He would cry out to God, telling God how he saw the situation but then he would always turn that bad report into faith statements. He never ended by declaring the power of the enemy to win. He concluded with declarations of God's faithfulness, superiority, power, strength, compassion, competence, character, etc. David chose to pray faith instead of fear-faith and he won!!

Fear-faith cries out to God declaring negative after negative.

For instance, David was real about facts as he saw them: he told Father God how bad things felt in the natural. But he demonstrated speaking faith as he chose to conclude with faith statements instead of doubt and fear statements. Instead of saying, "I am so defeated today that I can't pray scripture. I can't ... I can't ... ," faith will say "I am severely attacked today, BUT I am trusting God that Christ in me will overcome and I chose to persevere until I can pray according to scripture." As you learn to speak in faith, you won't only say "I was totally distracted when I tried to watch a NowFaith.TV video yesterday" BUT also "I believe I have the victory to operate in faith today." Your determination to keep your faith and joy will speak, "In Christ, I choose to move forward, never speaking doubt, persevering in His power no matter what and I will outlast the devil!" If you commit to speak faith, the Holy Spirit will lead you.

Fear-faith is not faith at all but just agreements with the spirit of fear voiced in a way that may sound like prayer. Real faith prayer always praises God for the coming victory and repents of bitter expectations that things will be as bad today as they seemed yesterday. Godly faith is responsible to speak in agreement with God and never speaking that the devil has power over me.

You may think you don't know how to break this habit.

The first step is to allow time to really pour out your heart to Father God: including doubts, fears, worries, hurts etc. Second, ask the Holy Spirit to reveal which parts were fear-faith instead of faith. Third, repent of giving power to the enemy by agreeing with him. Fourth, ask forgiveness in five ways: for doubting God, judging others, your own sinful reactions, forgive yourself and forgive others. Fifth, choose to let the Holy Spirit transform your speech into faith speech.

David's Psalms model his pattern of pouring his heart out to God BUT then agreeing with God's Truth. You can invite the Holy Spirit to convict you when your conclusion is based on fear-faith instead of faith. They say it is most important what you say after the BUT! You can say the battle is heavy today BUT conclude that the victory will be even better. You can express valid feelings of hurt BUT choose to take them to Jesus in faith for healing. You can express legitimate anger without sin BUT finish by confessing God's truth over others and yourself. You can tell Father God how frustrated you are BUT choose to submit to God's will, God's way and God's knowledge.

God is calling us to make big choices in these last crucial days and is revealing to us who the object of our faith really is. Many of us say "In God we trust" but we really trust more in our own resources.

I was studying the life of George Mueller, who ran an orphanage and ministry for sixty-six years on God's provision alone. I came upon an article on the Internet, "George Muller: How to Strengthen Faith" at www.pathtoprayer.com. This concise article reminded me of several characteristics common to people who have a lifestyle of living by "faith in God." I have added these to other points that he taught.

1. **Dependence upon the goodness of God, not ourselves.** Our right standing with God is based on the righteousness that the Lord Jesus Christ gave us as a gift and is the only ground for any claim of undeserved favor. We **choose** a child-like abandon to Him as our Provider, while we fulfill His purposes in agreement with His heart.
2. **Separation from all of our former idols and crutches**. Sin can be defined as choosing to get our needs met outside of the will of God. God is our Source and we **choose** absolute reliance on Jesus Christ, 100% obedience, and choose to stay in position under the fountain of His blessing.
3. **Faith in God's promises** as confirmed by His Word. We know that we are little and He alone is BIG; not to believe Him is to make Him both a liar and

fallible. We **choose** to lay aside every crutch formerly used to substitute for His provision and to run ahead of His timing. We **choose** to lay aside our doubts and fears; we **choose** faith that honors Him.

4. **Asking in accordance with what is on God's heart.** We **choose** Godly motives and must not seek any gift of God to consume it upon our own self-centered lusts. We **choose** to agree with God. As we seek His Kingdom first, to be done on earth as it is in heaven, "all these things will be added unto us" (Matt.6:33). As we lay down our own goals, we enjoy an immunity from frustration because we are content with His will, way and timing.

5. **Waiting on God and waiting for God.** We **choose** not to focus on any other source of provision, not to focus on the challenges or blocks, or any doubt or fear that has built a wall between us and God in the past. We **choose** to trust God's perfect timing. While we say that we are waiting on God, many times God is actually waiting for us to come into agreement with Him.

George Mueller reportedly had several practices he called "prayer secrets":

- He kept a journal of daily petitions and specific answers.
- He believed that nothing was too small to pray about.
- He also thought that laying up stores or hoarding money was inconsistent with a life of faith. (Keep sowing.)
- He believed four hours of work after an hour of prayer would accomplish more than five hours of work without prayer.
- He prayed for more orphans more than he prayed for more money, for a house, for helpers, furniture, etc.
- He created a "memory reminder" to help him to recall God's faithfulness.

I can only add that we cannot ask to live a life with supernatural intervention unless we will allow God to bring circumstances into our lives that require His supernatural intervention. So let's choose to trust Him and enjoy the voyage!

George Mueller's prayer to increase faith

One of the mightiest men of prayer of the last generation was George Mueller of Bristol, England, who in the last sixty years of his life (he lived to be ninety-two or ninety-three) obtained the English equivalent of $7,200,000 by prayer. But George Mueller never prayed for a thing just because he wanted it, or even just because he felt it was greatly needed for God's work.

I also found "Two 'Prayer Tips' from George Mueller" at www.hopefaithprayer.com

1. When it was laid upon George Mueller's heart to pray for anything, he would search the Scriptures to find if there was some promise that covered the case. Sometimes he would search the scriptures for days before he presented his petition to God. And then when he found the promise, with his open Bible before him, and his

finger upon that promise, he would plead that promise, and so he received what he asked. He always prayed with an open Bible before him.

2. After meditating on scripture he was more able to experience a meaningful prayer time.

You can use this space to journal your prayer plan as the Lord directs.

Fatherhood Issues

In my opinion, one of our greatest problems today is that people are going into life, into ministry or leadership of some kind without ever having been mentored or fathered themselves. I believe that the role of fathers today has been degraded in the public eye to the point that we have almost lost the vision for the critical role fathers play.

Appropriate affectionate touch and affirmation from a good father who is also a spiritual father, are probably the largest factors in building strong personal spirits into our lives. Without the affirmation of our fathers, we may wander through life, looking for our identity in many other places and pattern our behavior on performance-acceptance.

It is on our father's knee that we learn that we are the apple of his eye—and God's eye as well. We learn that we are a delight, a pleasure and that we are desirable to be with. A godly father communicates our value as a contributing member of the family, the community and the body of Christ. Feeling accepted by him gives us the confidence we need to live fully out our true identity in Christ. We have courage based on what our Heavenly Father says about us instead of performing to win the approval of everyone else.

We are not easily lured into sin with flattery, because our godly father has affirmed our God-given purpose, gifting, talent and callings in life. We are secure in bonded relationships and able to trust God when Satan's cheap, easy counterfeits come along to lure us with empty promises. We are able to minister out of health and stability that is based on God's truth because this is what we have been taught and seen modeled by our godly fathers.

If you have been blessed with such a father, please let him know how fortunate you are. If you are hurting as you read this, it's not too late to ask God for a spiritual father (or mother) to re-parent you and love you with God's *agape* love. Ask God for discernment to know who has a fathering heart, so you will be blessed and loved to life rather than rejected again.

You can pray for your own father or spiritual father by loosing him from fleshly traits and binding him to the heart of God and to His character, in Jesus' Name. If you have been hurt by an uncaring religious leader, ask God for a good leader who is a true spiritual father.

If you are afraid to choose a spiritual father for yourself, this comparison between a spiritual father and someone who is just a religious leader may help you to discern a true father and their godly motivations. These thoughts are taken from many sources on fathering and including *Mentoring and Fathering* by Schultz and Gaborit and some from *Restoring the Christian Family* by John Sandford.

GOOD SPIRITUAL FATHER	FLESHLY FATHER
Takes his own wounds to Jesus for healing	Takes his hurts out on the nearest person
Takes his fleshly reactions to the cross	Automatic reactions w/o leading of the Spirit
Forgives others, God and himself	Holds resentment, judgments, bitterness
Takes responsibility for sins he has sown	Blames others for what he is reaping
Honors and respects his authorities	Undermines his own authority with dishonor
Is flexible and led of the Holy Spirit	Under fleshly inner vows in his own strength
Believes the best, believes in you	Has bitter expectations that you will fail again
Confesses the sins of his fathers	Repeats the sins of his fathers and more
Touch, time, gifts, help, on your side	Loves you the way he wants to receive love
Hears God, is in agreement with Mom	Controls, dominates, competes, pouts
Appreciates/respects the opposite sex	Undermines feminine contributions
Encourages you for your own good	Flatters you and manipulates for his agenda
Finds time to be available to you	Is too busy to spend quality time
Will bless you when you are led to leave	Will cut you off if you are led to move on
Prays for you without ceasing	Will pray if you ask him
Willingly imparts spiritual gifts and wisdom	Doesn't want to lose (spiritual) advantage
Sees potential gifts, talents & callings in you	Only sees you as you are now
Trusts you to step out (with room to fail)	Will not release you for fear of your failure
Isn't afraid to discipline or correct you	Will either avoid correction or will overreact
Has a heart to restore the brokenhearted	Withdraws from high-maintenance children
Will pay a debt he does not owe	Will hold your debts over your head
Will fellowship with other fathers	Will hide from accountability to his peers
Moves toward the current move of God	Weds you to his beliefs, past moves
Is not threatened by your other relationships	Tries to control who you hear or who you serve
Teaches you dependence on God also	Keeps you dependent on him
Teaches you truth from God's Word	Teaches you his doctrinal bias
Has the heart of a true worshipper of God	"Attends" or sends you to a worship service
Is happy when you succeed more than he	Is threatened when you succeed more than he
Has the 'team' concept of service	Has a 'golfer caddy' idea of your service
Makes you feel comfortable / protected	Threatens to expose you or attack you
Helps, wanting nothing in return	Expects something for helping you
Willing to admit his weaknesses	Will not admit weakness or mistakes
Is interested in what you are doing	Only what he is doing / his vision
Is relationship oriented and sensitive	Is task oriented
Communicates well and listens well	Feels bothered and put upon by you
Hears God and leads by the Holy Spirit	Influences or controls for his own agenda

What if you are the father, wanting to learn how to model godly behavior?

So much about being a good father to a child can be summed up by knowing and speaking the child's love language. A good father knows whether his child receives love best as giving affectionate touch, investing quality time, by affirming words, offering to help them, or by giving gifts. You can learn about this valuable tool by reading and studying "The Five Love Languages" by Gary Chapman.

Affectionate touch may be the most crucial building block of good parenting. Loving touch must be modeled by a godly father in front of his children and also to his children in order for them to understand and recognize appropriate touch from other sources. As a father, do you show affection to your wife in front of your children? Do you hold your children on your lap, hug or kiss them, giving them affectionate touch appropriately?

You can invest quality time by taking an interest in their hobbies, driving them to school, taking them out for some special time alone with just them, or listening to them describe their day each night. Do you enjoy being with your children; do they enjoy being with you? Are they your priority? Does your schedule include things to do with your children that they enjoy?

As a godly father, you can build your relationship with affirming words when you teach your children to speak to you and each other respectfully by your good example. Do you affirm their successes and minister to their weak points? When your son or daughter comes running to you when they have been hurt, are they comforted by your affirming words? Do you calmly and gently train your children in the way they should go, without yelling or screaming? Do you tuck your children into bed at night with an "I love you," affirming words and by praying with them?

Do your children know that you are their best source of help or are you too preoccupied with your own agenda? Do you make breakfast for them or help them with their homework or school projects? When you give your children chores, are you there to help them if they need it? Do you lead by demonstration or do you just tell them what to do?

You can express your love by giving little inexpensive but thoughtful gifts. Do your children know that you believe in them and are happy to invest in them and their future? Are you providing opportunities for them to develop their talents, gifts and calling? Are you verifying their precious value with your wallet as well as all the above?

Prayer to become a godly father

Dear Heavenly Father, I receive you as my Heavenly Father and allow you to heal every hurt and wound so that I will be healed and able to partner with you to heal others. Please forgive me for every way that I have dishonored, condemned and resented my father, authorities and religious leaders. Forgive me for questioning, doubting and blaming you, God. I choose to forgive myself for all the ways that I have sinned against fathers, religious leaders, spiritual fathers and you Heavenly Father.

Please forgive me for all the ways I have let my view of human fathers, leaders and authority figures taint my view of you, Father God. I repent of thinking that you have weakness, attitudes, behaviors and tendencies similar to the humans who have let me down. Forgive me for all the ways I have doubted your faithfulness, your character, your intentions or your perfect love for me.

I know that every good thing comes from you. I now choose to trust you now, to heal every hurt, to redeem every hurtful experience and to leave me with the wisdom I gained. I ask you to bring trustworthy spiritual fathers into my life who will re-parent me with your power and love. I receive your discernment and the mind of Christ to make wise decisions and to choose spiritual mentors. As I meditate on this teaching on spiritual fathers, I ask you to a true spiritual father through me to everyone who is part of my assignment.
Amen

Use this space to write a few spiritual goals, whether about being a good spiritual father or about finding a good spiritual father.

Fear and Doubts about God

Fear can come in many shapes and sizes. Some people have a fear of God, a fear of losing their place in heaven, a fear of evil, a fear of the future, a fear of losing control or a fear of getting a debilitating disease. Some people, like Charlie Brown in the *Peanuts* comic strip, have pantophobia—a fear of everything!

If you had an emotional evaluation today, how well would you do? Are you really thinking God's truth about Him, yourself and others? Who do you really believe God is? Are you holding onto the truth by faith or are you falling for the deceptive lies of the enemy?

How many of the following beliefs really live in your mind? If you commit to praying these declarations as a prayer strategy for forty days, you can learn to overcome your fears and doubts and believe God's Word about His love for you.

- God never condemns His children, so I have no fear of condemnation (Romans 8:1).
- It is His desire to equip all believers with spiritual authority and power (Luke 4:6).
- He trusts me as a good steward, making me ruler over many areas (Matthew 25:23).
- His love for me is perfect, casting out all my fears and doubts (I John 4:18).
- Father God carefully protects me from the power of evil (Luke 10:19).
- He calls to me and desires for me to dwell in the secret place with Him daily (Psalms 91:1).
- It is His pleasure to continue to purify my heart of selfish fleshly desires (Matthew 5:8).
- He wants to visit me and to reveal His beauty, so I will inquire of Him (Psalms 27:4).
- God is more than willing to deliver me because He delights in me (Psalms 18:19).
- He has chosen me to take dominion over the earth, as His ambassador (Genesis 1:26).
- Father God freely gave me spiritual authority to forgive and to command healing (Luke 5:20-24).
- Father God cherishes me as His joint-heir and we will be glorified together with Christ (Romans 8:17).
- My passion is to know Jesus and to grow in His character and fruit (Philippians 3:10-15).
- My soul thirsts to be in right relationship with Jesus (and godly authorities) (Psalms 63:1).
- He has already equipped me with gifts; I can lift Jesus up (II Timothy 1:6).
- He invites me to stir up the spiritual gifts He has lavishly given to me (I Timothy 4:14).

- He commissioned me to proudly serve a Kingdom that cannot be shaken (Hebrews 12:28).
- We partner as true peacemakers who confront evil versus compromise (Matthew 5:9).
- Christ in me is powerful to take the Kingdom by force and take action (Matthew 11:12).
- He fills me with confidence to be faithful to do all His says to do (Jude 3).
- His strength enables me to endure hardship as a good soldier in His army (II Timothy 2:3-4).
- Christ in me discerns false teaching; I overcome error with God's truth (Romans 12:21).
- He rejoices as I step out in my gifts in the full measure they were given to me (Ephesians 4:7).
- He fills me with grace for the effective working of His mighty power (Ephesians 3:7).
- In gratitude, I share the gospel with His love, power and authority (I Corinthians 9:16).
- He gave everything for me and I expend myself to feed His sheep (Ezekiel 34:18-22).
- He sows liberally into me and I multiply the abilities that He gives to me (I Peter 4:11).
- He ministers through me, encouraging others in their spiritual gifts (I Corinthians 12:23-24).
- His hands are in my hands as I lay hands on others, spreading the gospel (Acts 6:6-7).
- His mind is in my mind, filling me with love, power and a sound mind (II Timothy 1:7).
- The Holy Ghost is one with me, filling me with power to be a witness (Acts 1:8; I Corinthians 6:17).
- The Lord is my encourager and strength and I am not afraid (Psalms 27:1).
- God resists the proud but gives grace to me, when I am humble (James 4:6).
- I say what my Father says to say with great boldness of speech (II Corinthians 3:11-12).
- The Lord is on my side; I will not be afraid because He will never leave me. What can man do to me? (Hebrews 13-5-6).
- He promotes me; I don't compete for position or prestige (Luke 22:24).
- Jesus has given me power over demonic spirits; they are subject to me through His name (Luke 10:19-20).
- Jesus took my shame and gave me favor, blessing and a double portion (Isaiah 61:1-7).
- Jesus made me worthy, holy, blameless and righteous in Him (Ephesians 1:4; Romans 5:21).
- He makes me overcome by the blood of the Lamb and my testimony (Revelation 12:20).

How do you minister to someone who fears that God has moved away from them? Or the Holy Spirit has left? What do you say to someone who is afraid and asks you, "Why does God seem so far away? I feel like He has abandoned me."

This kind of fear can result from many causes: rejection, hurts, disobedience, harsh teachings or preaching, legalism, spiritual abuse, false preaching, etc. What would you say causes this feeling? See if any of the following sentences reflect some thoughts of your own or of those seeking your help in being released from fear.

- I have begun to doubt my salvation.
- I think I have quenched the Holy Spirit.
- I have a fear of the devil and evil.
- I can't perform well enough to earn God's love.
- Religion is not satisfying to me anymore.
- My prayers just bounce off the ceiling.
- I can't get into reading the Bible every day.
- I don't have a "personal" relationship with Jesus.
- I don't think anybody can "interact" with God.
- I don't have time to spend time with God.
- God let my _____ die and I can't forgive Him.
- I can't seem to receive God's unconditional love
- I disappointed God and He has abandoned me.
- God asks more of me than I can do.
- I have sinned too many times and can't change.
- The devil keeps saying my life has no value.
- I am better off dead than screwing up like this.
- My only worth is to be used and abused.
- I can never measure up to the church's standard.
- I am a failure and deserve to be punished.
- This is just the way I am and there is no hope.
- I don't want to surrender to God's control.
- If God loves me, why didn't He protect me?
- God is uninvolved and unpredictable.
- I can't be addicted to drugs, etc., and still be a Christian.
- If God has the power to heal, why doesn't He heal me?
- I can never be good enough to go to heaven.
- I live a life of guilt, unable to get God to forgive me.
- No one can be sure they are going to heaven.
- I can never forgive myself or others; it's too hard

We have to pray more specifically with people who have an overwhelming fear of evil. Many people are frightened and alarmed with the overgrowth of cults, Satanism, new age, Wicca, witchcraft, Scientology and other religions founded by the devil. People who are highly motivated to come for prayer ministry often have areas in their life where it feels like devils are in control and there is no getting the victory over them. They may feel helpless and hopeless and believe they cannot win.

Believers who have not owned their spiritual power and authority in Christ have more faith that the devil will win than they have faith that Jesus Christ inside them will win. They report that they have tried to believe scripture but the devil still has them in captivity in certain areas of serious doubt and unbelief.

People may confess the power of evil over them, giving devils more and more power as they agree with them and their deceptions instead of believing God's truth. Evil has no power except what we give to it by agreeing with it. The main power that devils have is to threaten us with an ILLUSION that they will do something. If we agree with them, they will then have our permission to proceed.

Do you have more faith in the power of Jesus Christ inside you to win or more fear of the power of the evil one to win? Do you walk in fear or in faith? Do you speak worry, doubts and fears or command devils to go in Jesus' name?

Prayer to defeat fear and doubt

Father, I confess that I have been deceived by the enemy and have hesitated to believe in you for who you really are and for whom you say I am in you. I choose to believe what the Word of God says and to begin to enjoy my relationship with you to the fullest extent.

I covenant with you for forty days to declare the scriptural truths as given in this chapter. Open my heart to believe what my mind already knows. Break the power of fear that keeps my spirit imprisoned behind bars of unbelief. Set me free through the resurrection power of Jesus within me.

For a more complete deliverance, I promise to pray the Cross Walk Prayer and to ask for forgiveness in five ways. I ask for forgiveness for any judgments and condemnations I have pronounced over others, for my own sinful reactions, for any way I may have blamed you, to forgive anyone who deliberately frightened me or encouraged me in my sinful reaction of fear, and also to forgive myself for my unbelief.

Using the weapons of spiritual warfare that are mighty through God to the pulling down of strongholds, I tear down the strongholds of fear and unbelief through the power of the resurrected Lord Jesus. I declare that I belong to you alone and you have not given me the spirit of fear, but of power, and of love and of a sound mind. I loose myself from every stronghold of the enemy and bind myself to all that is in Christ, bringing every thought into obedience to the Lord Jesus.

I give myself body, soul, mind, and spirit to you as a living sacrifice and believe I am your temple, where you dwell. I am your bond-servant forever. Amen.

Financial Issues

Few of us ever complain about having too much money; it's almost always the other way around. Even when John D. Rockefeller was asked how much money was enough for him, he was quoted as saying, "Just a little bit more."

Since God owns the cattle on a thousand hills, we may sometimes wonder why He doesn't sell a few and give us the money. But we would be missing the point. Everything belongs to God, including everything we have. All that we possess is really a gift from God; we are just stewards of His riches. Instead of thinking we need more money, we should be asking God how He wants us to use His resources.

Financial needs can be a reminder that we are dependent on God and should rely on Him rather than a bulging bank account. Having wealth to spare is God's way of saying He trusts us to share His resources with others. Paul said he had learned to be content whether he was in need or had plenty because he looked first to Christ Who strengthened him (Philippians 4:11-13).

The secret is putting God first, trusting in His strength and His wisdom to provide what we need, when we need it. God's plan was that we would inherit blessings, but the sins of our ancestors may have brought on His disfavor. In Genesis 20:5-6, the Bible says the sins of the fathers go down to the third and fourth generation if no one ever renounces those sins. But His mercies and grace extend to a thousand generations to those who love Him and keep His commandments or choose to break the power of the generational sin and resulting curses.

Curses may still be limiting your prosperity.

Even if you are in agreement with God now, if you have never repented of and renounced your previous agreements with the author of lies, the devil. Ask the Holy Spirit to reveal the times when you have sown disobedience and reaped poverty and or some type of ineffectiveness.

Curses from a demonic source will bring mental torment, afflictions, disasters, misfortune and patterns of loss or they will at least weaken your business, income, ministry, effectiveness or reproduction. The intention of demonic curses is to cause you to be so discouraged, disillusioned, defeated or depressed that you will be intimidated and give up. If you give in to helplessness or hopelessness, you will not possess, occupy and multiply what God has promised to you.

Luke 11:21-22 says, "When a strong man, fully armed, guards his own palace, his goods are in peace. But when a stronger than he comes upon him and overcomes him, he takes from him all his armor in which he trusted, and divides his spoils." This scripture teaches us that in order to break the power of demonic assignments and resulting curses, we must bind the strongman that is assigned to devastate our family, finances, businesses or ministries. When a demonic strongman takes over our house, he is in peace and we are not. When a stronger than he—Christ in us—overcomes, we take it back.

Satan wants to cause you to lose faith and to violate God's principles by causing you to disobey God. When you agree with spirits of fear, doubt and worry you have opened doors to demonic interference and curses. The enemy's goal is to cause you to doubt God's faithfulness and promises to you.

The devil wants to convince you that you do not have the spiritual power and authority to defeat demonic agents hindering your prosperity and effectiveness today. He knows that if you defeat the strongmen, then every demon under them can be cast out as well. If he can cause you to sin and prevent you from repenting, he has the power to maintain curses over you and your finances.

Generational sins, curses and demonic interference can have a great deal to do with financial problems, but money troubles stem from inner sources as well.

Are you stingy with the contents of your wallet? Are you a hoarder? You may harbor a false belief that God won't be faithful in providing for your needs.

Do you have the opposite problem of using a heavy hand with your credit cards so that you're heavily in debt? You may have made an inner vow to never be without something you want or say you need.

Are you always bailing your children out of financial difficulties? You may be enabling their dependence on you because you crave being needed, even if it's only for a handout.

Do you find that there always seems to be more month left at the end of your money and you just don't have any to give to your church or another ministry? You may be avoiding personal responsibility to God, to yourself, and to your family.

Malachi 3:10 encourages us to prove God and take Him at His Word.

He will rain down blessings on you as you hold to His truth, tithe and obey His commands. Pray the Cross Walk Prayer repenting of past false beliefs, inner vows, bitter root judgments, generational sins and curses, and for allowing yourself to fall for the lies of the enemy. Repent and ask forgiveness in five ways to break the power of downward financial spirals.

Once you have repented of violating God's financial laws, you are free to sow good seed and reap a good harvest. When you declare God's Truth in faith believing, you will see good results. Angels will respond and be activated to carry out God's Word.

Once old patterns are broken, it can still take time to renew our minds with Scriptural Truth. I suggest that you proclaim the following Godly beliefs and scripture for forty days and watch God work in your life and in your financial issues. If Jesus said, "It is written…" for 40 days, it can easily take 40 days to win the war in our minds. As you declare these truths, other lies may be flushed out as well.

WE TRUST GOD FOR SEED TO SOW, TO EAT, TO MULTIPLY AND TO GIVE
II Corinthians 9:10: "Now may He who supplies seed to the sower, and bread for food, supply and multiply the seed you have sown and increase the fruits of your righteousness."

WE REPENT OF AGREEMENTS WITH THE ENEMY AND BREAK OFF HIS CURSES IN JESUS' NAME
Malachi 3:11: "'Then I will rebuke the devourer for you, so that it will not destroy the fruits of the ground; nor will your vine in the field cast its grapes,' says the LORD of hosts."

WE REPENT OF IGNORING OPPORTUNITY TO GIVE TO YOUR SERVANTS WHO MINISTERED TO US
I Timothy 5:17-18: "Let the elders who rule well be counted worthy of double honor, especially those who labor in the word and doctrine. For the Scripture says, 'You shall not muzzle an ox while it treads out the grain,' and, 'The laborer is worthy of his wages.'"

WE REPENT FOR NOT GIVING WHOLE-HEARTEDLY WITH REJOICING
I Chronicles 29:9 "Then the people rejoiced because they had offered so willingly, for they made their offering to the LORD with a whole heart, and King David also rejoiced greatly."

WE REPENT OF DISOBEDIENCE WHEN GIVING WAS A CHALLENGE AND WE CHOOSE TO EXCEL IN THE GRACE OF GIVING
II Corinthians 8:7 "But just as you abound in everything, in faith and utterance and knowledge and in all earnestness and in the love we inspired in you; see that you abound in this gracious work also."

Use this space to write corrections to your budget, priorities and financial goals.

Heart of Stone and Inner Vows

"I will give you a new heart and put a new spirit in you; I will remove from you your heart of stone and give you a heart of flesh" (Ezekiel 36:26 NIV).

Counselors of all types will tell you that one of the biggest challenges in healing emotions is to get past the walls or defenses the person has put up to defend themselves from being hurt again. When we are hurt or disappointed, we tend to develop a negative expectation that it may happen again and we may seek to protect ourselves and our hearts from further hurt or damage by making inner vows.

Inner vows create a self-fulfilling prophecy; what we expect tends to happen. When it does, we may develop a false or ungodly belief about being hurt, about others, about ourselves and even about God. Many times this false belief produces a heart of stone that continues to influence our lives, causing us to make unhealthy choices for years to come.

Many of us have believed that we were inadequate, inferior, unattractive or unacceptable—when in truth we were not. We may have tried to hide, to perform for acceptance or forget the past, "re-decide," manage our emotions, modify our behavior, cope with our illness, or talk our issues to death in analysis. When these efforts are not effective, we tend to feel like there is no hope for real change. Our alternative is to defend our unhealthy choices or to build higher walls of self-protection and the false beliefs and inner vows become a stronghold in our minds.

We end up walking down the same sidewalk, tripping over the same cracks. Why doesn't secular counseling have lasting effects? Because you can't fix your heart with your head! Analyzing the problem or making new choices does not make us immune to the law of reaping the seeds we have sown.

What we have experienced as truth tends to override logical truth in our minds.

Unfortunately, no amount of logical truth can replace experiential truth, even if that experiential "truth" is actually made up of lies. These lies hinder the healthy choices that we would like to make in our Christian walk.

So what's the answer? Replace the experiential false belief, inner vow, or root of bitterness with the truth that the God of the universe loves each one of us and wants to have a life-changing relationship with us—and that He has provided the way of forgiveness through His own Son. What an amazing God we serve!

Jesus came to offer us new life in our body, soul and spirit and to touch our defenses, walls, negative expectations, sinful choices and even our false beliefs. We invite Jesus to come into our heart to replace our "experiential truth" with His truth, healing the hurt and removing the pain from our experiences, leaving us with the wisdom to make Godly, healthy choices.

Prayer ministers partner with God to get healing truth not only to our hurts but also to our walls or defenses. Once the walls are down, Jesus, the Spirit of truth, will be able to access any area that needs healing on an ongoing basis. Prayer ministers don't just give us a fish; they teach us *how* to fish so that we can continue restoring relationships with ourselves, with others and with God. Not only does Jesus make us free but He also enables us to partner with God in offering healing to others.

Finally, we can live in harmony with our own body, soul and spirit and with the Spirit of God at the same time! Another result is that we are also able to live in harmony with others as Jesus makes us free to make healthy choices to fulfill our destiny in power and joy.

Do you know how to discern if someone has a heart of stone? Do you know how to minister to someone with a heart of stone? Hard-hearted people are lonely people who have made fleshly pledges, or inner vows, in an effort to protect themselves from being hurt or to isolate themselves from the world.

Test yourself first to see if you have a heart of stone, have built walls of resistance or have made inner vows. Let Jesus first set you free so you can partner with Him to set others free.

A heart of stone or making inner vows:

- defends my heart with a wall that keeps out both good and bad
- began with a sinful response to hurts or neglect
- deadens, insulates and isolates my hurting spirit
- shuts down my mental capabilities and objectivity
- prevents me from opening my spirit to be vulnerable if it might hurt
- was formed in childhood and was mostly forgotten
- blinds my spiritual eyes and deafens my spiritual ears
- isolates me; keeps me from receiving needed ministry and healing
- prevents healing on the inside even after the outward relationship is restored
- lies hidden behind a warm and friendly exterior
- stops the love and communication that is needed for my healing
- resists change for fear of increasing vulnerability
- refuses counsel and ministry for myself because "I am fine"
- but readily reaches out and ministers to others
- fears that it might melt and avoids warm, nurturing people
- triggers habitual resistant behaviors or ways of the flesh
- vowed to "never be like" the one(s) who hurt me
- vowed I will "never act like that"
- is childish or reactive when my "buttons" are pushed
- avoids feeling real emotions by focusing on compulsive behaviors
- stubbornly resists obvious steps to intimacy in relationships
- vows "I'll never share my true self with anyone again"

- would rather "get even" than reconcile with the perpetrator
- makes inner vows not to let the force shield down
- interprets transparency as a potential setup for hurt
- unintentionally blocks out the healing power of God
- prevents restoration as it agrees with strongholds or deception
- misses lost relationships but blocks reconciliation
- blames God for not healing my body, mind and emotions
- uses valuable energy to protect myself from expected criticism
- makes me feel like no one cares about me or even knows I exist
- destroys my immune system as I war against feeling my own needs
- makes me vulnerable to cheap thrills or affairs
- accuses me of being defective or undesirable
- shuts down emotions I need for real interaction of heart and soul

From this list, which is certainly not all-encompassing, we can see the negative effect inner vows make on the human heart. We pledged never to allow ourselves to be hurt again, but this just shuts up our hearts to avoid friendships and become insensitive to the needs of others. Inner vows of self-protection make our hearts less responsive to others and even to our Lord. We become afraid to love and receive love in return. Our hearts turn to stone.

Someone who has a heart of stone has to be led to renounce their inner vows and forgive themselves and others so that God can heal them and replace their hard heart with a heart that responds to His love to them and to the world around them. Once they learn to forgive, they can release any injustices to the Lord and let Him take care of their vindication in His own way and in His own time.

Prayer to renounce inner vows or for having a heart of stone

Father, I ask that you show me if I have a heart of stone. Show me the fleshly inner vows that I have used to protect my heart that stunt my growth in faith. I bring my fleshly protective structures to the foot of the Cross and ask you to bring these structures to death and raise up instead unshakable faith in your truth. Remove the walls I have built for my own protection and give me a heart of flesh that trusts you.

Because you forgive me, I choose to forgive those who have hurt and wronged me. In the past, I used them as an excuse to make inner vows and wall up my heart against any further hurt, but I only hurt myself in the process. Lord, guide them to know your love and your power. I pray for healing for our bodies, minds and emotions. From now on, I choose to give you access to all my relationships. I trust you to lead me to people who will encourage me to follow you.

Please forgive me for blaming you, Lord, when my relationships didn't work out. I see how I sabotaged my own friendships and drove wedges between me and family members. It was my fault, not yours.

Lord, I ask you to forgive me for judging others with condemnation. Show me where I have had sinful reactions to hurtful, unkind things that were done to me. Show me how I have walled out meaningful relationships and help me to receive the ministry healing I need.

I repent and ask your forgiveness for blocking your work in my life. It shames me to admit that my heart of stone also blocked others from pursuing deeper faith in you. Please restore the blessings and rewards that I have caused myself and others to miss.

Lastly, I forgive myself for blocking good and godly relationships and for treating people with suspicion rather than a welcoming attitude. I apply the blood of Jesus to my sinful reactions, humbly asking your forgiveness. I regret my foolishness for all the times I defended my sinful reactions and behaviors. My stubbornness opened doors to allow the enemy entrance to my heart.

Lord, connect me with a spiritual authority who will pray with me to break the power of the fleshly inner vows I have made. Release me to be led of the Holy Spirit in all relationships and to rest in your discernment and your choices for me. In Jesus' name, amen.

Use this space to list your inner vows and those you made have walled out.

Illegitimacy, Prenatal or Early Childhood Wounds

Many people believe they have already worked through their childhood hurts –until Mother's Day or Father's Day**.** They have endeavored to forgive, to stop blaming and condemning others or themselves. Yet on that day, their buttons are pushed again and they realize there are still walls protecting unhealed areas in their hearts.

One of the areas where many of us have experienced the most wounding, need the most prayer and are the most uneducated about is the issue of wounds caused by parent-child relationships. Many times we still have an unhealed wound that dates back to our earliest years. We may have the same mental distortions from the perspective of being the child and again from the perspective of being an adult.

Not rarely, not seldom, but OFTEN the Lord shows me that people are only partially healed because no one knew to pray about the root problem, which began before or just after birth. Whatever God reveals, He will also heal if we give Him access. He is not a time creature and He is able to heal all the way back to conception.

From research done on "crack babies," we know that even a new baby can be born with a spirit of addiction to drugs or alcohol. But how about a spirit of rejection and worthlessness or suicide because of being unwanted? Even very young children can experience a sense of abandonment when they are put up for adoption. Research also shows that unborn children can hear, taste, feel, develop attitudes, have expectations, become nervous, irritable, feel rejected, feel unwanted, reject a parent, or sense that they are not the preferred sex. Some are born with sexual confusion because a parent wanted them to be the opposite sex.

Why do we pray for healing for things that happened years ago?

We usually don't, unless they have caused hurts that still need healing. If we still struggle with the same lies of the enemy, the issue is current, not old. Studies have proved that unborn children have an understanding, learning ability, discernment and memory. They can have doubts, fears, worries, anxieties and negative attitudes about being born into this world!

Not only do unborn babies have spirits, but Hebrew mothers like Mary and Elizabeth would take the first 3-5 months off from regular chores to spend that time nurturing their unborn child's spirit with scripture, nurturing words, spiritual songs and music. Today, universities are forming classes to teach mothers and fathers how to speak life and strength to their unborn children.

Hurting people may come to you, needing healing because their mother planned or attempted an abortion. They may be depressed at that same time every year for no known reason. Thoughts may come to their mind of attempting suicide - even in the same way - with sharp instruments or drugs. These "anniversary dates" can be broken and they can be healed with prayer.

Many also feel somewhat separated from God because of the bruises left on their personal spirits by those hurtful experiences in the past. Their ability to trust was stunted. Their ability to hold their heart open in new relationships was hampered by the guilt, estrangement, rejection, fear of punishment or the neglect in their old relationships. They have been forgiven and have forgiven others, but still need the healing touch of Jesus to actually give them a new heart, in order to celebrate Mother's Day or Father's Day with joy and freedom.

Although their minds may be willing to accept God's truth and love, their personal spirits have unbelieving areas deep inside their heart. When memories are triggered, they quickly shrink back into a little "turtle shell" to hide or they harden like an "armored tank," ready to attack.

Many of us were deeply bruised, even as babies, and went into rejection before we could talk. Some of us were bitter because our home was divided by divorce, alcohol, disease or death. Unfortunately, some of our beliefs today, years later, are still based on beliefs we developed during traumatic times in our childhood.

Some of us wish that we had been better parents, but we ourselves were not taught how to really love and nurture because our parents did not model godly behavior. Through the finished work of Christ on the Cross, I declare that we can be healed and set free to comfort others! Remember, whatever the devil has stolen from us, he will have to repay several times, and God will be glorified as He is strong in the very areas that were our weaknesses.

Have you had any of these prenatal or early childhood wounds?

- I was not planned; I have to prove that I have a right to be here.
- My mother tried to abort me; each year at that time I feel depressed.
- I was always in childcare; I don't know how to bond with people.
- My father didn't care; I don't know my value or true identity.
- My mother was anxious, insecure and fearful; I have to fix it for her.
- I was afraid of my father; authorities don't have my best interest at heart.
- I was potty-trained with abuse; I am uptight, nervous and high-strung.
- I wasn't allowed to say "No;" I can't set and enforce my boundaries.
- I was not allowed to be "me;" I am defined by their values and needs.
- My father abandoned me; I am not valuable or loveable.
- My parent didn't take care of me; I have to take care of myself.
- My parent was not affectionate; I can't give and receive affection.
- I was constantly criticized and misunderstood; I don't belong.
- My parents bought me with things; I must buy people and their love.
- I could not live up to my parent's standards; I have to earn acceptance.
- I wasn't allowed or trusted to make my own choices; I am indecisive.
- My parent was a perfectionist; I procrastinate if I can't do it perfectly.

- My parents were horrible; God must not love me like He does other people.
- My father was simply not there for me; God is not there for me either.
- My parents didn't listen to me; God doesn't answer my prayers.
- I was not allowed to share my feelings; it's not okay to be real.

If you could relate to any of the above and can see how these bruises are still hurting in you today, accept Jesus' offer to take the pain out of your experiences and replace these lies with His truth. He is ready to restore your disabled heart with a new one and to enable you to relate to your Heavenly Father and others in wholeness.

Prayer for healing prenatal and early childhood wounds, illegitimacy

Prayer Minister: *Our heavenly Father, we bring this wounded soul to you for healing in such a depth as only you can touch. Speak to this one's spirit and reveal your everlasting care that you knew all about the circumstances of birth, that it was planned for in your will and you delighted in this new life, not as a mistake or an accident but as a joyous gift to the world.*

Lord, you promised that if your believers agreed *on anything according to your will and asked it in the name of Jesus, it would be done for them. We ask now that this one be set free from suffering, from rejection, depression and bitterness through the power of the resurrected Christ and the inner healing of your Holy Spirit.*

Dear Heavenly Father, I ask you in the name of Jesus, *to tell _____ that they are chosen, planned and are the apple of your eye...... that you have dreams and purposes for them....... that you came to redeem every hurtful experience ..... and to make those weak places strong..... that they are a joy and delight to you, precious in your sight.*

I ask you, Holy Spirit, to pour healing oil *into all their wounds and massage it in until they stop hurting....... to hold them until they accept your embrace and rest in your strong arms...... I ask you to rewrite their identity with the truths of your unconditional love and acceptance. Forgive them for every unforgiveness, judgment and bitter expectation that they sowed, so that they will not have to reap them. Help them to forgive themselves for buying into these lies all these years. Loose them now from all the effects of these wounds and give them new hearts and new ground to sow new seeds into.*

Dear Father, enable them to receive your heart to restore them *from all the injuries that the choices of others caused. Give them the courage to choose to receive your love, restoration and YOUR PLAN for their life now. May they know the fulfillment of being your child, who is loved and accepted, totally forgiven and fully pleasing to you. Take their shame, guilt and fears, Lord, and give them a double portion of your vision and blessing. Thank you, Jesus*

Prayer for healing prenatal and early childhood wounds, illegitimacy

*Prayer receiver: **Lord, I need your help.** I'm so used to being angry or humiliated about my birth, it will be hard to allow you to break down the walls I've built. But because of what Jesus did for me on the Cross, I choose to repent of my past actions and attitudes and let you live your life through me. Because Jesus has taken every curse on Himself, we say that the curse on illegitimate births has been broken. (Deuteronomy 23:2, Galatians 3:13)*

***I freely forgive my parents for their sin** against you and against me, for not modeling godly behavior, for not cherishing me, or for placing on me the shame of illegitimacy. I know you understand what that feels like because you were accused of the same thing.*

***In humility, I ask you to forgive my own sin of judging my parents.** In my mind, it was their fault that I felt unloved and unwanted. I thought that if they had done right, I would have been fine. Now I see that blaming others for their shortcomings or sins does not benefit anyone and is wrong in your sight.*

***I also judged other people who contributed to this false identity** by calling me names, teasing me, or gossiping about me. I lived a life of loneliness because of this, pushing family and friends away, in my false belief that if they really knew me, they wouldn't want to be near me. I'm so sorry for bringing this pain and isolation on myself and others.*

***Lord, your Word has shown me the truth** of who I really am—a redeemed child of God, adopted and chosen in love. Please forgive me for blaming you for the circumstances of my birth. This was not a surprise to you. you knew all about me and loved me in spite of everything. Remove the shame of illegitimacy from me, that I no longer struggle with the guilt of being born at the wrong time, of causing my mother health problems or being a financial burden, of feeling unwanted and unwelcome or even of being born the "wrong sex."*

***This is a hard one, Lord. I forgive myself** for any wrong actions or hurtful words spoken out of bitter anger, for hugging my false identity in clenched fists instead of coming to you for liberty and peace, for hardening my heart to your love, for believing all the lies instead of resting in your truth.*

***Father, empower me to become the person you planned for me to be**. Lift from my heart any hint of deception, any wound of having been lied to, any feeling of being betrayed by my parents and replace these with a sense of value and purpose.*

***I trust you now, to cut any cords holding me back--from conception on.** Let me see myself for who I truly am in you. Build my faith on the firm foundation of your truth and freedom. I am your treasured child, protected and loved with an everlasting love. Amen.*

Illicit Sex, Immorality and Sexual Sin

John and Paula Sandford, Founders of Elijah House International, taught that most of the problems we have today can be traced to people's negative reactions to their fathers. They said that judgmental, condemning attitudes and dishonor (even toward absent, neglectful or abusive fathers) affect how life goes for us today.

According to Deuteronomy 5:16, we are to honor our parents as God has commanded. The blessings that go along with this obedience are twofold: that we may have a long life and that it may go well with us.

Bitterly condemning a wayward father will bring the same judgment down on our heads, as the judgmental seeds we sow become a harvest of immorality later on in our own lives. Because of the law of sowing and reaping, every judgment we sow will be a harvest we reap more and later, in ourselves or others.

Besides dishonoring and judging a father who modeled immorality, there are many other reasons a person might choose immoral actions, including but not limited to immoral sexual activities. The following are just a few.

- lured or forced into illicit sex or a promiscuous lifestyle
- participated in premarital sex out of curiosity as a teen
- felt shy or unpopular and went along with the crowd to be accepted
- felt confused about true identity, so chose a new one
- felt the need to "escape" situations at home or work
- had an addictive personality hooked on the thrill of getting caught
- had trouble maintaining relationships without immoral means
- already felt rejected or devalued, immoral choices won't make things worse
- was molested, abused or fondled as a child

An immoral lifestyle can take many forms: sex outside of a faithful marriage, deliberately lying or deceiving others, spreading gossip and slander, murder without repentance and remorse, leading others into sin, amassing wealth through dishonest means, envying and stealing—anything from shoplifting to bank robbery.

It doesn't matter whether immoral people are mostly innocent or mostly guilty; the solution is the same. Whether they are in denial or confusion, self-condemning or blaming others, or even medicating their pain with food, sex or drugs, there is hope and healing in Jesus.

II Corinthians 7:10 "Godly sorrow brings repentance that leads to salvation and leaves no regret."

Godly sorrow is the key to repentance. People who are ready to renounce and forsake their immoral lifestyle, have to face their sin, ask for forgiveness and bring it to Jesus for Him to nail it to the Cross and put it to death. When they invite God to touch any area of their life that needs forgiving and healing, it is an awesome thing to see (or sense or hear) Jesus come in, identify the area, bring truth to it and then lead them into the freedom they need.

Do we know how to help those who want release from their immorality?

It's not enough to say, "The church steeple is up; people know where to go to find forgiveness." Expecting someone else to take care of the needs that we ourselves see is essentially spiritual irresponsibility.

People stuck in an immoral lifestyle already feel condemned and damaged; it's unlikely they will risk further condemnation by approaching a church that may be full of self-righteous, "perfect" Christians. It takes courage to open up and be vulnerable to others, especially when there is little or no evidence that anyone will understand or be able to help.

Many truly repentant people exhibit feelings of shame, guilt, anger, depression and helplessness regardless of the reason for their initial immoral choice; childhood rejection, abuse or forced prostitution, divorce, or simply a need to belong or be accepted by peers. They are confused, having believed the devil's lies for years, and they need to find a safe, confidential place to share.

We need trained prayer ministers who can reach out and identify with people who have been struggling alone and need supportive healing prayer.

In cases of sexual immorality, God wants to restore the joy of godly sex that was lost due to some corrupting influence. God wants us to give gifts of healing to those who were "imprinted" with traumatic understandings of sexuality because their first sexual experience was incest, molestation or a violent rape. Many believers have never told anyone, but they want to be released from the shame and fear that has isolated them and led them into wrong choices.

God wants us to give gifts of deliverance to people who are tormented by impulses to escape with sexual addictions. When we confess to one another, take responsibility and become accountable to others, we gain freedom from bondages that interfere with the deep satisfaction that only godly intimate relationships can provide.

God wants us to give gifts of forgiveness and to those who have hidden guilt from sexual sin or unspeakable regrets from abortion. Many are tormented by memories, dreams, reactions, depression, flashbacks or depression. He wants to cleanse the past, replacing the guilt and shame with honor and His gift of righteousness.

God wants to heal relationships where the woman has traded sex for "being taken care of." Men need healing of resentment because "she sold herself to me" and both need forgiveness and hope that when they confess, God will bless with a covenant relationship of true love and appreciation so that their marriage beds can be infused with holy passion and purity.

Sexual immorality usually begins with similar lies: that someone else could love us better than God, that we know what we need better than God, that His love for us is somehow inferior or at least not as good as what we get from human companions. How His loving heart must be injured when we consider His infinite love as fickle as human love that can fluctuate according to our physical attractiveness, popularity, talent or success. In truth, no one can bring us happiness like the Creator of sex and sunsets, life and beauty.

If we practice awareness of His Presence, He will speak to us as clearly as any human companion. There may be times when we wish He would speak louder, but it's really us who need to listen harder, to pay attention that still, small voice we hear during the hours we spend alone with Him.

When we are wounded by relationships, we will also be healed in relationships.

In cases of other kinds of immorality, God wants us to demonstrate faith that will give others hope that their slates can be wiped clean, thoughts can be untwisted, defilement can be cleansed, addictions overcome, and true identity realized. He wants to visit our hearts and give each of us a new identity of wholeness, as He makes our "weak places strong."

We don't have to battle sin in our own strength, try to change our lives and "turn over a new leaf" on our own; Jesus already triumphed over sin and death on Calvary. We don't have to prove ourselves worthy to God; He has made us worthy through our faith in His Son. We are free to enjoy life as God's beloved children and He keeps us on His righteous path.

When we make Jesus Lord of our lives or give Him control of our lives, He fulfills all our needs and gives us His eternal love. There is no sin too great for His grace to forgive. No matter what we have done in the past, our immoral choices can never nullify His power or His promises.

In I Corinthians 6:18, immorality is described as a sin against our own bodies. But Jesus promises to redeem every harmful experience we have ever had, taking the pain out of the memories, healing thoroughly, leaving us with wisdom and comfort that we can in turn pass on to others one day. He died so that we can live in restoration rather than regret and fulfill the destiny we were designed to fulfill.

I believe that the enemy attacks us in the very area that he knows we will be called to minister. Each of the areas where God heals us become testimonies of the supernatural power of God to bring hope and healing. God will take the shame and impart an ability to comfort others as He has comforted us.

What we give God, He will take. What He takes, He will cleanse. What He cleanses, He will use.

Prayer for forgiveness of sexual immorality

Father, I repent of sinning through sexual immorality. *I stand before you on the grounds of your infinite mercy and the finished work of the Cross of Christ. I have no other right to ask your forgiveness. In the name of Jesus, I submit my spirit, soul, my desires and my emotions to your Holy Spirit. I ask that you break any bonds or ungodly soul ties that may have been established between me and my partner(s) in sin. Through the power of Jesus in me, I renounce and refuse any inappropriate heart, mind, body, soul, and/or spirit ties. Uproot all the seeds and seedlings of sexual immorality. Cleanse my heart and my hands of all unrighteousness.*

I freely forgive my partner(s) in sin for all participation *in my act of rebellion against your holy law. The only person I hold responsible for my sin is myself. Believing I knew what I needed better than you did, I arrogantly dismissed you and your offer to give me the strength to say "no." Please bring deep healing to our damaged hearts. Father God, set us free; cleanse our minds so that our memories will not usher in bitterness to our spirits or bring up false guilt that you have already washed away.*

Lord, please forgive my judgmental attitude *toward those who tried to help me disentangle myself from the clutches of sexual immorality. In my pride, I saw them only as sinners like myself, who had no business telling me what to do. The double standard I thought I saw was my own wrong interpretation of their honest intentions, a lame excuse for justifying my sinful actions. My sin has hurt many people. Give me the courage to seek their forgiveness.*

I am so sorry I misjudged you, Father, *in falsely thinking you could never forgive me for what I had done. I deeply regret the time wasted in refusing to return to you, opting to fear your judgment rather than comprehend your love. Please help me regain the sensitivity of my conscience to hear and heed your voice.*

Finally, I forgive myself for choosing to act against your holy law *and for giving in to my weakness. I confess to letting my guard down over my thought life and of being lax in my walk with you. It was my own wrong choice to refuse the heavenly grace you offered, Lord, to resist temptation and so allow myself to degrade my standing as your child. I petition for the redemption of every person I have polluted through my sinful behavior.*

Through the finished work of Christ on the Cross, *I believe I am wholly forgiven, that you remember my sins no more. Thank you for cleansing me from all unrighteousness and delivering me from evil. From this moment on, I commit myself completely to you. By your grace, keep me holy in my spirit, soul, and body. Thank you, Father! Amen.*

Illnesses, Infirmities and Spiritual Roots

Although we are not saying that every illness or infirmity has spiritual roots, here are a few examples of some conditions that CAN have spiritual roots versus just natural causes:

heart attacks, aneurysms, strokes, hemorrhoids, varicose veins, epilepsy, cancer, leukemia, ulcerative colitis, Crohn's disease, diabetes, lupus, rheumatoid arthritis, psoriasis, histamine disorders, fibromyalgia, Chronic Fatigue Syndrome, multiple chemical sensitivities, environmental illnesses, allergies, asthma, breast cancer, ovarian and prostate cancer, PMS, osteoporosis, osteoarthritis, addictions, anxiety, stress, fear, panic attacks, alcoholism, dissociative disorder, SRA (systemic rheumatoid arthritis), STDs (sexually transmitted diseases), acne, colic, irritable bowel syndrome, thyroid dysfunctions and depression.

Mental health issues may be more easily traced from spiritual issues to physical symptoms. Witchcraft and demonic oppression can cause some mental disorders, such as bipolar and epilepsy. Rebellion against God's will can also open the door for demonic curses or influence. Once you unite with others in prayers of agreement to break demonic power then mental torment along with many mental disorders, will have to leave. (see Colossians 2:15).

Looking over the following examples may help you to understand how the body and the immune system can be affected by wrong reactions to the stress of living.

- Depression causes a reduction in the production of serotonin.
- Chronic depression may have roots in lack of self-esteem or anger, often due to a lack of nurturing in childhood that leads to a deficiency of serotonin.
- Paranoid schizophrenia is a malfunction of neurotransmitters: imbalance of serotonin, dopamine and norepinephrine and can be rooted in rejection.
- ADD (Attention Deficit Disorder) can start with a perceived personality deficiency, low self-esteem, rebellion, dealings with the occult.
- Migraines can stem from guilt, self-hatred, fear and anxiety, imbalance of serotonin, histamine, swelling of blood vessels pressing on sensitive nerves.
- Hypertension is basically cell wall rigidity causing vasoconstriction, from fear or anxiety or too much calcium.

Regardless of the illness, the answer is the same: get into agreement with your Creator. Recognize the root, repent of your negative reactions, renounce the lies, release truth and resist the temptations that would block your own health.

Scriptural promises of healing are usually conditional on our obedience. This is why we need to be discerning while praying for and visiting with those who are sick. We must also discern whether they need to forgive others or themselves or perhaps seek guidance from Holy Spirit in some area of disobedience in their lives.

Unresolved interpersonal conflicts not only lead to decreased immunity but also open the door to what we call "blocks to healing." Let me give you an example. Think of someone who has injured you badly. Feel that ping go off in your chest or stomach? Unresolved conflicts not only leave spiritual blocks in our bodies but also in our souls and spirits. We must do what we can do to resolve interpersonal conflicts.

"Etiology unknown" is a common red flag denoting that an illness may have unknown causes or spiritual roots. When there is no known medical cause or cure, it may possibly be psychosomatic or spiritual. It has been suggested that more than 80% of all illness has a spiritual root component. Actually, this should give us hope. We don't have to settle for disease management or medical cures.

Our goal is the prevention of illness by understanding how spirituality affects our body-soul-spirit connection.

It seems that we are looking everywhere for healing for our incurable "etiology unknown" or our spiritually rooted diseases. People are turning to New Age modalities for spiritual healing and allopathic medicine to manage symptoms with medications. How many have spent thousands but still have the same illness? All of our treatments for diabetes and cancer have barely extended life expectancy.

In reality, God's most perfect will is NOT to heal us; God's plan is to prevent disease in the first place through Godly responses and Godly ways of life. "My people perish because of a lack of vision (purpose, destiny, hope)" (Hosea 4:6).

I am amazed that some believers say God made them sick to teach them something. Well, then, if God gave you the illness, don't go to doctors!! Don't pray for healing if you believe that God wants you sick! What do you believe about your heavenly Father? There are about 150 references to healing or curing in the Bible. Of course, if you choose to believe that God will not heal you today, don't worry, He won't!

God's Master Health Plan is rooted in love. Deuteronomy 6:5 says, "Love the Lord your God with all your heart ... love thy neighbor ... as thyself." Often instead of being able to love ourselves, we are blocked by self-doubt, self-hate, self-rejection, self-accusation, etc. Thus we are unable to love our brothers well because we do not know how to love ourselves. I John 4:20 states, "If anyone says, 'I love God,' yet hates his brother, he is a liar. For anyone who does not love his brother, whom he has seen, cannot love God, whom he has not seen" (NIV).

There are many spiritual roots to our inability to love. Many families appear to be intact but the children are still basically fatherless. Many who are married are actually spiritual widows or widowers. Some are able to release the situation or individuals to God but some carry resentment, bitterness, jealousy, rejection, fear, judgments, etc. like a ball and chain all their lives.

Yet some are well adjusted in spite of these challenges. Some learn to respond in healthy spiritual ways instead of reacting negatively and becoming bond slaves to their own unhealthy reactions.

So we see that it's not what is done to us, but rather how we react to stress, hurts and trauma that makes us sick.

It is separation on three levels that destroys our immune systems, resulting in spiritually rooted illnesses (SRI):

1. Separation from God. (Father God doesn't love me like _____.) Lie: God made me sick because He is trying to teach me something.
2. Separation from self. (Do you like yourself? An autoimmune disease usually has roots of self-hatred or self-bitterness.) Lie: I will never forgive myself.
3. Separation from others. (Is hurt just a memory or do you still carry the emotions of hate or resentment or bitterness?) Lie: They ruined my life.

Healing begins with making peace with God, self and others. You can begin to prosper body, soul and spirit as you renew your mind (Romans 12:1). When the church attacks itself, it is opening the door for spiritual autoimmune disease in the whole church body. Bad roots grow bad fruit, both in individuals and corporately.

Here are some blocks to healing and some spiritual roots to illnesses:
- Strife while praying and fasting; God blocks His ears (Isaiah 58).
- Blaming others for our sinful reactions versus taking responsibility.
- Fear that prevents love, power and a sound mind (I Timothy 1:7).
- Many are weak, sickly and die because they do not discern the body rightly (I Corinthians 11:30).
- Roots of bitterness spring up to trouble you and defile others (Hebrews 12:15).
- "Eye for an eye" living; philosophy of "Don't get mad—get even" (done away with by Jesus in Matthew 5:38-44).
- Cursing yourself: "This is killing me! I am sick and tired of ..."
- Grudges, resentments held against one another prevent worship in spirit and truth (Matthew 5:22).

Many today are still settling for substitutes for healing or for palliative care, even though adverse reactions to prescriptions are the fourth highest cause of death in the United States. Side effects can be worse than the illness. For example, blood pressure medications and Prozac can cause impotence, which certainly does not help one to feel better about himself!

Our discernment and conscience can also be dulled by prescription medications. We have emphasized nutrition more than resolving our conflicts, maintaining healthy relationships and repentance for our negative reactions. These issues have left harmful residue in our lives that block our path to healing and health.

Proverbs 17:22 says that "a merry heart does good like a medicine but a broken spirit dries up the bones." God's plan is healing broken hearts, delivering us from captivity, healing our illnesses and setting us free from bondages (Isaiah 61). Where did this plan break down? You might ask yourself, "Who broke my heart? When did I begin to be separated from myself, others and God? What is blocking my ability to love?"

Looking for the spiritual roots in the Bible, we find that there is cause and effect in the spiritual realm just as there is in the natural realm. Just as laws of gravity are impartial, so are spiritual laws. We reap what we sow, unless we repent. What we condemn, we reap more of—more and later than we sow.

Carlotta's Testimony of Healing

When I first married, I was a strong young nurse who had been able to consistently work six night-shifts a week. Little did I know that one of my patients had tuberculosis. The doctors did not test for it until after she had died. By that time all the staff were infected and forced to take a prescription, INH, to prevent TB from developing. Back then, they did not know to monitor the damage to our livers, and I became very sick—not from TB, but from the INH. This was the beginning of my damaged immune system.

Before long, I had miscarried my first child, had to resign from nursing and was requiring about eleven hours of sleep a night. Back pain plagued me and, unlike pain from a temporary injury, this back pain would last for many years. Chiropractic was a tremendous help, as muscle testing showed that 2/3 of my muscles were now weak. I had to stop my birth control pills as they made my body even more toxic.

Where I was once working overtime without giving it a thought, now just walking up a flight of stairs seemed like work. For years, I wondered what was wrong.

Finally, I was diagnosed with **Chronic Fatigue Syndrome**. CFS is a persistent, relapsing or debilitating fatigue that does not improve with bed rest and reduces or impairs average daily activity level by more than 50 percent. I had most of the symptoms: concentration problems, sore throat, joint and muscle pains, interrupted sleep, post-exertion malaise, brain fog and the feeling that I had a virus. No amount of rest enabled me to feel rested.

(Chronic Fatigue Syndrome is usually rooted in self-esteem issues due to internal conflict between your own soul and spirit. I was striving was, driven…to perform, to know my true identity, to prove myself, to earn approval or to get away from a cloud of guilt. The inability to love myself was rooted in an inability to receive God's love. CFS is usually accompanied by hypoglycemia (low blood sugar) by pushing ourselves with sugar and caffeine maybe.

But that wasn't all. I also developed **fibromyalgia**, which is a chronic disorder that causes pain and stiffness throughout the tissues that support and move the bones and joints. Pain and localized tender points occur in the muscles, particularly those that support the neck, spine, shoulders and hips. The disorder includes widespread pain, fatigue and sleep disturbances. Fibromyalgia had me hurting around the clock.

In fibromyalgia, there is an inability to "rest" and the muscles carry the tension continuously without relief. While I may have looked calm on the outside, I listened to spirits of anxiety, fear, distrust, worry and doubt that attacked me on the inside. I could go to sleep right away but could not rest well. I carried tension in my shoulders, my back and feet muscles twenty-four hours a day for years and years.

My endocrinologist then prescribed Synthroid because I had developed another illness: hypothyroidism. It is often rooted in anxiety and fear. My adrenal glands attempted to compensate, but eventually, they became weak too. Because my endocrine system was now out of balance, my gynecologist put me on injections to prevent the recurrence of ovarian cysts. Because my immune system was compromised, I developed new problems like allergies, sinusitis, kidney infections and a hip joint infection.

As we attack and accuse ourselves spiritually in self-rejection, self-hatred, and self-bitterness, our body turns against itself as well. Instead of the white blood cells attacking infection as they were designed to do, they attack our own cells, paving the way for various disorders, including chronic inflammation, heart and autoimmune diseases, and even cancer.

As I pushed myself to try to be productive again, new calcium problems left me with bunions, spurs, arthritis and a severe case of osteoporosis with scoliosis and kyphosis. I was tested at Emory University Hospital in Atlanta, GA., but they could not find the cause. Probably due to the medications, I developed gastritis, overly thin blood and low blood pressure. Then there were a few other ailments "common to man."

Fortunately, I was introduced to Shaklee vitamins and their nutritional teaching. Dr. Shaklee said that your body rebuilds itself every three to four years and I began to rebuild mine. I chose Shaklee vitamins because they have live enzymes, have never been heated and are made from real dehydrated food instead of synthetic petroleum products.

The vitamins helped a great deal, but I still hobbled along pacing myself and had lots of TLC from understanding family and friends.

At this point, many people settle for being satisfied with their progress in healing. Yes, they are still somewhat sick or in pain (and may enjoy the attention they get from being sick.) Their pain may seem to fulfill some deep inner need that is not being met. If you ask them, they will say that above all they want to be well, but do they really mean it? Here is where a trained prayer minister can help people discern between true illness and a tendency toward hypochondria.

Unfortunately, I was not a hypochondriac; I had twenty-four diagnoses and documentation to prove it. I had prayed for my healing with only occasional symptom relief until I began to hear about the spiritual roots of illnesses. If there was a spiritual solution, I wanted to align my thinking with truth from the Word of God and get into a position to receive the healing that Jesus died to provide for me.

The Word of God showed me that my physical healing was also provided with my salvation. "He forgives all my sins and heals all my diseases" (Psalm 103:3).

One day as I listened to a Christian tape, I heard how Jesus had to fight the devil even though He was perfect. He declared, "It is written..." for forty days (Matthew 4) and was victorious. Interesting—even Jesus had to fight a good fight using the Word of God! I realized that I shouldn't immediately feel condemned if I found out that my illnesses had spiritual roots. Knowing Jesus had to fight using scripture suddenly made me realize there was hope in declaring Truth from the Word of God. In fact, Jesus had already paid for my healing by His death on the Cross. Prayer was a lot less expensive than doctors and prescriptions.

I began to study how to tear down personal fleshly strongholds by praying in agreement with scripture. Next, I collected sixty pages of Bible verses to renew my mind and declared them as I prayed daily against one of my personal strongholds: bitterness (unforgiveness, resentment, judgmental attitudes) jealousy, unloving spirits, rejection cycles, fear, accusation, religious spirits and pride. I also prayed against assignments of witchcraft against me and my family. As I continued to agree with scripture, I began to make some real progress in healing.

I have to be careful here. I don't mean to say that spiritual factors are the sole cause for all diseases. Physical illness is not necessarily a deficiency in character or an indicator of disobedience or unbelief. In John 9:3, Jesus said that not all infirmity is because someone sinned.

Our fleshly structures and illnesses can have multiple spiritual causes: generational sins and curses, ungodly beliefs, partially healed hurts, judgments on others, bitter expectations, inner vows, the sins we have sowed, rebellion against God's plans, inability to receive God's love and a false identity from believing the lies of the enemy.

In my case, exposure to TB + INH = liver damage = compromised immune system. Driving myself, false guilt, performance anxiety, etc. was probably more a result of poor health than the cause of it. I prayed scriptures against the strongholds in order to cooperate with God for my healing.

I certainly don't have all the answers. I can relate to the blind man who said, "ALL I know is that I was blind and now I can see" (John 9:25). I just know Jesus died to heal all of our diseases and I chose to line my thinking up with His Truth and to receive His healing—body, soul and spirit.

Thank God, the medical world is finally recognizing the body-soul-spirit connections! Research studies have proved the power of prayer and meditation on God's Word to heal. Hopefully, the church will minister more effectively to the body, soul and spirit too.

As we are beginning to believe God's promises again, He forgives all our sins and heals all our diseases, as stated in Psalm 103:3. 1 Thessalonians 5:23 clearly points out the body-soul-spirit connection. Because of these truths, we can pray for the healing of incurable illnesses with integrity. We can expect to discern spiritually rooted illnesses along with their spiritual roots.

Doctors had officially diagnosed me with many illnesses, like hypothyroidism, ovarian cysts, gastritis, allergies, sinusitis, low blood pressure, kidney infections, bladder infections, hip infection, weak adrenal gland function, hemorrhaging, fibromyalgia, chronic fatigue, bunions, spurs, painful calcium deposits, arthritis, plantar warts, common warts, many fractures and more.

I give God the credit for supernaturally healing me of all the above. The key was simple. I chose relevant scriptures and began to pray like Jesus did: "It is written ... It is written ..." After 3 months of declaring the scriptures with faith believing I was healed, I suddenly realized most of my symptoms were gone!!!!! I was healed by agreeing with and declaring the truth of God's Word. Whether I was sick from natural exposure to illness, ungodly reactions and attitudes or side-effects from medications, God healed it all! The Bible has not lost its power. Truth from the Word of God never comes back void! Here are some Bible verses on healing:

- Psalm 34:19: He delivers us from all our afflictions
- Psalm 103:3: He heals all of our diseases
- Psalm 107:20: He healed them with His Word
- Isaiah 35:3-6: He heals weak hands, feeble knees, fearful hearts, blind eyes, deaf ears, lame legs and mute tongues
- Isaiah 40:13: He renews our strength
- Isaiah 53:4-5: He bore our griefs, carried our sorrows, our chastisement and we are healed by His wounds
- Isaiah 57:18-19: He heals and gives comfort
- Jeremiah 17:14: Heal me, Lord, I shall be healed indeed
- Matthew 9:35: He heals sickness and disease
- Luke 4:18: He is anointed to heal the brokenhearted
- Luke 13:12-13: He heals our infirmities
- James 5:15: The prayer of faith shall save the sick
- I Peter 2:24: By His stripes (wounds) we are healed

When Jesus died on the Cross for us, He provided for both our salvation and our physical, mental and emotional healing. It has always been Christ's passion to provide for our healing and salvation.

Isaiah 53:4-5: "Surely He took up our infirmities and carried our sorrows. He was pierced for our transgressions, He was crushed for our iniquities; the punishment that brought us peace was upon Him, and by His wounds we are healed."

Prayer to heal the spiritual roots of illnesses (prayed with a partner or team)

Father God, I worship you as the Source of all love and power in the universe. I plead the blood of the Lord Jesus Christ over me, my pets, possessions, property, everything and everybody I care about. I surrender to your authority in every area of my life and receive my inherited spiritual power and authority. I confess my sins and ask you to reveal any unrighteousness that would give the devil a foothold in me.

In the mighty name of Jesus Christ, the Anointed One, my Lord and Master, I cancel every assignment of the enemy to affect me, block or hinder me. I break every agreement, known or unknown, that I have had with the enemy and refuse him any further involvement in my life. I say that no demon can even see or hear what I am praying or doing here today. I loose the Spirit of truth on all demonic influences so that they will know and proclaim Jesus Christ is Lord.

Father, you alone are all-knowing, all-powerful and are present everywhere. I receive your keen discernment, words of knowledge, words of wisdom and prophetic words to discern any demonic spirit in me, on me or around me. In the name of Jesus, and because of your blood and finished work on the Cross, I say that every demon has to leave me and go to the dry, uninhabited places and never come back. I declare that only the Holy Spirit can affect me and I am in a safe place in Him where no weapon can harm me.

I welcome you, Holy Spirit, and submit myself to your strategies to enforce the Word of God in my sphere of influence. I ask for wisdom, knowing you will give it liberally. I choose to partner with you, Spirit of truth, and release you to fall upon me, in wisdom, knowledge, understanding and truth to make me free in you.

Holy Spirit, I receive your conviction of sin and deception. I repent for every way I have given any place to demonic spirits and I forgive all who may have influenced me to sin. Show me my areas of weakness that need your life-changing power.

Please forgive me, Father, for the times I foolishly blamed you for not healing my illnesses. I didn't realize all the work you needed to do in my life before healing could take place. It wasn't only my body that needed your touch; it was also my heart, mind, and will. I invite you to go into the back rooms of my soul and heal, deliver or cleanse everything that is not of Father God.

I forgive myself *for the pain and limitations I have allowed demons to inflict upon me when I did not repent of my sin right away. I renounce mindsets that allowed demonic influences to build strongholds that blocked the knowledge of you and your truth, O God. I pray for both healing and deliverance. (See Luke 1-9.)*

Now, through the power of the shed blood of Jesus Christ*, I own my spiritual authority and command every demonic spirit to leave me now. I command them to go to the dry uninhabited places and never come back. No longer am I under the influence of the enemy and his lies.*

I choose the crucified life and take my flesh to the Cross. *I renounce all ungodly beliefs, fleshly inner vows, judgments, bitter expectations and word curses spoken by me or over me and ask for the fullness of the Holy Spirit to fill me today.*

I ask you to help me write new godly beliefs *that align with your will, way and timing for me. I receive your faith to believe you will fulfill your plans and purposes through me, as I am 100% healed. Thank you for creative miracles that will enable me to be a testimony and glory to your name. Lord Jesus, as I speak your Truth, send your Word and heal me from head to toe. Amen.*

You can use this space to list all of the healings and creative miracles you need.

Judgmental or Critical Attitude

"Set a guard over my mouth. O Lord; keep watch over the door of my lips" (Psalm 141:3). There are few of us who can say honestly that we have never gossiped about someone else or tried to make ourselves look superior by cutting another person down. Whether we use words, actions, or attitudes, it's easy to fall into the trap of being both judge and jury.

Since the devil's main goal is to undermine God and His Kingdom of righteousness, it should come as no surprise that the devil is out to undermine us too. The enemy sets many traps for believers, but one of the biggest ones involves the tendency to criticize or judge another person.

In Luke 6:37, the Bible warns against a judgmental attitude. We will be judged in the same way we judge others. James 4:11-12 says not to speak evil against others because when we criticize others we set ourselves up as a judge when the only true Judge is God. Who are we to be sitting in His chair?

There is a difference between judging and discerning.

We are given the authority to discern between right and wrong in order to discern sin in our own lives and in the lives of other believers. But we are not to use discernment to blast another Christian and rake him over the coals. We are to restore the repentant believer gently, always being on guard against sin in our own lives and not to think we are above others (Galatians 6:1-3).

James 5:16 teaches that we should confess our faults to one another, rather than giving the impression that we are perfect Christians who never succumb to temptation. There is great strength in a small group of close friends who humbly admit their weaknesses and pray for one another.

Very gifted spiritual people can easily fall prey to the deceptions of critical spirits. True spiritual discernment can suddenly become a critical judgment or condemnation if we walk after the flesh. Prophetic intercession can give way to accusation if we begin to agree with the enemy, who would say our security is threatened by what someone else does or says.

The enemy sets us up to speak his lies about others by making us afraid of their impact on us. Instead of seeing others as God sees them, we listen to the deceptions of the enemy. We rebel against what God says about them and speak what demons say about them. Instead of loosing them from sin, we bind them to it as we speak the devil's deceptions, accusations and criticism.

How does the enemy tempt you to criticize? He hooks into a fleshly area and tempts you to think your needs will be better met if you criticize. A critical spirit cannot attach unless there is critical attitude in you that will agree with it.

Here are some ways the devil may speak through believers:

- speaking false accusations
- repeating gossip or an innuendo
- exposing another's weak points to others
- criticizing, not motivated by love
- judging another's hidden motivations
- twisting the truth to a critical slant
- distancing ourselves from another's "sin"
- bruising another versus bearing all things
- defining others by their sinful strongholds
- destructive vs. constructive criticism
- helping the enemy accuse the brethren
- minister condemnation vs. intercession
- tearing down versus restoring one who falls
- assuming we are another's judge and jury
- undermining their authority to lead
- choosing leaders then rebelling against them
- dishonoring authority figures or parents
- sowing criticism but expecting to reap good
- undermining those whom we envy
- proudly criticizing those who curse us
- quenching Holy Spirit's work or resisting
- reacting sinfully to immaturity in others
- claiming we are victimized by them
- name calling and labeling it prayer
- discrediting someone's success
- judging other's actions versus perceiving their need
- wishing punishment on them instead of grace
- competing with others for righteousness
- sabotaging by suggesting suspicions
- stirring up strife by telling tales
- tearing down versus building another's confidence
- confronting even though God said to pray
- coming against people versus renouncing critical spirits
- speaking failure over their vision or calling
- activating demons by agreeing with them
- speaking of another's past as if it is still current
- refusing to overcome evil with good
- refusing to let love cover a multitude of sins

- judging them for the same sin over and over
- refusing to bless those who persecute you
- slandering with either facts or lies
- judging by their natural ability versus discerning anointing
- envying others, envying God's blessing on others
- taking offense when God chooses others
- rejecting or excluding the one who succeeds
- refusing to forgive and forget another's sin
- accusing others but excusing ourselves
- projecting our standards onto others
- imagining others have our sinful attitudes
- expecting more from others than ourselves
- forgiving others as poorly as we forgive ourselves
- refusing to focus on Christ in us or in others
- refusing to minister the heart of God
- driving others back to "salvation by works"
- refusing to humbly impart the grace of God
- proudly presenting ourselves as another's "fixer"
- competing with the new insights of another
- upstaging the work of the Holy Spirit
- believing the worst without checking it out
- rebuking an elder without respect

Do any of these sound familiar in your life?

Prayer for the release of a judgmental or critical attitude

*Lord, I repent of speaking criticism instead of intercession and choose to operate in true spiritual discernment. I **confess** my sin (and if appropriate, my ancestor's sin) of judgmental and condemning attitudes. I **ask forgiveness** for any way I have doubted, criticized, judged or blamed you, God. I **forgive** those who contributed to my forming these judgmental critical attitudes including myself. I ask you, Lord, to **forgive** me for living my life by them and for any way I have been a stumbling block to others and defiled them. I **forgive** myself for misusing my discernment to tear down instead of to build up. I **renounce** and **break** my agreements with deception, the power of darkness, and with demons. In Jesus' Name, I **cast out** all critical judgmental spirits to the dry uninhabited place, to never come back.*

Once you have cast out all demonic influences through the authority of the name of Jesus Christ, ask the Holy Spirit to keep watch over your words and actions. Giving God complete control of your life, mind and tongue will ensure that you always "speak the truth in love" when dealing with others so that you build up others instead of tearing them down (Ephesians 4:15-16).

Legalistic Thinking

Legalistic thinking bears the stigma of fear: fear of losing your own salvation, fear of rebuke from others if you don't follow all the rules, fear of not being able to adequately obey a self-imposed list of dos and don'ts, fear of not being able to please God no matter how hard you try.

Perhaps your parents brought you up under the strict umbrella of legalistic thinking, or maybe you attended a church with legalistic leanings. Some churches allow no freedom in spirit to worship God. They insist that their members follow a pattern of the accepted form of worship. There may also be an enforced lifestyle with little or no joy or life. Most sermons covertly or overtly give the message that Jesus saved you just so that now you can try to please God with your good works even better.

They seem to imply that if you are busy keeping the law, you will bear more fruit for God. In other words, if you obey their standards, you are guaranteed to live a good Christian life. You may get worn out trying to force yourself (and other poor souls) into their mold so you can earn acceptance and feel worthy of carrying the name of Christ, but that's okay with them. In their eyes, you are producing good fruit as you "burn out" for God even though you are actually getting exhausted trying to conform to their fruit-bearing standard.

This is not the way God says we bear fruit for Him.

Striving to conform to a set standard of Christianity in our own efforts is useless. Keeping the law makes us obedient to the law rather than to God's freedom. John 15 makes it clear that if we abide in Him, we will automatically be fruitful. There's the guarantee—life in Christ that flows through us and out to others.

Romans 7:4-6 tells us something that is seldom heard from the pulpit of legalistic churches: if we become dead to earning righteousness by keeping the law and we are joined to Jesus Christ, we bring forth fruit for God out of our oneness with Him as our Bride Groom. Good fruit is conceived and born out of His strength, not our own.

According to Romans 5:6-8, before we invite Christ into our lives, we are helpless sinners, enemies of God and bankrupt of anything we could bring to Him in hopes of making us worthy of forgiveness. We have to come to the realization that our salvation is totally dependent on receiving abundant grace and the free gift of righteousness through Jesus Christ (Romans 5:17). It's nothing that we do. Jesus has done it for us. Likewise, we bear good fruit as we release Jesus to live through us.

Romans 5:20 says that when we sin, God's grace abounds even more than our sin. It can be hard to grasp the enormity of the grace of God that abounds "even more" than our sin. This is great when we see our need for grace, but can we see our need for God's grace to overcome legalism? After all, it only seems fair that those who are trying to do good works should get more grace. Shouldn't doing good works earn more righteousness in our heavenly bank account? What does Jesus want from us? Don't we have a debt to pay to Him for all that He has done for us?

If we insist on following legalistic thinking, we are like the synagogue leader in Luke 10:25-29. He was a lawyer, a scholar of the Jewish law, who knew every nuance of the law thoroughly. When he asked Jesus what he needed to do to inherit eternal life, Jesus told him he could keep on keeping the law. But the man knew this was an impossible task and sought to justify himself.

The entire Sermon on the Mount emphasized that people could take the law route to God if they wanted to try, but they couldn't skip anything, they couldn't be imperfect or even have bad thoughts (Matthew 5, 6, 7). Jesus warned them that they had to do a better job than the self-righteous, legalistic Pharisees sitting among the group of listeners. In other words, it can't be done (Romans 3:20).

What we could do for ourselves in our own strength, Jesus did for us.

He kept the law of God perfectly and so fulfilled it entirely. The sixth chapter of Romans is all about how believers have died with Jesus, were buried with Him and then raised to live a life free from the law of sin and death.

Romans 7:1-6 parallels this law of sin and death with the law of marriage. A wife is bound to her husband as long as he lives, but once he is dead she is free to marry again. We are no longer bound by the law and the "old man" because our old nature has been put to death with Jesus on the Cross. Old things are passed away and all things are made new (II Corinthians 5:17).

Of course, our flesh (that survival instinct that yells, "Me first!") remembers the old programming when we were bound or married to the law, But we don't owe that "old man" anything; the old nature is dead. We are joined to Jesus now. We are filled with His life and that life in us will birth His fruit.

Why is it we slip back soooo quickly into thinking we have to earn our acceptance and approval from God? Or that there is even any way we can?

So then what does Jesus really want from us?

He wants us to acknowledge our old husband, righteousness by the law, is truly dead and to be married to Him (Romans 7:4). He has come as our Bridegroom and wants us to finally accept His proposal to provide us with a new identity as His bride. He doesn't want us to live our old life "for" Him; that old life is dead. He wants us to receive His new life in and through us.

Jesus said He came to give us a whole new personal spirit. "He that is joined to the Lord is one spirit with Him" (I Corinthians 6:17). In John 17, He prayed that we would be one with Him as He is one with the Father. Is that possible? It is not only possible, but if we will die to legalism and trying to earn our own righteousness, we can receive our new identity and be joined to Jesus to partner with Him. The whole point of Christianity is dying to the old man who married us to the law and being joined as a new creation to Jesus, Who bears fruit for God through us.

The entire first chapter of Ephesians lists what Jesus has done for us, that no good work on our part could ever do. He alone has made us holy and blameless. Apart from Jesus living His life through us, we can't live the Christian life at all.

Legalistic thinking is also separated thinking.

We think that we can and must do good works in our own strength and then offer it to Jesus, Who is "way out there" in heaven someplace. Instead, we should be thinking that He lives within us, ready to do good works through us in His power.

Jesus just asks that we present ourselves to Him and He will prove what is the perfect will of God as we let Him live His life through us (Romans 12:1-2). As we die to our own separated strength to keep the law and allow God to join us to Jesus, He will bear good fruit through us. We will be brides, impregnated with His life, and a new birth of good fruit will come forth. In fact, it always takes a union to cause reproduction of new life, doesn't it?

Christ in us is the mystery of the gospel and our hope of glory (Colossians 1:27).

Prayer for freedom from legalistic thinking

Father, I thank you for your good law *and for the understanding I now have to see how I abused it. I missed the goodness and blessing built into your law, seeing only an endless list of dos and don'ts. In striving to keep this list, I see now that I was trying to gain your approval and a good standing among your people.*

Mostly, I was seeking my own justification, that by being "good" in my own eyes, I was somehow better than other Christians. I didn't see that it was my own sin that turned your good law into an impossible burden. I didn't see your law as coming from a loving Father, designed to keep me, as your beloved child, close to your grace and strength.

Please forgive me for judging others for not following your law as well as I thought they should. Let my self-righteousness be exchanged for your righteous life in me. I'm so sorry for looking down on others when they failed to keep your law perfectly. I didn't understand how sowing and reaping affected my life, how my judgment locked me into the same attitudes I condemned in others. I became a mirror for what I most disliked.

I forgive myself for my own fruitless endeavors *and for relying more on people than on you and then becoming angry, bitter, and disillusioned when they let me down.*

Lord, forgive me for the times I blamed you *for being such a harsh taskmaster, insisting on holiness in your children. I didn't understand that holiness could only come through the power of your Holy Spirit and that He was ready and willing to live out that holiness in me.*

I saw your law as many things: a rigid pattern to be followed *with fearful steps, a way to earn favor with you and other Christians, a path to my own self-righteousness. But your law showed me what my sin truly is and that I was doomed to failure in my own strength. Now I understand that, because of the cross of Christ and His blood shed for me, there is no kind of condemnation due those who follow you (Romans 8:1).*

By the resurrection power in me, I am now free *to choose to let you live out your law of love in me so that others will see your goodness flowing through me and want to follow you as well. You will do through me what I could not do for myself.*

Thank you for this freedom and for the truth of your good law *and how it offers your children security and safety as they trust in you. It isn't an impossible burden; it is a mighty gift from an all-powerful and loving God. Thank you for showing me this truth that sets me free. Amen.*

You can use this space to write a note to self, giving yourself permission not to perform to earn acceptance and approval through legalism.

Lonely, Unloved or Rejected

Did you know that Jesus said the "greatest commandment" included loving yourself? In Luke 10:27 He said to "Love the Lord your God with all your heart and with all your soul and with all your strength and with all your mind; and your neighbor as yourself." Yes, your ability to LOVE is far more important than any gift, talent, skill, calling or impressive resume.

God's plan is for us to love Him and to love others *and* to love ourselves. His plan is to reconcile us to Himself, to others and to ourselves in a new oneness. The problem is that most of us have not received Father God's love and do not know how to love ourselves. We measure ourselves by our performance and we tend to measure others with the same performance-based yardstick.

Can we truly love our neighbor as much as we love ourselves if we really don't feel loved but rather feel lonely or rejected because of a false belief, an inner vow or bitter root of expecting the worst from people?

The devil's plan has always been to separate us from others, from God, from ourselves and ultimately to destroy our ability to love. He seeks to erode our love by attacking us through others and through our own minds. Usually, how we see God has been distorted by our perceptions of human father figures around us. If our earthly fathers have failed us, we may anticipate that God will do the same. Remember, the devil's goal is **to block us from seeing God's love and seeing ourselves as God sees us.**

The devil also speaks through "unloving spirits" that barrage us with lies about who we are or what people think of us and lies about what God thinks of us.

When I went to Pleasant Valley Ministries in 1998-1999, Dr. Henry Wright taught us about unloving spirits that are assigned to undermine our self-esteem and our ability to trust in a loving God. I took copious notes, but I have summarized a brief working definition for each one. Test yourself for these spirits. Do you relate to any of these voices who would prevent you from loving yourself?

- **self-rejection** - Says I am the non-person of the family, calls me names, says my opinions and preferences are not important.
- **self-hatred** - Uses my voice to tell me that I hate myself, then my body/soul/spirit connection reacts with infirmities, autoimmune illnesses and diseases of unknown causes.
- **competition** - Says I must always win and manipulate for self-promotion. I cannot defer to others easily as Jesus taught in Matthew 5,6 and 7.
- **self-pride** - Causes me to lust for a position, a relationship or material things to complete myself or to maximize my potential.

- **selfishness** - Makes me hypersensitive to whether I am getting my share (i.e. of the love) when I want it and how I want it.
- **exalted "I" and "I will"** - The devil suggests that I can do it independently, by myself, in my own strength, with my own talents, gifts and resources like Lucifer did in Ezekiel 28.
- **rebellion** - I reject God's original choices for me: i.e. my IQ, appearance, body, parents, race, birthplace, etc.
- **attention-getting** - I demand attention from people before they even have a chance to offer their love or at least before they can reject me. I am easy prey for counterfeit love.
- **excessive talkativeness** - Drives me to dominate conversations with my opinions, needs, feelings, knowledge or just chit-chat.
- **insecurity** - Sets me up to be easily offended, to overreact, to feel devalued and to take things personally.
- **fabricated self** - I prematurely create a niche for myself and tend to project myself as more qualified than I really am.
- **unworthiness** - I fear that I am unworthy of blessing (based on my performance.)
- **self-deprecation** - I torture myself by calling myself names, cutting myself down (i.e. with humor), minimizing my strengths and maximizing my faults.
- **self-comparison** - Causes me to measure myself negatively in contrast to the progress, blessings, gifts, talents and accomplishments of others.
- **self-assertion** - I am not just asking for what I need; I demand with pressure, control or manipulation.
- **self-deception** - I rationalize that sinful reactions, beliefs and behaviors are okay; I defend them when others try to tell me the truth.
- **self-questioning** - I constantly doubt God's truth about myself, my perceptions, and my abilities and tend to believe that I will choose unwisely.
- **self-indulgence** - I am addicted to ineffective coping mechanisms, like overspending, binge eating, kleptomania, drug abuse or therapy that "never seems to take effect."
- **self-idolatry** - I obsess about my agenda, my needs, my successes and my glory instead of God's purposes and plans.
- **perfection** - Says that I can only feel good about myself if my performance meets the standards of others, my own unreasonably high standards or is perfect (and of course, it is not).
- **self-accusation** - Refuses to acknowledge the progress or growth in my life; identifies me with my past failures and projects my past onto my future.
- **self-condemnation** - I "am" a failure, inadequate, inferior, unattractive, to blame and unlovable. I believe that I am shameful because I am basically defective.
- **self-bitterness** - I keep a record of my failures, withholding forgiveness from myself, and resenting myself for being imperfect.
- **unforgiveness toward self** - False humility tells me that it is more holy not to forgive myself and that I should punish myself.

- **need for approval** - I try to earn "unconditional love and acceptance" (oxymoron) by meeting the supposed expectations of others.
- **not necessary, not needed** - I agree with devaluating condescending lies and conclude that I am not valuable and that my contributions are not worthwhile.
- **self-doubt and unbelief** - I disqualify myself, settle for less, believe I am the most unlikely to be chosen and cannot believe that God could love me.
- **self-denial** - I tend to exclude myself, isolate myself and to suffer instead of asking for what I need..
- **self-absorption** - I obsess on analyzing myself, my interests, my needs, figuring out my own way or ruminating about my issues.
- **self-abuse** - I blame myself, drive myself with drugs or unrealistic demands, deny basic needs, volunteer for martyrdom, victimize myself, am addicted to self-destructive behaviors.
- **self-pity** - I accept the identity of a victim, stuck in the past, who is not healed and I insist that I should be pitied rather than believe that I can release my pain to Jesus to heal.
- **self-sabotage** - I "shoot myself in the foot" because I am afraid to receive promotion, compliments or great opportunities. I disqualify myself when I am afraid of succeeding; I push love away for fear of inevitable rejection.
- **self-annihilation or elimination** - I have a plan to kill myself, make suicidal gestures or actually attempt suicide.

If you find that these spirits have implanted lies in your mind, you can pray, repent and renounce your agreements with them. Use the Cross Walk Prayer or the prayer at the end of this section as a guide.

Now, it is equally important to receive God's truth about you instead of each one of these lies. You need to know and accept how much God loves you. If you will look yourself in the eye (in the mirror) and agree with God, He will begin to delete the lies and replace them with His truth about you.

Are you familiar with the "Father's Love Letter" online? If you will declare Father's truths from this love letter for forty days, God will "re-parent" you and renew your mind! The Word of God will arm you with truth to defeat the accuser and you will walk in new confidence and victory! Try it! See the classic Father's Love Letter online at www.fathersloveletter.com.

Prayer to dispel feeling unloved, lonely, or rejected

Prayer minister: Dear Heavenly Father, I ask you in the name of Jesus *to tell _____ that they are chosen, planned and are the apple of your eye, that you have dreams and purposes for them, that you came to redeem every hurtful experience, to take the pain and shame and to make those weak places strong. Invite them to climb up in your lap and hear that they are a joy and a delight to you, precious in your sight.*

I ask you, Holy Spirit, to pour healing oil into all their wounds *and massage it in until they stop hurting, to hold them until they accept your embrace and rest in your strong arms. I ask you to rewrite their identity with the truths of your unconditional love and acceptance.*

Forgive them for every time they have withheld forgiveness *and for every judgment and bitter expectation they have sowed so that they will not have to reap them in their own life. Help them to forgive themselves for buying into these lies all these years. In the mighty name of Jesus, loose them now from all the effects of these wounds, and give them new hearts and fresh ground to sow new seeds into.*

Dear Father, enable them to receive your heart *to restore them from all the injuries and feelings of unworthiness from the past. Give them the courage to choose to receive your love, restoration and YOUR PLAN for their life now. May they know the fulfillment of being your child, who is loved and accepted, totally forgiven and fully pleasing to you. Take their shame, guilt and fears, Lord, and give them a double portion of your vision and blessing. Thank you, Jesus.*

Prayer receiver: Dear Lord Jesus, I recognize *that I have been believing the lies of the devil, and I repent for coming into agreement with him instead of believing your truth about me as I read in your Word. I forgive those who taught me these lies. I ask forgiveness for judging them, not forgiving them, for my own sin, and for doubting you, Lord.*

In the name of Jesus, *I renounce and break all agreements with the devil's lies and command all these unloving spirits to leave me, to go to dry, uninhabited places and never come back. I ask you to fill every empty place in me with you, with your life and your peace.*

I choose to receive God's truth about me: *Because of what Jesus Christ has done for me on the Cross, God sees me as righteous, holy and blameless in His sight. I stand on the truth of Ephesians 1:4 and Romans 5:18.*

I agree with God's truth that I am precious, *loveable, totally forgiven and unconditionally loved and accepted, completely apart from my performance. I choose to receive all the blessings that I have previously been afraid or reluctant to receive.*

Father, I ask you to restore me to your purposes and plans. *Please "restore all the years the locust have eaten." Father God, you love me and have promised you will never leave me. Amen.*

Love, True or False?

What do you do when you aren't being loved like you want to be loved? What if they show their love through touch or giving their time, but you want to be appreciated through words, loyalty or service instead? Or worse yet, did someone tell you they loved you while they abused you, implying that love includes abuse?

Did you learn a false definition of love because no one loved you rightly in your childhood? Perhaps you bought into the Hollywood version of love, with all the bells and whistles. In the real world, a symphony orchestra doesn't actually start playing on your first kiss.

Are you busy acting out love for your spouse instead of being you? Are you trying to change to please him or her and getting little or nothing in return?

Maybe your developing years were the beginning of your false definition of love. Did your parents' expression of love include things that were not loving at all? Are you unconsciously drawn to people who abuse or criticize like they did?

Other people are also affected by definitions of love drawn from their childhood, whether false or otherwise. Do family members or friends try to force you to love them like their mother or father loved? What if they accuse you of loving poorly like their mother or father loved poorly? How can you get the love you want?

Use the following checklist to see if you have a false identification of love.

- Do you find yourself expecting to get all your needs met by one person?
- Are people wounded because you don't appreciate the ways they show love to you?
- Do you feel measured, judged or compared to others who are more loveable?
- Do you use manipulation, exploitation, demand or control to get love?
- Are you more in love with "your picture of love" rather than a real person?
- Are people bitter and resentful because you don't fit their picture of love?
- Have people in your life made an idol of finding love, leaving you, your relationship or your marriage behind?
- Have you decided you didn't really need their love and you won't feel your anger, because you have given up on true love?
- Do you find that even when people love you your way, you feel unsatisfied or unsure that their love is genuine?
- Has a human being become your source in life? Are you looking to them to complete you rather than to Jesus Christ?

If you saw yourself or someone in your life in any of the above, you could benefit greatly from reading and studying *The Five Love Languages* by Gary Chapman. (Touch—words of appreciation—acts of service—gifts—quality time.)

How can we find a true definition of what unconditional love is?
It would take volumes to try to define love, but we can begin with biblical definitions. As we begin to meditate on 1 Corinthians 13:4-8, Holy Spirit will reveal to us how He wants to demonstrate His agape or unconditional love through us and to us.

1 Corinthians 13:4-8 Love is *large and* incredibly patient. Love is gentle and consistently kind to all. It refuses to be jealous *when blessing comes to someone else.* Love does not brag about one's achievements nor inflate its own importance. Love does not traffic in shame and disrespect, nor selfishly seek its own honor. Love is not easily irritated or quick to take offense. Love joyfully celebrates honesty and finds no delight in what is wrong. Love is a safe place of shelter, for it never stops believing the best for others. Love never takes failure as defeat, for it never gives up. Love never stops loving.

Obviously, only Jesus Christ in us and through us can love this way. But we can begin by releasing Him to love through us in supernatural ways on a daily basis.

Prayer to renounce false identification of love; to give and receive true love

Father, please know that I love you and want to be your beloved child. At the same time, I know that the picture I have formed in my own mind of what love should be is far removed from the truth. That picture has limited my ability to accept and receive your unconditional love.

Because of my smallness of vision, I have felt lonely even while surrounded by people I claimed to love and who professed to love me. Movies, books, the examples of others, and my own imagination conjured up an unrealistic picture of love. I nurtured this form of love and treated it like an idol to be sought after and adored. The more love I demanded, the less I was satisfied as I insisted on being loved my own selfish way.

Forgive me for the suffering I caused my family and friends through my tyrannical manipulation as I tried to force everyone else to love me MY way. No one, not even you, could measure up to this impossible standard. I see the many ways of showing and offering love that I denied because they didn't fit into my mold. How foolish I was!

I forgive my parents for any distorted examples of love they may have been and for any demanding or indifferent attitude they may have shown toward me. Forgive me, Lord, for judging them and being resentful and bitter because they couldn't or wouldn't love me according to my standard. Please bring healing to them for the times when I rejected their efforts to love me.

Father, I forgive anyone else *who may have contributed to building up my false definition of love. In turn, forgive all my bitter judgments toward people who tried to love me, but then I held up my measuring stick and found them lacking. Oh, forgive me for placing such an impossible burden on them! Forgive me for trying to fit others into my mold when you are their Creator.*

I ask you, Father, to reveal to me *all my false identifications of love and neurotic demands, whether they appear to look good or bad. I repent for expecting people to be my source and to meet needs that only you can meet. Open my heart to receive you as my source again and to renounce all my idolatry. Give me new faith to expect you to visit me in my quiet time and to receive your love and be an expression of your true love to others.*

I realize now that no one but you *could ever meet all my needs. I can't control or manipulate love. It is a gift offered in many ways. Open my eyes to see and appreciate those ways, that I may be aware of how others show love and learn to appreciate even small gestures. I forgive myself for the many times I overlooked love when it didn't fit my lopsided picture. Make me more sensitive to the many different ways that others want to receive love as well.*

Teach me to love your way, Father. *Teach me sacrificial love that chooses to give rather than demand. Take my false definition of love and bring it to death on the Cross of Christ. Resurrect my heart to newness of thought and response. Through your power within me, let me hear your words of love and grant me the courage to live for you and others, instead of for myself. I choose to trust you and rest in your constant, never-ending perfect love that casts out all my fears.*

Draw me out of my safe, comfortable space *to begin to see ways you want to love through me. I choose to receive your vision for love and your loving heart. Give me a new passion for you, Lord, and your compassion for others. Amen.*

Use this space to journal as you ask God how He wants to love through you.

Marriage Issues

While almost any issue in this book can affect our marriage relationships, this chapter is devoted to issues related to our view of marriage. What we expect before, during and after marriage will bear fruit according to our faith, negative faith or positive faith. According to Hebrews 11:1, our positive faith is the evidence and substance of what we do want to see (and our negative faith will be the evidence and substance of what we do not want to see.)

I had decided, "I will never remarry because I am a failure at love." "Every man who wants to date me turns out to be the bad apple in the bunch." My ungodly beliefs about marriage, myself and men were blocking me from God's best and from being led by Holy Spirit. While my ungodly beliefs looked like proven facts to me, they were not based on God's truth or His plan and purposes for me. The more I believed for the worst, the more I got the worst. Let me share some sample ungodly beliefs related to marriage.

Ungodly beliefs about men/women:
1. Men/women are the problem.
2. They all want to marry me for the wrong reasons.
3. All they want is someone to help support them.
4. They don't really accept me for who I am called to be.
5. They will try to limit my opportunities and spiritual gifts.
6. All they want is a cook, maid and sex partner.
7. They will want to control every decision I make.

Ungodly beliefs about marriage:
1. Romance is a trap that leads to a marriage without romance.
2. The best part of marriage is dating before marriage.
3. I cannot fulfill God's purposes and be married.
4. I cannot submit to God and be in agreement with my spouse.
5. I will have to do my responsibilities and theirs too.
6. You can't get a good conversation from a spouse like you can from your friend.
7. They only want _____ , not true intimacy, heart to heart, spirit to spirit.

First, you can choose to ask forgiveness in five ways and break the power of these ungodly beliefs. Biblical forgiveness is not only forgiving others but also asking for forgiveness for our own sinful reactions and behaviors, five ways.

Ask Holy Spirit to reveal your sinful reactions, beliefs and behaviors, and write them here.

Then break their power through prayer.
I repent, asking forgiveness in five ways.
Father, forgive me for my sins of:

- not asking others to forgive me
- judging and not forgiving others
- my own sin and sinful reactions
- blaming or doubting you God
- not forgiving myself

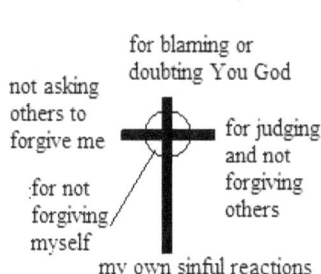

Second, after you take responsibility for your own sin, you will be able to hear God better for His plans and purposes for you. As you speak the truth in agreement with God's truth about yourself, others, God and your future, you will receive the fruit of your own lips. Third, if you will decree godly beliefs daily, you will be transformed by the renewing of your mind! Let's trust God to give you godly declarations that enable you to fulfill your destiny for this year. But, you may have bitter expectations that marriage will surely lead to abuse (if it hasn't already.) Here are some examples of ungodly beliefs you can renounce and some godly beliefs.

Ungodly beliefs	**Godly beliefs**
Submission means tolerating abuse.	Godly submission can still say "no" to abuse.
Exposing abuse only makes it worse.	God will connect me with wise counselors.
I resent people who take advantage.	I repent of resentment and set healthy boundaries.
I am to blame for the abuse I get.	I reject false guilt and sow/reap genuine respect.
Don't share, tell, talk, ask or be real.	Godly counselors give me healthy perspectives.
I shouldn't get angry about manipulation.	I am assertive and I express anger without sin.
Their choices will ruin my destiny.	Their choices do not limit God's faithfulness to me.
Everything I do and say is wrong.	I have the mind of Christ to make wise choices.
I will never have normal relationships.	I believe God for loving Spirit-filled relationships.
I am shameful and damaged used goods.	God is redeeming every experience and healing me.
I have to take them back regardless.	I require counseling before reconciliation.
All I get is empty promises or lies.	I exercise keen discernment for true repentance.
Divorce is the unforgiveable sin.	As I submit to God, He will confirm His will to me.
I can never get back on God's plan A.	God forgives all my sins and restores my soul.

My testimony: Although I had a series of failed relationships, I was just sure that the other person was the main problem, until I noticed that in many of my relationships, I seemed to experience almost the same pattern. I had already tried marriage counseling of all types. Finally, I admitted that I was simply reaping dishonor that I had sowed against my parents and authority figures. I had to admit that my dishonoring, judgmental and critical attitude was the factor that kept this cycle going, and my repentance was the key to successful marriage counseling.

So I forgave them, asked God to forgive me for dishonoring them, released God from the blame I had placed on Him, asked God to forgive me for my judgments and dishonor, and forgave myself for sowing this awful pattern into my life. If there was bad fruit on my tree, the bad root was in me! This unlocked my relationships, and they have been different ever since. Hebrews 12:14-15 says that I was defiling them with my bitter root judgments and expectations! When I truly repented, either they changed or my defiled perceptions changed. It sure felt better either way. The pure in heart can see God and others better.

More testimonies of healing for relationships through Restoration Prayer Ministry

MARRIAGE AND FAMILY COUNSELING
I learned that condemning judgments and dishonoring of parents can cause the problem to come back on you and your marriage. Since I have learned the Cross Walk Prayer, I am praying it all through the day, and I am teaching it to my three children. We have already experienced real change from so many things. I now say "I got the power!" [God has made it so easy: in every area that you truly repent of dishonoring your parents, those same areas will begin to go well in the whole family!]

I WAS 50% OF THE MARRIAGE PROBLEM!
For years, we had strife at our house, which was devastating to all of us. We had tried deliverance and several Christian counseling ministries with only very brief relief. My spouse had almost given up, and I was desperate. Then I began to understand my 50% of the problem. I was able to get enough healing so that I could begin to trust God with my spouse's problems as well. One of us had to be spiritual first! The first month, I saw positive changes in both of us even though I was the only one receiving counseling. Now we are both moving forward in faith and able to SOW the love into our marriage that we have always wanted to REAP! [It works! Repent of your judgments and dishonor of your parents so that you do not have to reap those things anymore. Now, sow what you want to reap!]

MY FAMILY CHANGED TOO!
My parents had always been undermining and hateful to me, treating me like I was a problem. I prayed to forgive them, release God from blame and forgive myself for receiving their rejection. My mother has changed, and so have I! I took her on a day trip, and we both enjoyed each other as if we had never hated each other. I have new peace and joy. God is truly transforming our family! I will be careful to honor my parents from now on. (Eph.6:1-3)

MY BITTER EXPECTATION DEFILED HER!
I had always thought my sister was irresponsible, lazy and mooching off my family. I prayed to release her from my judgments against her and asked God to forgive me for having bitter expectations that defiled her. (Romans 2:1-4, Hebrews 12:14-15) Mom says that she has gotten

her own home, a job and is taking care of her children. All these changes happened within a month of my prayer of release. [Our judgments of other people help to keep them from growing the very way we would like them to.]

DON'T JUDGE YOUR SPOUSE!

I was not aware of how my judgments of my spouse had affected my marriage and my children. When I repented of judging my husband, he became attentive immediately. When I got home from the counseling session, he had already begun to change. He had fed and bathed our children and had them in bed asleep. Now he is asking me to be more involved in the family! We are a new couple! Restoration Prayer Ministry works!

FREEDOM FROM BONDAGE

This is my testimony of how Restoration Prayer Ministry released me from many spiritual structures of bondage that I had prior to the 18 hours I received from Prophetess Carlotta Waldmann. Each step of the process peeled back an area of blindness that I had not understood until I completed each step. Asking for forgiveness and repentance in many different areas allowed me to progress to new areas of growth in Christ.

The Christian life is one of going from glory to glory and the restoration prayer ministry format gives you the breakthrough to maintain a steady state of overcoming as you face each challenge in your life. Restoration prayer ministry equipped me with a Biblical format to walk in victory.

Thank You Carlotta for all you do for the Kingdom.
Sincerely

See more information at www.pprpm.com/restoration.html

Men: What Do They Want?

I have never described myself as a marriage counselor, but I do know a bit about what not to do. During my years in the wilderness, I never had a problem attracting a man, I just wasn't good at attracting a man that I could respect over time. I used to say I was attractive to men because I was able to tell a man "no" and would never live with a man outside of marriage. (Men liked that, actually.) But I was like most women in that I didn't understand what men want most.

If I tell you that I think men want respect more than anything, you might immediately say, "OK, sure, I respect him." But I don't think most women understand **what men mean by "respect."** I am not a man, but let me try to define it by comparing respect to what I think men don't want.

Men want genuine love and respect without fear of you:

- constantly being disappointed in them
- manipulating them with lots of drama or tears
- invading their privacy or phone in a search for dirt
- embarrassing them in front of friends and family
- probing their past relationship history for sexual sin
- complaining about their shortcomings in public
- trying to control them with pressure and guilt trips

Ouch! I can remember doing stuff like this in previous relationships. No wonder many men have an inner vow, "Never tell a women anything she can hold against you." Does his heart safely trust in you? (Proverbs 31:11) Men hate hypocrisy, like when a woman preaches love and acceptance and then they talk behind their back. Who wants to live with someone who is paranoid or suspicious, investigating for evidence that they should not respect you? They also don't want to marry a wife who wants to mother, smother or coach them.

Sometimes, women are too analytical, over-interpreting every expression, glance or gesture. Men tire of being challenged to prove their love again and again. Who wants a beauty if she is also high maintenance, self-centered, demands compliments and still needs to attract attention from other men? Why do some men pretend to prefer staying single?

As the Admission Nurse of a large hospital, I observed many couples who came in for treatment. I have to admit that I wondered how some women who were so unattractive kept their men for a lifetime. How did that woman have a happy marriage and a happy husband? And I thought most men could see better than they could think!!

What does motivate a man to trust a woman? I was trying to remember when my husband-to-be suddenly changed from Mr. Mysterious to wanting to see me every evening. We had gone to the same church and elder's prayer meetings for seven months, and he had never asked me for a date. But on Christmas Eve, we took a long walk in freezing weather, and I prophesied to him– his potential in Christ, his strengths, his future successes–and his heart melted. I think he suddenly realized how much I respected him and was sure that I believed in him. Within one week, he asked me out. Within two weeks, he told me he wanted to spend his life with me! NOTE: I am not suggesting manipulation with prophecy or flattery.

How do you know if your man has taken the padlocks off of his heart?

- Would he fight to defend you and support your mission in life?
- Is he sure that you are on his side? That you have his back?
- Does he listen when you share your dreams? Do you listen when he shares his?
- Is he loyal to you no matter what? Faithful to a fault?
- Does he look forward to the deposits you make in his heart every day?
- Is he proud of you? Amazed by you?
- Does he find you to be irresistible? (Men go after what they want.)

I began to research what men want, and here is what they told me. They like a woman who is:

- Content and at peace with who she is in Christ
- Complete in Christ, not half empty all the time
- Confident and self-assured but humble
- Believes in herself and Christ in her
- Knows her strengths and operates in them
- Virtuous and whose dress is attractive but modest
- Strong but not aggressive or competing with him
- Compassionate, generous and serving others
- Healthy and vibrant in body, soul and spirit
- Trusting God to transform them and their man

Men are pretty easy really. Give them genuine respect, admiration, appreciation and a little affection and they are happy. Single women need to make their non-negotiable list of what they must have in a man, and then never forget why they chose those traits in their man. Spend your life appreciating those same qualities and respecting him out loud.

Men like to be a hero who is meeting real needs and whose service is appreciated. When I first married Louis, I was still a little too independent. But as I began to allow myself to be more vulnerable and dependent on him, I realized how much I need his strengths. Like anyone else, men want to be needed. God designed them to be hunters who want to earn your love and admiration. They study you and memorize your likes and dislikes. Then they set out to prove they are the most worthy of your devotion and that they will love and cherish you forever.

You may be thinking of qualities in your man that you do not respect. But you have the power to choose to focus on his good qualities. You have the power to turn your relationship around by sowing respect, admiration, appreciation and affection. Your man just wants a true friend who honestly accepts him as he is and trusts God to transform the rest. Try being more transparent and vulnerable. The hero in him loves to protect the real you that he chose, too. Let him hear that you have been talking behind his back, praising his strengths. Build him up by bragging on him. Show him glimpses of the real you that fascinated him in the first place.

Now! Are you ready for ideas for sowing respect?
Kay Price and I came up with this list of ideas for wives.

1. Provide a favorite meal or dessert for them.
2. Write a special note of how you admire them.
3. Improve your appearance before they come home.
4. Praise them in front of the children, family or others.
5. List their strong points and thank God for them all.
6. Tell your spouse that you love them deeply.
7. Ask them for advice and then appreciate it.
8. Buy them a little gift or make something for them.
9. Ask them to pray for you or about your problem.
10. Respond with understanding when you disagree.
11. Sow respect for them and your children will too.
12. Demonstrate your admiration for them in public.
13. Respect your spouse's authority in the home.
14. Never intimidate with loud condescending remarks.
15. Don't give ultimatums when you don't get your way.
16. Want to be with them; suggest "let's do it together."
17. Express confidence in their leadership and style.
18. Patiently allow time for them to hear from God.
19. Verbally appreciate their perceptions and insights.
20. Appeal to their intelligence and knowledge base.
21. Ask them to help you solve your problems.
22. Ask them what their top three needs are.
23. Respect them from your heart, mind and body.
24. Repent of rejecting them with negative body language.
25. Keep communication open and want to understand.
26. Pray for your spouse daily and trust God to answer.
27. Pray for insight, spiritual maturity and pure motivations.
28. Thank Jesus for working in your family and marriage.
29. Ask them to pray for your heart and attitude.
30. Expect Jesus to lead you through your spouse.
31. Keep an ongoing growing list of their strengths.
32. Defer to them because you truly value them.
33. Respond to their loving advances with great enthusiasm.
34. Sincerely want to hear their confidences and concerns.
35. Ask for clarity versus challenging their choices and views.
36. Ask Jesus to purify your critical or judgmental thoughts.
37. Choose to quit doing what you know irritates them.
38. Choose to be supportive of them even if their plan fails.
39. Sow the same grace you want to receive from them.
40. Resign from being the judge and jury over them.

"… and the wife must see to it that she respects her husband." Ephesians 5:33

Nurturing Your Personal Inner Spirit

Dr. Mark Virkler once said that we are just dust fused to God's glory. But do we always feel like we are fused to God's glory or do we feel more like dust under His feet? Do we really believe it when the Word of God tells us the resurrection power of Christ is available within us, that we are the temple of the Holy Spirit who dwells within us, that God actually wants to work through us to accomplish His purposes?

When our personal inner spirits have not been taught to believe in God's truth, we tend to have a personal spirit that is not nurtured. This means that our innermost being is hungry because we don't know or don't believe what God says about Himself and about us. Even though we are sitting at a banquet table laden with nourishing food, we still have hunger pangs because we don't think the food is real or provided for us to eat.

A malnourished personal spirit leads to an ineffective Christian walk. This is often a result of a lack of true spiritual teaching in the home. Children may listen to what their parents tell them, but they watch to see if their actions mesh with their words. If parents and church leaders don't model godly behavior and teach God's truth, what is raised up is a generation of people with apathetic spirits. They may actually be hungry for God, but they remain unresponsive to the gospel because they are not aware of its life-changing power.

So how do we move into that place of living out of full spirits?

How do we go from malnourished spirits to strong personal spirits? Can we command our rational minds to bow down so we can live in the spiritual realm? How do we release the Holy Spirit, His gifts and His fruit through our lives 24/7?

The answer is to meditate on God's truth, accepting it as truth. It's not a matter of simply trying harder, volunteering for more church committees or attending more spiritual seminars. We need to get down to business with God, spending time with Him in His Word and letting His promises and blessings nourish our personal spirits so that we finally believe what He says is true.

Even Jesus said He could do nothing on His own (John 5:19). If Jesus needed to rely on the power of God within Him, why should we think we don't need it too? In order to nurture our personal spirits, we must choose to live in the spiritual realm with Him. We must grasp the truth that He has all the power of the universe and He lives within His children.

Meditate on the following scriptural truths, and let the Word of God nourish and nurture your inner personal spirit

- My old man is dead, and Christ lives in me (Romans 6).
- I am partaker of a new divine spirit (II Peter 1:4).
- I abide in Him; He abides in me; together we bear much fruit (John 15).
- I am joined to the Lord, and I am one Spirit with Him (I Corinthians 6:17).
- I release the Holy Spirit to love others through me!
- My old spirit is dead, nevertheless, I still live, and I am not alone; Christ lives through me and is even the faith through me (Galatians 2:20).
- He has all the strength and might in the whole world, and He lives through me (Colossians 1:16-17).

We receive our true identity as a container and an expression of Jesus Christ, who is the fullness of the whole Godhead who came in the flesh. He now lives through our mortal body. Our new divine spirit desires to be one spirit with the Holy Spirit and it can be. We turn our eyes on Jesus within and focus on Him instead of on ourselves.

We receive who we are in Christ; we see ourselves as spiritual creatures.

As we think "one with Him," we remember that we are complete in Him. Out of our union with Christ, good fruit is birthed (Romans 6:22).

Can you see how a malnourished spirit could learn to rejoice while feasting on these profound truths? Here are some more spiritual entrees and side dishes to load on your plate:

- I am a temple where the Holy Spirit chooses to live (I Corinthians 6:19).
- I am a temple of the Holy Spirit and choose to live out of His power through me, in His anointing.
- I am bought by God, and I invite Him to live through me (I Corinthians 6:20).
- I am grafted into Him, the vine, and I invite His sap to flow through me. He has all the power, and without Him, I can do nothing and cannot bear fruit (John 15:5).
- As I choose to live out of His flow, I have everything I need for life and godliness and I am called for His glory (II Peter 1:3).

Through the finished work of Christ on the Cross, we are free to live by the law of the Spirit instead of the law of sin and death (Romans 8:1-2). He is our all in all and we have everything we need inside us. God is sovereign and His Holy Spirit is always in control. This is a one power universe. He is omnipotent, omniscient and omnipresent. He always wins. He knows no limits and He lives within us.

He is the Head and we are part of the body. We receive orders from Him each day. As we submit to Him, we release Almighty God, His power, His anointing through our lives. We have the mind of Christ in our mind, His hands in our hands and His feet in our feet. As we submit to His authority, we walk safely, owning our spiritual power and authority in Him.

If God says it, it is already. He is not a time-limited creature. We can choose to live in the spiritual realm because we are primarily spiritual creatures. Christ in us knows no natural realm limitations. He is our limitless pill. (smiles)

Here are some other wonderful truths to ponder about:

- I am crucified with Christ; I live out of my spirit, one with His Spirit.
- I die to self-power every day and choose to tune my spirit to the Holy Spirit (John 8:26-28).
- I hear God's thoughts and see His pictures; I do and say what the Father says.
- I thirst to drink His living water into my spirit; I live in the river (John 4).
- My priority is to come to Jesus expecting living water, communion, visions and impartation (John 7:37-39).
- I take time to drink from His flow every day; His river of living water flows out of my innermost being (John 4).
- I choose to enter into God's rest and cease from searching for what I already have in "Christ in me" (Hebrews 4).
- I receive new revelations as I quiet myself, focus on Jesus, tune in to the flow of the Holy Spirit and journal what He reveals to me.
- Jesus said, "My sheep hear My voice (John 10:27)." I hear His voice and see His pictures, dreams and visions (Acts 2:17).
- As I delight in God, He gives me the desires of His heart as my own desires and fulfills them in me (Psalm 37:4).
- I repent of dead works, works done without tuning into the Holy Spirit (Hebrews 6:1).
- I repent for trying to meet my own needs outside of God's plan and provision. I receive the blessings of Abraham by faith (Galatians 3:14).
- God is love; as I abide in Him, God's perfect love casts out all my fears and loves others through me as I am one with Him (I John 4:16).

Be childlike; release Jesus to live His joyous life through you! Learn FUN creative ways to feed and nurture your personal spirit. God is at work in you, strengthening you to do His pleasure (Philippians 2:13; Colossians 1:11; Ephesians 3:16-19).

Give yourself three months to declare these truths. Practice to walk and talk with God and you will do it the rest of your life! Learn to be still before God and you will be able to walk the walk. Let the Holy Spirit energize you and give life to your body (Romans 8:11; Jude 20). Spend hours with God in fun ways and you will only need minutes for everything else (Romans 8:5-6, 9). Learn to tune in to the mind of Christ to release divine wisdom (and get over trying to figure everything out).

Walk and talk with Father in the garden, as He wanted all mankind to do. Listen for creative ways that you can feed your personal spirit or the personal spirit in others as you develop a fun relationship with Jesus. Learn to tune in to the flow of God and

His pleasure in you. Relax, agree with God and speak your future into being according to His Logos and Rhema Word. Receive it; speak it; live it.

God is more fun than you think. Walking in His Spirit is GREAT JOY!

Prayer to care for my own personal spirit

Lord, my spirit is weak and hungry, *like a body that has been starved or inactive. Your Word teaches that people who trust in you for strength are happy and spiritually blessed. When I rely on my own strength, I find that it's not enough. I thought I could handle whatever life dished out, but without you, I can do nothing. I need to learn to tune into your Spirit, to be one with your Spirit, to allow you to flow through me and to empower me with your fruit and your gifts. I cannot stand alone in this world. I need you and your people to encourage me.*

I choose to receive your definition of my personal spirit*: a new creature, a divine nature, a temple for you to live in and through. Lord, show me how to receive who I am in spirit, a spiritual creature. I command my soul and body to bow to my spirit, which longs to be one with your Holy Spirit and to bear fruit out of that union. I thank you that as I abide in you, the branch, you release your "sap" to flow through me, making my spirit strong. I choose to invite you to live through me in all your mighty power, anointing and unconditional love. Out of your abundance, I have courage, life, the mind of Christ and living water that springs up inside me.*

Please forgive the many times I judged my parents *or others in the church for not nurturing me and letting me down. I wanted to know you, but I feel like my spirit has been walking around in a fog, unable or unwilling to appreciate your creation and your gifts. I kept to myself and didn't ask for help because this was what I was taught through the example of my parents and others in the church. And so I forgive them for their lack of spiritual nurturing, for not knowing how to teach me communion with you, true spiritual worship, for not building a close-knit family and for not knowing how to build strength into my spirit.*

I forgive the other people in my life *who influenced me to avoid you and your people by pointing out the hypocrisy and disunity in the church and insisting I could fill my spiritual emptiness with materialism or life experiences. I forgive those who wounded my spirit and left me bleeding. I lay down all that I think I know about quiet times and prayer and invite you to teach me how to really commune with you.*

Father, to my shame I also blamed you *for seeming to be far off and uncaring, when in reality it was my choice to hold you at arm's length, not accepting your love and your life. Show me your intense desire to abide in me, to nurture my spirit and to express yourself through me.*

Lastly, I forgive myself for my participation *in weakening and wounding my own spirit by not seeking you or nurture from your people. In running after material things to feed my hungry spirit, I didn't appreciate the beauty of your creation. I didn't take time to be still before you and learn of your plans for me. Right now, I choose to make my first priority of every day communion with you, hearing your voice, seeing your vision and walking with you in the garden.*

Because of the power in the blood of Christ *to cleanse, redeem, and make whole, I now choose to live out of my spirit which is one with your Spirit. Be creativity in me to build the spirits of my children/family so they will not reap the dust I've sown in the past. Build my family so we can all rejoice in knowing you and your salvation. Open my eyes and my heart to the wonder of life and the magnificence of creation, that my hungry spirit may feed on the abundance you provide. Make me a vessel of joy, filling their spirits with peace. Teach me how to be fun and childlike again.*

Give me the courage to ask for what I need *instead of running away to pursue something else that only brings emptiness. I invite you to nourish my spirit with your truth, your Word, your Holy Spirit, as I linger in your presence as a bride and groom would linger together unrushed. Help me share this amazing life with others and enjoy the fellowship of dedicated Christians as together we grow in faith and an ever-deepening intimate relationship with you, Lord. You are the apple of my eye.*

Let me always find my strength in you*, boldly asking for the grace I need to be an expression of you with all my spirit, soul and body. Increase my trust in you. Fill me with your joy and strengthen my spirit to fully accept the gift of life. I reckon my self-powered life is dead and I am finally truly alive as you live your life through me and in me. Amen.*

Performance Orientation

Many believers have dropped out of regular church attendance because they just couldn't perform the Christian life. (I used to say, "I couldn't pass the physical of being at church every time the doors opened!") They have become wanderers who are searching for other ways to get their needs met because they didn't find fulfillment in church. Some tried and tried but felt they were only producing "wood, hay and stubble" (I Corinthious 3:12) and never finding the key to living a victorious Christian life. They finally got off the religious treadmill, weary of trying to meet the Christian standard to earn acceptance or trying to produce "good fruit that remains" (John 15:16).

What is the secret to living the Christian life?

The key to living the victorious Christian life isn't to keep on striving to attain that perfect list of dos and don'ts. It's to end striving and rest in the ability of Christ inside you to work through you (Ephesians 2:8-10; Hebrews 4:9-10).

One of the hardest areas to bring to death is our perpetual drive to earn acceptance and approval instead of accepting God's unconditional love and acceptance, based on what Jesus has provided, by His death on the Cross.

Many of us have heard sermons on Romans 7:7-24 about the frustration Paul experienced when his spiritual performance was not what he wanted it to be. From the pulpit, we are told that we must try harder to be good. However, even the apostle Paul wasn't completely satisfied with how he lived his life for God.

Because of this performance-based mindset, we feel bankrupt when it comes to pleasing God. We have no idea how to live the Christian life or how to bear good fruit because we are already trying to do all we know how to do to be fruitful. And it isn't enough. Many of us erroneously see God as a strict father who commands obedience and then doesn't give us the power to do it.

The problem with preaching on Romans 7 is that there is more truth to be learned than just from verses 7-24. The seventh chapter of Romans describes the two things that are necessary to bear fruit for God, but most people, and preachers, miss it.

Do any of the following sound familiar?

- I was committed to keeping God's law but never succeeded.
- Tried to live the performance code of my church and family.
- Asked for forgiveness for the same things over and over.
- Felt like I was still helpless to overcome temptations in life.
- Heard many sermons exhorting me to do right but didn't know how.
- Felt like I had nothing to offer God in order to please Him.
- Tried to give my life to Jesus but kept taking it back.

- Kept doing the bad stuff when I wanted to do the good stuff.
- Doing the good stuff never gave me satisfaction.
- Performed better and better, but I never felt God accepted me.
- Couldn't ever be perfect enough to walk a life of holiness.
- Performed very well but still felt I didn't meet the standard.
- Thought my bad behavior proved I was not really a new creature.
- My main job was to improve myself with self-improvement.
- If my good deeds outweighed my bad deeds, I would be okay.
- I attended conferences to find out how to improve my performance.
- I read Christian self-help books to find out how to do better.
- I felt like I was still my "old man" fighting the "new man" inside me.
- I didn't believe anyone could live the victorious life here on earth.
- I was afraid I would get what I deserved based on my inconsistency.
- I didn't feel alive in Christ; I felt dead and defeated.
- I took unfair advantage of God's grace as I sinned more and more.
- I felt helpless to obey God and to keep His law.
- If I could perform better, God would love me more.
- God commanded us to be holy and blameless, but I can't.
- God commanded us to be perfect, but no one can do it.
- No matter how well I do, it will never be good enough to please God.
- I can't accept righteousness as a gift because I am unclean.
- I was defective and couldn't live the Christian life, so I gave up.
- I can't ever be weak, make mistakes or fail and expect to please God.
- The more I try to keep the law, the more I fall into sin.
- God could have given me the grace to keep the law, but He didn't.
- I can never feel good about my performance or myself.
- In order to earn my pastor's approval, I have to meet his standard.
- People who keep sinning and failing should be punished.
- God must not care about me; I will get my needs met the best I can.
- God is an indifferent, hard taskmaster like my father was.
- The church is full of hypocrites who pretend to obey God.
- God didn't give us the power to obey His law, so no one can.

This is an incomplete list containing some of the standards that we think people think or expect from us. We may not see any actual lists of these standards, but we are made painfully aware that they must exist, especially when we have been rejected. We just didn't meet their standards to earn acceptance or approval.

Sometimes the situation is reversed. We pressure others to perform.

Instead of trying to meet other people's standards, we strive to get others to conform to our standards of acceptable behavior. This is just as bad. We make other people mistakenly believe they are responsible to meet our standards or our needs, especially if we are significant to them.

Either way, someone is going to get exhausted from their own efforts to seek acceptance and value through controlling or being controlled by someone else. Conforming to the standards of another or seeking to conform someone else to your standards is no way to live!

Whenever a people pleaser fails to please a significant person in their life, they feel like a failure, a loser. It's a dreadful burden to seek our own value and worth from other people. The lists keep changing from person to person.

Instead, we need to consider what God's standard is and find our true identity in Him. With the proper insights and prayer, we can break the power of striving to please God and others in our own strength. Then we will be free to let Jesus live the Christian life through us while we enter into His rest and cease from our own striving for acceptance (Hebrews 4:9-10).

God's Word tells us who we truly are, and His list never changes. We must seek our value and needs from God. He will meet all our needs, and He will not refuse us when we believe in Him. We don't need to perform for God. He created us and He knows all about us.

God proclaims we are valuable, not because of anything we have done or haven't done but because He says it is so. He loves us because He loves us (Deuteronomy 7:7-8). Jesus died for us, not just for the salvation of our souls but also to give us freedom, grace and strength to live according to His plans and purposes for our life. He lives this life through us (Galatians 2:20).

When we walk according to our flesh (or own strength) and, either in the role of a god or expecting another person to be our god, we will not have the peace that Christ has promised.

Is this something in your life you need to repent of? Jesus said a tree is known by the fruit it produces (Luke 6:44). Examine the fruit in your most significant relationships with others. Do you pressure yourself or others to perform?

- Do you get angry if others don't do what you want them to do?
- Do you try to manipulate others to change?
- Do you play the blame game? ("If you would just _____, I wouldn't be unhappy." "Oh, you make me so angry!")
- Do you have a list of things others must do for you in order for you to feel accepted in their group or for you to accept them in yours?
- Do you sulk and give the cold shoulder to anyone who doesn't live up to your expectations?
- Do you challenge? ("If you really loved me, you would_____.")
- Do you use shame or guilt? ("I can't believe you did that!" "What's the matter with you?" "What will other people think?")

- Do you try to "fix" yourself in order to "fix" others? ("Once I get myself straightened out, then he/she will change.")
- Do you compromise yourself to be accepted?
- Do you spend more time examining the faults and shortcomings of others than of yourself?
- Do you use the Bible to try to force others to change?
- Do you check to see how well others are following the scriptures as compared to you?
- Do you pressure others to obey the scriptures you think they "ought" to be obeying?

Hebrews 10:23-24 teaches that we should indeed encourage one another in doing good, but our job as Christian spouses, parents and fellow believers is not to drive each other to perform well in order to be accepted. We are *already* accepted in Jesus. He alone is the way, the truth, and the life (John 14:6). Our job is to learn God's plan and apply His standards personally.

We are not valuable and acceptable to God because of our bank account, the clothes we wear, our social circles, our church attendance or faithfulness in tithing. What other people say about us may hurt sometimes, but they don't decide the truth about us; God does.

No human being is powerful enough to provide life and value to another. We weren't created by God to "fix" other people according to our own standards or to slavishly follow other people's standards. God alone determines the standards and Jesus lives those standards through us by the power of the Holy Spirit (Romans 8:1-4).

If we lead by example, others will follow, walking in freedom rather than by compulsion. We serve God out of love—because we *want* to, not because we have to.

Prayer to replace performance orientation

Lord, I have come to see my performance orientation. *I confess to you that although my head believes salvation is by grace, my heart strives to earn favor to be good enough, to present myself to others and to you. I admit that I cannot change myself. The fear of not being accepted or loved is so overwhelming it puts me into gear and I begin performing again. When acceptance is given with no strings attached, I cannot receive it.*

I ask you into my heart to do the work in me for me*. Bring my striving to death. I want to rest in your love. Help me remove the hindrances I have erected which prevent me from entering into your love. Bring all my fleshly self-effort to death on the Cross.*

Lord, I have been angry with you *for putting me into this (family, situation, team) I don't want my anger to keep me from you. So I ask that you restore my soul.*

I forgive *my (friend, family, Pastor, etc.) for _____(list the wounds that helped form performance orientation or fueled it).*

I ask your forgiveness for my angry responses*, my fear and insecurities, my impure motives, and for not believing the truth: You love and accept me unconditionally, when I perform well and when I don't.*

Lord, I renounce the family lies *_____ (name them specifically). I accept my true identity as your child. Help me learn how to live my true identity, according to your Word, in my daily life. Help me to know within me that success is being your child. Help me to be like you, Lord.*

I ask you to bring to death in me the structures*, the habit patterns, of performance I have created: I ask you to minister to the ambivalence in me when I want correction but cannot receive it or when I want and need compliments but cannot believe them. Likewise, be the Lord of my tongue so that wisdom and kindness permeate the correction and compliments I give. Help me take my eyes off my needs and fears and to focus on releasing Christ to live through me.*

Lord, I resign from managing the universe! *I give to you my compulsive need to control people and situations. I recognize I have wounded others by not affirming their contributions. I always had to edit, add or correct. Now I am reaping what I have been sowing. I could always do it better. Forgive me and guide me in restoring lost and damaged relationships.*

Lord, for both my insecurity and my arrogance *as well as for the wounds I have caused, I humbly ask your forgiveness. Help me believe I am not responsible for all that goes on around me. Forgive me for always being a Martha. And help me to hear when you call me to be a Mary. Show me where I have taken on jobs or duties for the wrong reason and give me the wisdom to resign from them if necessary. Each day let my prayer be: Lord, show me my assignment and I will only do what the Father says to do.*

Help me to fall in love with you Jesus*, so that what others think of me is not important. I no longer base my significance on what I think others think. You have said that it is you working in us that enables us first to will and then to act according to your good purposes. I want to be a good workman but only with your strength and your will. Help me to not only be like you, Lord, but also to yield to you so that YOU CAN LIVE YOUR LIFE THROUGH ME! Amen.*

(This prayer was adapted from "A Prayer to End Striving" in the "Elijah House Training for the Ministry of Prayer Counseling manual" section two, page 74. I was given permission to use the Elijah House manuals to teach Bible College courses since I am a certified facilitator to teach Elijah Schools.)

Pride

If it is true that pride is the root of all sin, why is it so hard to see it in ourselves? While we should be very alert to discern fleshly pride in ourselves, there is also a spirit of pride that the Bible describes as Leviathan, a monster that cannot be tamed. Leviathan makes us quick to see pride in others and slow to see it in ourselves. He looks down on all that are haughty; he is king over all that are proud (Job 41:34).

Pride offers to promote us but tears us down instead. Because the proud person looks to their own strength, they may react with jealousy or negative words to downplay the good work others have done, as they haughtily seek to call attention to their own work as superior. It may seem at first that others go along with the proud in getting their own way, but it doesn't take long for most discerning people to see through this smokescreen and they begin to avoid them.

People who are proud trust in their own self-effort.

They are comfortable with the knowledge that they have the necessary talent or gift to walk alone without aid from God or other Christians. They may arrogantly feel that others should also be like independent like them and fail to help out others or even stand in the gap for people in need of prayer.

Because we live in a material world with performance orientation as the short-term focus, it is not always easy for us to contemplate the long-term focus, which has an eternal perspective. If we continue in our pride after we are born again in Christ Jesus, we will even be proud that we have a new nature. We might presume that we can use our new nature to perform perfectly and to earn God's approval when actually are new nature is designed to be one with Christ (John 17).

Instead of acknowledging that we are all like plain melamine cups, only containers of Him and without Him, we can do nothing, we will try to compete to grab a bit of the glory in some way. But God said that it's nothing we have done, but rather it is His power working, from salvation to fruitfulness in His Kingdom (Ephesians 2:8-9).

We have been given everything we need for life and godliness (II Peter 1:3). The suitcase we are handed when we are born again is already full. Together with the Holy Spirit, we can unpack the resources we need for whatever God has called us to do. We already have it—as a gift from God. It's nothing we've done on our own and pride has no part in this gift.

Ready to see the many signs of pride that may already be taking root in your life?

Test yourself for the various ways pride interferes with your spiritual growth.

- Hinders prayer or causes the person to feel sleepy.
- Blocks believers from sensing the need to pray or seek God.
- Blocks sensing the need to ask for help or make supplication.
- Will speak harshly to others or in a prideful tone of voice.
- Will not enter into a covenant or mutual agreement.
- Rarely submits one to another i.e. in marriage under God.
- Is the spirit behind separation or divorce in most marriages.
- Blinds and keeps believers from honoring their covenants.
- Prevents from receiving/walking in covenant with Jesus.
- Denies the authority of the Bible to bind us to covenants.
- Causes comparison, competition and religious pride.
- Prevents from submitting to and serving under another.
- Sets you up to argue, fight and contend to get its own way.
- Will fight deliverance like no other demonic spirit.
- Causes hardening of the heart and resisting the Lord.
- Sets you up to stand against God's plan and purposes.
- Tempts you to exalt yourself and to resist God in rebellion.
- Manifests as arrogance, conceit, vanity and a haughty spirit.
- Leads to division, isolation, rejection, shame and fear.
- Basically insecure and fearful, wanting attention.
- Encourages self-righteousness and religious comparison.
- Quenches the freedom and work of the Holy Spirit.
- Hinders the gifts of the Holy Spirit from flowing.
- Divides with denominational pride and exclusive thinking.
- Shields self from discovery, transparency or true identity.
- Manifests with boasting, lying, cursing and defensiveness.
- Speaks arrogantly, arguing and disputing viewpoints.
- Is easily agitated, troubled, aggravated and offended.
- Stirs up strife to "get what you want when you want it."
- Has an angry heart; is self-important, provoking quarrels.
- Refuses to receive the current moves of the Holy Spirit.
- Refuses change or departure from tradition for the "new wine."
- Is not teachable, is unbending and will not submit to leadership.
- Claims its rights and is not humble to defer to others.
- Doubts God due to a deep lack of trust in God's character.
- Will not acknowledge that God is always faithful without fail.
- Causes backsliding, compromise and lukewarm involvement.
- Is spiritually dull without understanding or discernment.
- Refuses to receive God's fullness or baptism of the Holy Spirit.
- Is stiff-necked and refuses to heed correction or direction.
- Rejects the Holy Spirit's conviction to repent of sin.
- Causes scriptures to be forgotten and misunderstood.

- Prevents you from applying the Word of God to yourself.
- Mocks believers who are "fanatics," immature or carnal.
- Attacks new ministers who need more training or mentoring.
- Hinders your growth; puts you to sleep during anointed services.
- Causes agitated restlessness when God would give you rest.
- Promises you the world but kills, steals and destroys.

A humble spirit will always seek God's will and His righteousness rather than promoting self-righteousness. Humility will also view repentance and restitution as a gateway to future opportunities to help others.

Prayer to renounce pride

Father, I bring my pride before you *and ask for your grace and mercy in bringing this to your Cross to be put to death. Thank you for loving me enough to give your perfect life in exchange for my sinful one. I receive your resurrection life and power to transform and renew me. Give me the strength and wisdom to be able to deal with anything in my life that is not according to your will and destiny for me.*

Please forgive the many times I judged others *in my arrogance, criticizing them for not meeting standards of Christianity that I couldn't achieve myself. I saw only the faults of others but was blind to my own. I am ashamed of how I mistreated those who tried to help me. Show me what I must do to seek their forgiveness and restore the relationships ruined by my sinful attitude. Open their hearts, Lord, to receive your healing for the wounds I gave them.*

Father, forgive me for the times I judged even you *for not being the kind of God I thought you should be—as if I knew more about righteousness than you did. I know now that your ways are not my ways and I was foolish to imagine myself above you. From this point on, I relinquish my imagined reins of authority and acknowledge you as the Master of this one power universe. I've seen the reality that you are in charge of all things and I repent of wanting to be in control. All praise, honor and glory belong to you alone, Lord God Almighty!*

Please forgive me for my attitude of pride *and cleanse me from spiritual idolatry by putting myself before you. Keep me from judging another person according to my own impossibly high aspirations and help me to see the truth of your working in and through me, instead of my own self- efforts. Lord, your love is unconditional and eternal. You have given me a new past, present and future. I ask for an open heart to let your unconditional love flow through me to all you bring into my life.*

Through the power of the Cross, I forgive those *who encouraged me in my rebellious pride, who misled me into thinking I was the only person who could do the job right when there were people more qualified, who agreed with my haughty attacks on others and fed fuel to the fire of my willful, stubborn spirit. Father, they didn't understand what a wreck they were making of my relationship with you. In* *your mercy, please forgive them as you forgive me—not because we deserve it but because your Son has paid for it with His own blood.*

Lord, I forgive myself of defaming others *through my arrogant words or attitude, for trying to grab all the attention, for making myself look more competent or wiser than anyone else, for hardening my heart against correction, and for insisting on my own way. you made each of us unique and special to fulfill your plan and I had no right to demand that everyone should be like me. Put my pride to death on the Cross and raise up instead a humble acceptance of who I am in you and a deep appreciation for each of your uniquely gifted children n.*

Father, how good it is to be forgiven and beloved! *Because of what Jesus accomplished for me at Calvary, I am forgiven and no longer stand condemned in your sight. You meet all my needs and I do not need any other source. Please help me to give myself completely to you, to love you with all my heart, mind, soul and strength, and to love others as you have loved me.*

Thank you, Father, for your power and strength within me *to make all the changes necessary to live the victorious Christian life you intended. I choose to live my life so as to make a difference in this world according to your plans, purposes and vision for me. I choose to lay down all the weighty baggage of my pride and self-efforts and come back to your original plan for me. Show me your Kingdom purposes for my life and help me to be your love and power to others for your name's sake. Amen.*

Rape and Its Effects

Believers must learn to pray for survivors of sexual violence. Roughly 1 out of 4 females and 1 out of 6 males have suffered from unwanted sexual contact. This means that 20% of the people at your church, school, business, club, market, etc. need effective prayer ministry for healing from sexual trauma.

Sexual assaults can run the gamut of sexual contact from unwanted touch all the way to brutal rape. No matter what has happened, it still has an effect on the survivor. Every sexual assault hurts the mind, heart, and psyche on a deep level.

Secular therapists may say, "This incident has changed this person's life; it will never be the same." They insist that how well the person copes will depend on how willing the survivor is to move through "the process." They caution that this process is painful and difficult, but the survivor can become stronger and wiser for it.

This is true up to a point. It is necessary to go through some kind of healing process in order to face what happened and deal with the damaged emotions. The difference with effective prayer ministry is that the survivor will come through the process not only stronger and wiser but also victorious and able to help other survivors find their liberty in the healing power and love of Christ.

Finding the rest, freedom and abundant life that God has called us to have is bound up in knowing His true nature, His loving heart for us and accepting our identity in who He says we are. This involves more than just facing reality and dealing with damaged emotions. It means taking the risk to trust again, to love and be loved. It means renouncing the negative patterns picked up from the abuse and choosing to ask for forgiveness for my own sinful reactions and behaviors.

There are several choices that survivors of abuse must make.

These choices must be based on God's Truth as found in scripture. This is security they can hold on to with both hands. Let's take time to look at each one thoughtfully.

They can choose to forever blame God, run from His love and ride a downward spiral of despair, anger, stress, bitterness and self-centeredness, demanding answers and retribution from Him for what happened. Or they can choose to see God's great, loving heart breaking for the wickedness people inflict on His children. He weeps over His abused children, even when they blame Him for not rescuing them.

God never causes the abuse. He created mankind with a free will to either choose to follow Him or to follow their own evil ways. If God "took over" whenever there was wickedness, then there would be no free will and no way for us to follow Him with our whole heart. And that's why we were created with a free will—to choose to love

God with all our heart. In return, God wants to lavish His love on us as we learn to trust Him without any defensive walls.

Throughout His earthly life, Jesus showed us how to walk in the midst of suffering and He promises to be with us in all our suffering as well. He promised to never leave us or forsake us. Confident in His constant Presence within us, we can look forward to the future and cast our sorrows on the One who promised to carry them.

The right to choose is what the abusers stole.

Survivors can regain that lost ground through making a conscious choice to accept Jesus' payment for their sin and the sin of their abusers as well. Withholding forgiveness is a choice to follow their own way; choosing to forgive and to be forgiven five ways is a choice to be set free.

By choice, they can lay their hearts bare before God and let Him see what they can hardly stand to look at or admit themselves. They can choose to trust Him to remove all that hinders them from living the abundant life and take it all to the Cross to be redeemed into something good for them and glorious for Him.

Trusting and resting in God moves people from victim to survivor to overcomer to a thriving warrior in the battle against evil. But it requires choosing to believe what's written about Him in Scripture and choosing to accept who we are in Him, rather than who we think we are because of being abused.

A single choice can affect everyone around us like ripples in a pond caused by tossing in a single stone. Satan wants us to tolerate our own sinful reactions and behaviors after an assault and resist Holy Spirit's conviction and healing in our souls. As we resist Holy Spirit, Satan steps in to build sinful strongholds in our minds, will and emotions (like unforgiveness, resentment, bitterness, fear, rebellion, etc.) While we defend our rights to harbor these sinful reactions and behaviors, we are building walls. The trouble with these walls is that we are also walling out God's Truth and His power to heal us if we would align with Him instead of lies from the enemy.

Below is a list of negative beliefs and behaviors that we must choose to take to the Cross of Christ to be put to death. They serve us no good purpose.

- Submission to God means tolerating abuse.
- Exposing abuse only makes things worse.
- Forgiveness means they are no longer accountable.
- Forgiveness means I don't remember the pain anymore.
- I should resent people who take advantage of me.
- I am to blame for the abuse I get.
- Don't share, don't tell, don't ask, don't feel, don't be real.
- I shouldn't get angry at manipulation and control.
- Their reactions and choices will ruin my future.

- I may never have normal relationships.
- I am shameful, damaged and defective.

In this list, note how our choices of Godly beliefs and behaviors are redeemed and brought to life through the resurrection power of Jesus. These good choices lead us into living the abundant life God planned for us.

Godly beliefs and behaviors that bring healing and freedom.

- Godly submission does not mean to say "yes" to abuse.
- Spirits of intimidation thrive in darkness and secrets.
- Forgiveness means I release them to God to judge.
- Sincere forgiveness does not mean I am pain-free.
- I repent of resentment and set healthy boundaries.
- I am free to reject false guilt and to expect respect.
- Godly counsel will give me healthy perspectives.
- Abusive demons "back off" when I say "NO."
- Their choices cannot limit God's faithfulness to me.
- I have the mind of Christ and make wise choices.
- I believe God for loving Spirit-filled relationships
- God is redeeming every experience and healing me.

The only two things we can really control in life are our choices and our attitudes. Just like each destructive choice leads to hurtful consequences, so healthy choices lead to healing opportunities. The choice is up to us.

We need to face the truth of taking charge of our choices and attitudes, take anything that is not of God to the Cross to be crucified, and then trust God for everything else.

When we choose to risk laying our wounded hearts bare to God, He is faithful to heal us. His Presence will become our safe place, our resting place.

Survivors of abuse need this assurance that if they keep their eyes fixed on Jesus, give Him everything that holds them back from living a victorious life, and learn to forgive from the heart, that the pain of their past will be washed away. We can choose to believe Jesus for healing and restoration deep in our hearts and eventually we will be compelled by a heavenly love that is beyond anything they could ever imagine. He will make our weakest places into our strengths by His power.

When God touches them with His own heart in holy intimacy, they are forever changed and the devil and his lies are defeated for good. His resurrection life is a powerful force within them, a rare and precious gift no one and no memory can ever take from them. They know who they are in Christ and they stand with their Redeemer, confident warriors against all the fiery darts of the enemy.

God promises grace sufficient for anything we need. He is always with us, no matter what we face, whether we "feel" His Presence or not. He promises to heal the brokenhearted and to give us life abundant. What good news!

Prayer to heal the effects of rape or abuse

Lord, your Word says *in Isaiah 61:3 that you "will bestow a crown of beauty instead of ashes and the oil of gladness instead of mourning." I'm asking that you somehow turn the ash heap of what happened to me into something of beauty. Right now it seems an impossible task, but your Word says it may be impossible with man, but with God, all things are possible (Matthew 20:26). Even though I don't understand how, I'm believing by faith that it can happen.*

I know that healing starts with forgiveness. *Your Word says in Matthew 19:21 that we are to forgive 70 x 7 those that do wrong to us, so as an act of my own free will, I choose to forgive _____ for what he/she did to me. Lord, you know that I'm not feeling the forgiveness right now, but I do choose to speak forgiveness and trust that in time eventually I **will** feel the forgiveness and release on the inside. I understand that forgiving the other person in no way lessens what happened to me— it simply frees me from the final bondage of power and control that _____ has held over me. In the name of Jesus Christ, the Anointed One, I break the bondage of that final ungodly soul tie now and I declare that I am free!*

Lord, please forgive me the sinful reactions *I have had. Forgive me for any way that I have blamed you, for any way that I have believed the devil's lies, for any way that I have condemned others and forgive me for not forgiving myself.*

I refuse to be a prisoner any longer—*a prisoner who has been held by the bondage of hatred—hating the person for what he/she did to me, hating and blaming myself for it happening to me, hating and blaming you, Lord for somehow allowing it. I break the ties of the bondage of hatred that have held me, and declare freedom now in Jesus' name!*

I don't understand why it happened *but I know that according to your Word in Romans 8:28, you work all things out for good for those that love you and are called according to your purpose. I love you and I'm called by you, and I hold onto that hope, and trust that somehow, some way, some day, what happened will be worked out for good. In the meantime, I love you, Lord Jesus, and believe that you love me!!*

I speak your Word over myself *and say that you will make my weak places into strengths. You will take my pain, shame, guilt and false guilt on yourself and leave me with your wisdom and redemption. As I forgive, you will restore the blessings and rewards I have missed. You even restore the years I have lost.*

I choose to believe that you will connect me *with someone you have anointed to further minister your healing to me. I am believing you for someone who can truly* *mentor your healing and freedom and restore me—spirit, soul and body. Thank you, Jesus! Amen!*

See more info on restoration prayer ministry at www.pprpm.com/restoration.html

Rebellion: My Way or God's Way

We often face trials and tribulations because of our own willful wrong choices. But it is also true that God places us in stress-filled circumstances for us to learn His ways and understand His mindset. Jesus was led up by the Spirit into the wilderness to be tempted by the devil (Matthew 4:1). Our life journey is full of crossroads where we are supposed to stop, seek God's will and then make an informed, Spirit-led choice before we proceed.

Because God created us with free will, we can choose to follow His way or insist on doing things our way. Even believers sometimes make the wrong choice and move away from the direction God is leading. If we exercise this freedom of choice to move in the opposite direction to the guidance of the Holy Spirit, we follow a way that progressively leads further and further away from God.

Following our own devices is basically rebellion against God, and it is the path of bondage rather than freedom. This path may take the form of legalism (a form of religion without life) or lawlessness (a form of religion without obedience). Either way, we become conditioned to our own way of thinking instead of having the mindset of God.

Believers who follow this path of rebelling against God's plan will find that He often uses a process of trials and tribulations to bring us to the realization that we need to change. He puts more crossroads in our path to make us choose whether we will follow His way or our own way.

Since Cain and Abel, the great issue in life has been, "Will I do it God's way or my way?" Whether we are conscious of it or not, there is a constant battle of wills that provokes this question. But why can't we live our own lives as long as we make a positive contribution to society? Aren't all sincere efforts acceptable to God? Doesn't a benevolent end justify the means?

Here are some points for you to consider:

- God has a plan to reach mankind and to relate to us. This plan was first initiated by God. "For God so loved the world that He gave His only Son, that whoever would believe in Him, would have eternal life" (John 3:16).
- No one can reach God independently by their own plan. "There is none who does good, not even one" (Romans 3:12).
- Jesus offers eternal life as a free gift that cannot be earned by adopting a new code of ethics or meeting religious standards. "For the wages of sin is death, but the free gift of God is eternal life in Christ Jesus our Lord" Romans 6:23).
- Jesus doesn't just command you to live right; He offers to live inside you, empowering you to live the Christian life. "Christ in you, the hope of glory" (Colossians 1:26-27). "I came that they might have life and have it more abundantly" (John 10:10).

- Jesus isn't just another better-than-ever forgiveness plan; He is the power to live a godly life, His life, already built into us. "But we have this treasure in earthen vessels, that the surpassing greatness of the power may be of God and not of ourselves" (II Corinthians 4:7).
- Jesus wants relationship—to be one Spirit with us, as He is with the Father. "He that is joined to the Lord is one Spirit with Him" (I Corinthians 6:17). "That they may all be one; as thou Father, are in me, and I in thee, that they also may be one in us" (John 17:21).

Jesus births His new life into us, to live the Christian life through us.

He wants us to believe in Him and invite Him in as Lord, not just a ticket to Heaven. Only as Lord of our lives can He lead us in obedience to God's way.

Galatians 2:20 can be paraphrased like this: "The 'independent unsaved I' has been permanently crucified with Jesus; nevertheless I still live, yet not I as a separated being, but the Spirit of Christ lives as one Spirit with my spirit and the life I now live in my mortal body, I live by His faith as He uniquely expresses Himself through my personality."

Some believers may still hold out for choosing their way instead of God's way, for example, if they are philosophical, rational thinkers. They live more out of their thought life than their spiritual life. When someone shares a dream or a vision from God, they may say, "Let's be logical here. All we can know for sure is what the Bible says and in some cases, even the Bible isn't all that clear. We need to trust our heads more than our hearts."

Rationalism is the reliance on reason as the basis for the establishment of religious truth, a theory that reason is in itself a source of knowledge superior to and independent of sense perceptions. Since faith is the evidence of things not seen (Hebrews 11:1), it isn't difficult to conclude that believers who follow rationalistic thinking may not put a lot of stock in "blind faith."

Are you living out of a rational Christianity or spiritual Christianity? Does your knowledge of God come only from studying the "Logos" (written) Word of God? Or also from the "Rhema" (spoken) Word? Are you trying to heal your heart with your head? Does God also speak to your heart through visions and dreams and intuition? Are you living out of your spirit that longs for communion with God? Or are you satisfied with reading a few verses of scripture and calling it a day for your quiet time with God? Would you like to hear God to you speak every single day?

Is your heart guarded or does it actually have a padlock on it? Are there walls around it that were erected years ago? Would people say that you are "all heart" or that you live out of your mind? Are you known for your ability to trust God or your inability to let go and let God do as He pleases through you? Do you feel the need to control other people and circumstances for fear of failure or shame? Is your mind on the throne of your life instead of Jesus? Our minds always want to be in control.

Can spirituality truly be lived out of your mind? As I was preparing to teach "Communion with God" by Dr. Mark Virkler, I was faced with the question, "Are you believing in a Christian rationalism?" I began thinking about how much (or how little!) Christians really know about God. Do they usually just learn about God or do they truly experience Him? Is Christianity a matter of giving mental assent to the superiority of Christ or an exchange of our old spirit for a brand new one?

Of course, God created our minds, and a good mind is a good thing.

I am not suggesting that we ignore our intelligence and knowledge. The question here is whether our mind should control our lives or if our spirit should control our minds. Do you know God spirit to Spirit? Or do you just know about Him? Are you believing in rational Christianity (your way) or true spiritual Christianity (God's way)?

Can we actually command our minds to bow down to our spirit? Would you like to test whether you are living more out of your mind or your spirit? Let's see what best describes your approach to living the Christian life.

- I make decisions based on reason in my mind or as my spirit leads.
- I live mostly in this natural world or out of the spiritual realm.
- Reality is what my mind perceives or Truth from God's Word.
- My primary goal is to educate my mind or to nurture my spirit.
- I am controlled by my mind or by self-control, a fruit of the Spirit.
- Worship is a church service or worship is my communion with God.
- Prayer is a list of petitions or prayer is an interactive conversation with God.
- My emotions are fleshly or my expressions of the heart of God.
- I can only trust analysis or I can also trust impressions in my spirit.
- I think it through and figure it out or I am led by the Holy Spirit.
- Christianity is a code of ethics or an intimate relationship with Jesus.
- I pray to God in Heaven or to Christ inside me, abiding in me.
- I live a good life for Jesus or I invite Christ to live His life through me.
- Christianity is a one-time experience or experiencing Christ daily.
- Christianity is my philosophy is a lifestyle of encounters with Jesus.
- God's Word is only the Bible or is also hearing God's voice.
- Jesus lives in Heaven or Jesus lives His life through my humanity.
- I set goals for productivity or I do what Father God says to do.
- I lead out of natural leadership abilities or out of spiritual authority.
- I invest more in natural commodities or more in the Kingdom of God.
- I am comfortable in my traditions or as I am led by the Holy Spirit.
- My significance is based on people's opinions or on God's Truth about me.
- I have difficulty focusing on God or my passion is to know God.
- Wisdom is based on my experience or wisdom is applying God's Truth.

Did the above list help you to identify areas where your mind is still trying to retain control and has not yielded to allow your spirit to be in communion with God or His Holy Spirit? It may be that you need further training on hearing and discerning God's voice. The Bible makes it clear that we can hear and know God is speaking to us.

John 10:27: "My sheep hear my voice, and I know them, and they follow me."

Revelation 3:20: "Behold, I stand at the door, and knock: if any man hear my voice, and open the door, I will come in to him, and will sup with him, and he with me."

You may need more information about removing the blocks that prevent you from hearing His voice. I believe the Holy Spirit is ready to connect you with the healing and equipping you need in order to hear God's voice clearly. We are all called to minister God's heart to others and God desires to enable us to minister with new confidence.

As a prayer minister, there may be times when people come to you thinking they are believers when in fact they are not. Do you know how to lead someone to Jesus for salvation and healing? You can use the following paragraphs as a pattern for setting up a crossroads situation in their lives where they will have to choose either their way or God's way.

What does it mean to have a personal relationship with Christ, and in what way does it impact our lives? And how does someone go about making that kind of commitment?

Those are good questions and typical of someone who understands the significance of Jesus. Here is some information to help answer these and other questions you may have about Jesus.

Because of Jesus' resurrection, His followers do not honor a dead founder, as most religions do. They have a vital, personal relationship with Him. Jesus Christ lives today and faithfully enriches the lives of all those who trust and obey Him.

Throughout the centuries, multitudes have acknowledged the worthiness of Jesus Christ, including many who have greatly influenced the world. French physicist and philosopher Blaise Pascal spoke of people's need for Jesus when he basically said, "There is a God-shaped vacuum or hole in the heart of every man, which only God can fill through his Son Jesus Christ." (Original source still debated)

Can your God-shaped vacuum or hole be filled? Yes, it can! Because of God's deep love for you, He has already made all the necessary arrangements. Through the death and resurrection of Jesus Christ, God's Son, you can enjoy a personal relationship with Almighty God. Jesus made it possible to bridge the chasm which separates us from God.

When I was staff with Campus Crusade for Christ, I learned how to share the following four principles which will help you discover how to know Jesus personally and experience the abundant life He promised to believers.

The first principle is that God LOVES you and created you to know Him personally

John 3:16: "For God so loved the world that He gave His one and only Son, that whoever believes in Him shall not perish but have eternal life."

John 17:3: "Now this is eternal life: that they may know you, the only true God, and Jesus Christ, whom you have sent."

The second principle explains what prevents us from knowing God personally.

Man is SINFUL and SEPARATED from God, so we cannot know Him personally or experience His love.

Romans 3:23: "For all have sinned and fall short of the glory of God."

Romans 6:23: "The wages of sin is death [spiritual separation from God]."

Romans 8:6-8: "The mind of sinful man is death, but the mind controlled by the Spirit is life and peace; the sinful mind is hostile to God. It does not submit to God's law, nor can it do so. Those controlled by the sinful nature cannot please God."

A great gulf separates man from God. Man is continually trying to reach God and establish a personal relationship with Him through human efforts, such as living a good life, philosophy, or religion. But he inevitably fails.

The third principle explains the only way to bridge this gulf.

Jesus Christ is God's ONLY provision for man's sin. Through him alone we can know God personally and experience God's love

Romans 5:8: "God demonstrates His own love toward us, in that while we were yet sinners, Christ died for us."

I Corinthians 15:3: "Christ died for our sins, according to the scriptures."

John 14:6: "Jesus said to him, 'I am the way, the truth and the life. No one comes to the Father except through me.'"

God has bridged the gulf that separates us from Him by sending His Son, Jesus Christ, to die on the Cross in our place to pay the penalty for our sins.

The fourth principle reveals that it is not enough just to know these truths.

We must individually RECEIVE Jesus Christ as Lord and Savior; then we can know God personally and experience His love

John 1:12: "As many as received him, to them he gave the right to become children of God, even to those who believe in his name."

Ephesians 2:8-9: "For it is by grace that you have been saved, through faith. This does not depend on anything you have achieved, it is the free gift of God; and because it is not earned no one can boast about it."

Receiving Christ involves turning to God from self (repentance) and trusting Christ to come into our lives to forgive us of our sins and make us what He wants us to be. Just to agree intellectually that Jesus Christ is the Son of God and that He died on the Cross for our sins is not enough. Nor is it enough to merely have an emotional experience. We can only receive Jesus Christ by faith, as an act of our will. It may or may not be an emotional experience.

Jesus Christ is waiting for an invitation to come into your life. In fact, He says, "Behold, I stand at the door and knock; if anyone hears my voice and opens the door, I will come in" (Rev. 3:20).

Perhaps you can sense Christ knocking at the door of your heart. You can invite Him in by faith right now. God knows your heart so it doesn't matter exactly what words you use. Here's a suggested prayer:

Lord Jesus, I want to know you personally. Thank you for dying on the Cross for my sins. I open the door of my life to you and ask you to come in as my Savior and Lord. Take control of my life. Thank you for forgiving my sins and giving me eternal life. Make me the kind of person you want me to be. Amen.

If this prayer expresses the desire of your heart, pray it right now and Jesus Christ will come into your life, just as He has promised. Once you invite Christ into your life, He promises to never leave you.

Hebrews 13:5: "God has said, 'Never will I leave you; never will I forsake you.'"

To know God personally is the greatest decision you will ever make.

Reverend John Wesley, the founder of the Wesleyan Methodist Church, was a humble man who trusted God with his whole being. Below is a favorite prayer of his. Whether you are a Methodist or not, this prayer is a powerful prayer of covenant and a reminder of whose we are. It re-orders our life to focus on our mission from God and discipleship. Will you choose to dedicate your heart to follow God's way?

John Wesley's Prayer

I am no longer my own but yours.
Put me to what you will.
Put me to doing, put me to suffering.
Let me be employed for you or laid aside for you,
exalted for you or brought low for you.
Let me be full or let me be empty.
Let me have all things or let me have nothing.
I freely and wholeheartedly yield all things to your disposal.
And now glorious and blessed Father, Son and Holy Spirit,
You are mine and I am yours. So be it.
And the covenant now made on earth,
let it be ratified in Heaven.
(original reference unknown)

Prayer to renounce rebellion and choose God's way

Lord Jesus, I admit that I can never be good enough to earn your love and acceptance. I turn from trying to manage my life in my own efforts and choose to trust you to forgive my rebellious heart. Based on your death on the Cross for me, I ask you to live the Christian life through me. I cannot do it without your strength and wisdom.

Forgive me for being critical of others who tried to show me the error of my ways. I'm so sorry for my harsh words and condescending attitude. Help me to obey whatever you tell me to do to restore these people back into my life. I need discerning people to shine your light into areas that are slipping into darkness and I choose to listen to those you send to me as your voice from now on.

I'm sorry for rebelling against you, Lord. I thought I could do a better job of running my life. I command my mind to bow down to my spirit which is one spirit with your Spirit. I receive the mind of Christ which has all knowledge and power.

I forgive all those who told me I had a right to insist on my own way. I choose to speak your truth which has the power to revive someone else whose heart has been deceived by the enemy. Help me to show others how to choose your way.

Lord, I also forgive myself for refusing to see and accept your truth. I trust you and believe that you are inside me now, equipping me in every way that you want to express your heart in me and through me to a needy world.

I choose to yield to you day by day. *Your all-powerful grace and ever-present wisdom provide everything that I need. I choose to know you and agree with your plans and wonderful purposes for me. There is nothing more important to me than a relationship with you, Jesus. May we be one in spirit forever. Amen.*

Roots of Bitterness

In my opinion, the most common spiritual root would be bitterness lodged in the heart, as a result of judging with condemnation, resentment or unforgiveness. Most Christian workers who quit the ministry fail because they cannot get along with other workers. As a fellow minister to believers who need healing, it is imperative that you learn how to discern hidden spiritual roots (or not so spiritual roots) and help others discern and break the power of bitterness.

Invite them to use the following scripture prayer strategy and **pray scripture daily for forty days** like Jesus did during His temptation in the wilderness. He answered all the devil's tests with "It is written…" Let the power of the Word of God discern between their souls and spirits and the thoughts and intents of their hearts. In His own way, the Lord Jesus will show them their blind spots, hidden bitterness and judgmental attitudes.

Hebrews 4:12-13: "For the Word of God is living and powerful, and sharper than any two-edged sword, **piercing even to the division of soul and spirit, and of joints and marrow, and is a discerner of the thoughts and intents of the heart**. And there is no creature hidden from His sight, but all things are naked and open to the eyes of Him to whom we must give account."

Ephesians 4:31-32: "**Let all bitterness**, wrath, anger, clamor, and evil speaking be put away from you, with all malice. And be kind to one another, tenderhearted, forgiving one another, even as God in Christ forgave you."

Hebrews 12:14-16: "Looking carefully lest anyone fall short of the grace of God; lest any **root of bitterness** springing up cause trouble, and by this many become defiled."

Luke 6:43-44: "For a good tree does not bear bad fruit, nor does a bad tree bear good fruit. For every tree is **known by its own fruit.**"

Luke 6:45: "For men do not gather figs from thorns, nor do they gather grapes from a bramble bush. A good man **out of the good treasure of his heart** brings forth good; and an evil man out of the evil treasure of his heart brings forth evil. For out of the abundance of the heart his mouth speaks."

Romans 2:1-3: "**Therefore you are inexcusable,** O man, whoever you are who judge, for in whatever you judge another you condemn yourself; for you who judge practice the same things. But we know that the judgment of God is according to truth against those who practice such things."

Romans 12:17-20: "**Repay no one evil for evil.** Have regard for good things in the sight of all men. If it is possible, as much as depends on you, live peaceably with all men. Beloved, **do not avenge yourselves,** but rather give place to wrath; for it is written, 'Vengeance is Mine, I will repay,' says the Lord."

Romans 6:6-10: "Knowing this, that our old man was crucified with Him, that the body of sin might be done away with, that we should **no longer be slaves of sin**. For he who has died has been freed from sin. Now if we died with Christ, we believe that we shall also live with Him, knowing that Christ, having been raised from the dead, dies no more. Death no longer has dominion over Him."

I John 2:9: "He who says he is in the light, and **hates his brother,** is in darkness until now."

James 4:11: "Do not speak evil of one another, brethren. He who speaks evil of a brother and judges his brother, speaks evil of the law and judges the law. But if you judge the law, **you are not a doer of the law but a judge."**

I Corinthians 4:5: "Therefore **judge nothing before the time,** until the Lord comes, who will both bring to light the hidden things of darkness and reveal the counsels of the hearts. Then each one's praise will come from God."

Prayer to clear out roots of bitterness and judgmental attitudes

Lord, I come before you in humility, seeking your help with a problem I caused in my own life by my judgmental attitude. I cannot uproot this in my own strength. Because I sowed judgment against others for their sins and failures, I focused on the behavior or attitude I hated in them and now find the same thing cropping up in me. I am reaping a harvest of harmful roots of bitterness, resentment and anger.

Lord, please forgive me for the times I put the blame on you for not protecting me from the darts aimed at me by other people, even Christians. I thought it was your fault for having such lousy children. Now I see that my own sinful judgmental attitudes were defiling them. In my eyes, they became what I expected them to be. Lord, open my eyes to discern myself rightly and to remember the judgments I have sown long ago, so I can finally renounce them.

I need to change and I can't do it without the power of your Holy Spirit in me. Please forgive me my sinful reactions and judgments and for how I've hurt others through my own choices. Forgive me for enticing anyone else to follow the tangled path I laid out for others because of my own self-fulfilling expectancies.

By the power of the blood of Christ poured out on the Cross, I choose to forgive, letting go of my right to hold any offense against those who hurt me. Because Jesus paid the price for my sin and theirs, I choose to release my anger and bitterness to you, Lord. Please remove all traces of resentment and judgment from my heart and bring all the sinful seeds I have sown to death on the Cross so I can be free to sow new seeds into good soil.

You alone, Lord, are the Righteous Judge of all the earth. *The judgment I sent out was unjust and unwarranted, harmful not only to myself but to those around me. I forgive myself for allowing my own judgmental attitude to stunt my faith and give rise to bitter roots within my life. I ask you to bring my entire fleshly structure of judgmental reactions to death on the Cross. Weed out my bitter roots and cleanse the soil of my inner man. Make me a well-watered garden, full of the fruit of the Spirit, that my life would please you.*

I choose to sow good seeds of true spiritual discernment. *Help me to see myself and others through your eyes, persons in your process of transformation. Give me your heart to minister intercession not accusation, vision not criticism. I choose to partner with you, Lord, whenever needed to support your work in their hearts. May I be a person you can trust with the secrets of men's hearts because I rejoice in their potential in you. I choose to be humble, knowing that except for the grace of God, there go I. Thank you, for a ministry of reconciliation, not condemnation.*
Amen.

Use this space to list all the ways you have been critical and judgmental.

Self-Image Issues; True Identity

How we view ourselves depends on many factors, including past experiences, childhood traumas and reactions to present-day situations. Often our self-image is tied to beliefs we have held onto for years. Studies show that most of our personality is formed by the time we are six years old. Likewise, our view of God and ourselves was largely formed based on our pre-school experiences. It's time to update!

Self-image issues definitely affect our faith. For instance, do you believe God short-changed you when He made His original sovereign choices for you? Would you rather be dead than go through your life and circumstances again? Do you feel uncoordinated, as if your spirit and body are out of sync with each other? Do you believe God has not equipped you to live the Christian life He has called you live? Do you feel fragmented, both wanting God's favor but fearing God at the same time?

How about physical challenges? Do you often have auto-immune illnesses or symptoms with no known cause or cure? Have you rejected your sexuality, not believing you can be a blessing as a spouse or to a spouse? Have you had difficulty with learning, dyslexia, space, time, language and sequences? Do you have trouble with inversions of letters, words, numbers or differentiating between right and left?

Rebelling against God's choices for you can affect your body, soul and spirit. Think about it. Can you joyfully follow God's leading and plan for your life if you feel God made a mistake when He made you, and you don't really believe that you are fearfully and wonderfully made? **Is your spirit going forward with God while your mind, will and emotions resist him?** Are you afraid to trust God and His choices for your future and destiny?

Ask yourself these questions:

- Would you choose the same century God chose for your birth?
- Would you choose the same neighborhood and country again?
- Would you choose to be born into the same race and economy?
- Would you choose the same father and mother God chose?
- Would you choose the brothers/sisters God chose for you?
- Would you choose to be the same gender, if God asked you?
- Would you choose to have the same face, body and appearance?
- Would you choose the same mind, memory and intellect?
- Would you like to have the same personality and character?
- Would you like to have the same gifts, talents and abilities?
- Would you finish living this life if God gave you a choice?

What changes would you have made if God had said it was OK?

As Christians, many of us are so tied up in negative self-image issues that we never allow the power of God to flow through us to change us and our world. We don't really know who we are and have never understood or accepted our true God-given identity. We feel powerless against the enemy because we are trying to fight in our own limited strength, not knowing that we have Almighty God Himself and all of heaven's armies to back us up.

I clearly remember interviewing a former witch who impressed upon me the importance of really believing who we are in Christ. She said that witches have their own discernment and they could discern that maybe only one or two people in an entire church "really knew who they were in Christ."

I was never so motivated to start really believing all that the Word of God says about my identity in Christ, as I have been since that night in 2000. Yes, I know the Bible and have been a Christian counselor for years, but there were times I still managed to say, "Yes but…" when God wanted to do greater works through me (John 14:12).

It takes faith to believe that we will do greater works than Jesus did, whether we are believing for our daily bread, praying for healing or working miracles. It can be even more challenging to believe what the Word of God says about who we are in Christ: righteous, blameless, holy, unconditionally loved and accepted, totally forgiven, called and gifted. But this *is* our true identity in Christ if we are born again.

Do we believe that born-again believers already have everything we need?

We really have all the fruit of the Spirit inside us in Christ already. We are rooted and grounded in Him, regardless of our circumstances and perceived needs. He allows challenges in our lives so He can show us that He is greater than anything that may challenge us. He has all the power in the universe and He is all that power inside us!

Needs are just stages set for a miracle from Father God.

As we abide in Him, we acknowledge that He is our all in all. He has already answered every prayer, provided for every need, solved every problem, equipped us for every task, discerned every situation and prepared every connection we will need to bear fruit that remains.

Negative self-image issues tie us to the natural law of trying to do what is right in our own strength—and failing. Through faith in the resurrection power of Jesus Christ within us, we are set free to live supernatural lives as we release Christ to live His life of righteousness in us. This is true success. "Therefore, my brethren, you also have become dead to the law through the body of Christ, that you may be married to another—to Him [Jesus Christ] who was raised from the dead, that we should bear fruit to God" (Romans 7:3-4).

By His death, Jesus has done His part—provided forgiveness for every sin, freedom from every bondage, truth to replace every lie and has taken on Himself every curse that could come against us. As we do our part—accepting Christ as Savior, confessing our sin, become born again and filled with His Spirit and appropriating each promise in scripture—we die to trusting in our own ability to bear fruit by keeping the law. Through faith, we experience all that Father God has promised His children.

As long as we think we can get our needs met by ourselves or by others, God will let us pursue this fallacy until we find out that, ultimately, no other person or thing can meet our needs. God gave us the law as a tutor to point us back to His love and grace (Galatians 3:24). We don't need (demonic) spirit guides to assist us in life because God's Holy Spirit inside us is all we need. He is supernatural wisdom, knowledge, counsel, power, strength, love, etc. inside us.

We must learn to trust Father God 100% to complete us and that in Him we are always complete. As we continually confess the Word of God, our spirits will eventually receive God's truth: believers really are holy, righteous and blameless in Christ, as Ephesians 1 and Romans 5 say. Through grace by faith (Ephesians 2:8-9), we receive God's truth that we are totally forgiven, loved and lovable, chosen and the ideal place for Jesus to live.

We have access to Him 24/7 because He is inside us every moment.

Let's choose again now to receive God's truth about ourselves. He intends for us to allow Him to live His life through us without stressing over deceptions and lies that say we are incomplete, inadequate, insufficient and insignificant. Father God says we have everything we need to live His life in godliness (II Peter 1:3).

The reason we have everything we need is that we have it all in Jesus.

According to John 15:4, apart from Him we can do nothing—but as we abide *in* Him, we truly have everything we need to do all He asks us to do. When we abide in Him each day, we are filled automatically with all the wisdom, knowledge, power, insight, love, gifts, fruit—everything we will need for the day or the night!

Our negative self-image problems stem from believing the enemy's lie that we are somehow missing something. But Jesus has not withheld anything we need for life and godliness. If we have received Jesus Christ as our only Lord and Savior, we are complete in Christ (Colossians 2:10). We simply choose to abide in Him and to agree with Him as He abides in us.

We hear His will and we speak in agreement with Him, speaking His supernatural provision into the visible natural realm. As we believe He has given us the very desires our heart should have, we ask and speak, believing He told us to ask and has provided the answer already (Luke 11:9-10). Every need is already met in Him.

Are we supposed to ask for gifts and fruit? Or more of the Holy Spirit? When we see other believers doing miracles, seeing visions and living a victorious life, do we believe God is more faithful to them than to us?

We need to discern with our double-minded thinking about God and ourselves.

Long ago, most of us experienced some rejection and began to wonder if we were inferior, inadequate or somehow less than others. The enemy set others up to criticize us and reject us, hoping we would believe his lies about who we are and what we can do. Ultimately, the devil planned to hit a triple play: he wanted us to reject others, ourselves and God.

Many people acknowledge that God has equipped some people to fulfill their destiny but believe He may never equip them fully. If you asked them if they think God favors others but has short-changed them, they may say "no" with their mouth but "yes" with their eyes. In their spirit, they may want to believe God, but their mind says, "Look at the facts; God has not given you all the gifts and fruit of the Spirit that you need to succeed."

Other believers once sensed a calling on their life in the past but find it hard to trust God for it now. They may fear that they have been disqualified or even rejected by God. Others believe they have to earn God's acceptance with good behavior before He will equip them. Some believe God accepts them but find it impossible to accept themselves. They can't seem to just enter into God's rest and stop trying to earn His acceptance.

Despite what they read in the Bible, Christians often believe the accusations of people and the enemy rather than believe what God has said about them. They can't receive His truth about who they are: unconditionally loved and accepted in the beloved, totally forgiven, the righteousness of God in Christ Jesus, holy and blameless and fully equipped to fulfill their God-given destiny.

Read Romans 5 and the first chapter of Ephesians. They are full of blessings for God's children. Listen to the truth in these verses—this truth is for you.

The New Testament says Christ died to make us worthy and acceptable.

"To the praise of the glory of His grace, wherein He hath made us accepted in the beloved" (Ephesians 1:6). In the Old Testament we are assured that if we will give God our shame, we shall be called His priests and ministers, He will give us an inheritance in the nations and give us a double portion: "But you will be called the priests of the LORD; You will be spoken of as ministers of our God. You will eat the wealth of nations, And in their riches you will boast. Instead of your shame you will have a double portion, and instead of humiliation they will shout for joy over their portion. Therefore they will possess a double portion in their land. Everlasting joy will be theirs" (Isaiah 61:6-7).

In fact, II Peter 1:3 says God has given us everything we need for life and godliness. Would God call us and then refuse to equip us? Of course not!

So what's our problem? Is it that we see God as we saw our human fathers? Do we project rejecting attitudes onto a holy God? Have we believed false teachings that say God will reject you if you don't do everything just right? Are we on a quest to become complete even though God says we are already complete in Christ? Is our problem that we don't believe we have what God says we have in Christ? Or are rejection cycles blocking us from walking in the gifts and fruit that we already have because the Holy Spirit is inside of us as born-again believers?

The best way to root out areas where you do not believe God is to pray related scriptures daily until your doubt and unbelief are exposed in the light of the Word. I encouraged you to collect the scriptures that are the most difficult for you to believe, especially scriptures related to who we believers are in Christ. We can believe our true identity in Christ because of what Jesus did for us on the Cross.

This will take commitment on your part, but you will begin to believe you are the mighty man or woman of God that God says you are. What a great way to start and end the day! Agree with the Word of God like Jesus did for forty days saying, "It is written…" The Word of God will not come back void.

Prayer for healing and freedom from self-image issues

Lord, I admit that in the past I have not accepted *the life you gave me. I rebelled against your choices for my mind, appearance, circumstances, my family, my personality, my own body, etc. I never saw myself as a gift to the world but rather wondered if I were a burden. But now, because of your love and the sacrifice of Christ, I choose to embrace life. Help me to accept your wise choices for my life—and to trust you to redeem my past, present and future.*

For a long time, I've been angry with you, Father, *because I believed the lies the enemy whispered to me--that you didn't have my best interests at heart, that you were weak and couldn't help me, even that you didn't care about me or the pain I suffered. There were times I wanted my life to end because I couldn't bear the thought that no one cared, not even you. But it wasn't true. I see that now and I release you from any blame I hurled at you in my despair when you didn't answer my prayers in the way I wanted.*

I confess that I have judged other people *for wounding my spirit. I saw my family members and even authority figures as incapable of wisdom and sensitivity, as unworthy of being in leadership. In judging them, and you, I viewed others as deficient as myself. In sowing dishonor, I reaped a harvest of trouble in my own life* *and I have seen the weeds of damage I've caused in other people's lives as well. I'm so sorry. Let my repentance bring healing to the wounds and help me to sow good seeds that will blossom again with healthy relationships.*

Lord, I also forgive the people who supported my rebellion *and self-pity, buying into the lies of the enemy right along with me and agreeing that you had shortchanged me and that I was right to reject your choices for me. I choose to trust your designs for my life. Help me and them to see your truth that sets us free.*

Even though I don't feel like the gift you say I am, *I choose to trust your truth and not to let my emotions run my life. In faith, I choose instead to be grateful for my life, to accept myself as a blessing that will bring glory to you and be a help to others. I turn my spirit toward your light; I have walked in the darkness of my own making too long. I choose to believe for blessing and divine favor with you and with man.*

I forgive myself for wallowing in misery, *frustrated with what I saw as my own inability and limitations. I regret the many opportunities I wasted while running from the disappointment of my life. In rejecting myself, I rejected you and your plans for me. I choose to receive your creative design and purposes for my life, my talents, gifts and even the weaknesses you gave me. I believe that you are carefully orchestrating my training and connecting me through divine appointments so that I will have every opportunity to fulfill my destiny.*

Father, please open my eyes to your power within me. *I invite your Holy Spirit to fill every part of my body, soul and spirit. I allow your abundant life to flow through me, bringing joy in knowing you and accepting that I am "fearfully and wonderfully made." I am not broken, I am not defective and I am not a mistake. I am your child, redeemed by the blood of Jesus Christ, who loved me and gave Himself for me.*

I join the Great Commission Army with a permanent commitment. *I choose to be loyal to my fellow soldiers and to obedient to you, my commanding officer. Your orders will be welcomed with confidence in your wisdom and loving care. Thank you, for the courage to believe that you are divinely equipping me to fulfill my calling, as we build your Kingdom together.*

Show me, Lord, how I can also believe in your design for others, *also supporting them and their calling in life. Enable me to sow into their ministries and to reap a good crop as I invest in them. As I sow favor, I believe I will reap favor and blessing, more and later. I receive my assignments, those who will be my prayer partners, co-laborers in ministry and those who will invest in our vision and mission outreaches to make disciples and to teach all nations. In Jesus' mighty name, amen.*

You can use this space to write your vision.

Slumbering Spirit

Have you ever wondered, "What's up with that believer? Are they asleep to what the Holy Spirit is trying to say to them? Not only are they not tuned into God, sometimes they don't even seem to have a conscience!" They may defile the body of Christ with their irresponsible business practices, immorality or ministry methods—without remorse. They seem to sleep right through the most Spirit-filled services.

Or maybe you wonder if your personal spirit is not really awake like that of other believers. You wonder if you hear God, sense His Holy Spirit, tune into worship, the spiritual realm, or even to other people spiritually like some believers do. All believers have the Holy Spirit but some feel dry in their own personal spirit.

For one thing, the art of fathering has been so lost that many believers have slumbering spirits in this "fatherless generation." Fathers who were not fathered have not known how to nurture their children's spirits. Children used to be nurtured by the entire extended family, but now many children have only one parent or none. Many adults still need to be nurtured to life. God wants to turn the hearts of the fathers back to their children to love and pray with them.

Where can we find help when so many have the same problem?

Their personal spirits have not been loved to life by loving, affectionate fathers. The quality of fathering has a direct influence on the strength and fiber of our society. Seldom are children fortunate enough to have fathers who teach them, much less love them enough to pray with them. Gangs are a direct result of little or no nurturing and fathering. How do we restore the hearts of the children? Personally, I was in my forties before I found someone who would nurture my spirit to life.

Learning to discern a slumbering spirit is one of our most powerful tools because it is a major root of the powerlessness of many believers. Many believers are sincere and know verses about an intimate relationship with God but have trouble actually tuning in to Father God. On the other hand, you may have known of ministers who could even go from their own services immediately into serious sin. How can they mix gross sin into their ministry without repentance—or even remorse? Is their heart so hardened that they can exhort, evangelize and minister to others, while continuing in gross sin themselves?

The first function of our new spirit in Christ, our personal spirit, is to relate to and be one with the Holy Spirit. Some believers testify that they were reborn in Christ, filled with the Holy Spirit and called to ministry, but in practice, their walk talks much louder than their talk talks. They go through the motions of ministry to others while only imparting the motions but not life in the Spirit, life in Christ.

Without these teachings, many of you might rush in to pray deliverance prayers, thinking this person is captive to a demonic spirit that prevents them from receiving the conviction of the Holy Spirit. While this may be one aspect, I would like to teach you the difference between a captive spirit and a slumbering spirit.

A slumbering spirit has never really been awakened to life in Christ.

They may have been filled with the Holy Spirit at one time, but now have a hardened heart. They may minister to others but are like a rock inside, not receiving the ministry of the Holy Spirit to themselves. They are now dead to it. It's like They feel more born again in mind than in spirit.

We must ask Holy Spirit to teach us to discern these basic signs of someone whose spirit needs to be loved to life versus someone who primarily needs deliverance from a captive spirit. For instance, when we minister to someone with a slumbering spirit we must hear Holy Spirit suggest many ways that we can father or mother them to life through His love and that they will be able to:
- Sense the presence of God in cooperate worship
- Experience God daily in their private quiet time
- Receive revelation as they hear God's voice
- Receive dreams and visions from God
- Thrive in their natural health and immunity
- Flow with new insights and inspiration from God
- Rejoice in relating to God in their past, present and future
- Communicate with others with real empathy, heart to heart
- Experience the glory of marriage union in body, soul and spirit
- Be sensitive to Holy Spirit conviction of sin versus only remorse
- Father/mother others to life and fruitful membership in the body
- Bring the presence of God with them everywhere they go

You may discover that you need to allow God to restore your own soul and spirit so you can impart strength and energy from your spirit to others. Begin to receive nurture from Father God for YOU. Let the Holy Spirit impart His glory through your spirit so that others can tune into the heart of the Holy Spirit and develop an intimate relationship with Father God.

I pray you will earn how to pray effectively and to love people to life, to awaken their personal spirits, to impart life and the ability to relate from deep within their souls and spirits. You will be able to minister more out of your spirit, awakened by the Holy Spirit, rather than only with eloquent words. You will be more able to empathize with the personal spirits in others, to partner with Father God and to nurture what He is raising up in their personal spirits.

It may also be necessary to work with a team of people who will commit, over time, to love that slumbering one to life. Ask God for a team of people who can receive and release God's heart of love and an appropriate interactive intimate relationship.

Prayer to awaken a slumbering spirit

Lord, I realize now that my spirit is not fully awake, *is asleep, is not aware of your presence or is not fully functioning in this life you've given me. I am not able to tune into your Holy Spirit when I worship like some do. My devotional time with you seems dry toast instead of fresh bread. I don't often hear or see you or get the fresh revelation from your Word that you have promised believers. My spirit has been too weak to even sustain my own health. I need total healing—your divine healing—for my physical body.*

I am not satisfied with copying others. *I want to believe you for original insights, inspiration and supernatural creativity, straight from your Spirit to my spirit. I want a more intimate relationship with others too, relating spirit to spirit. Send me those fathers and mothers in the Lord who will parent me again. Send me mentors who know how to activate my personal spirit in the power of Holy Spirit.*

Lord, please awaken my spirit and conscience *to desire your will and way before I fall into sin (or fall again.) Something was always missing in my spiritual life, but I wasn't sure what. Was my spirit ever really in tune with you? Was I like Jonah, who fled from your plan? Or was I like the one whose spirit was never loved to life in the first place? Either way, I have hidden my light under a bushel basket and it has caused trouble.*

I am so happy to hear that your heart's desire *is to Father me, to breathe life into me and to bring people into my life who will love my spirit to life. Right now, I choose to receive their nurture even though it will be a challenge to open my heart to trust for unconditional love and acceptance. I choose to receive a new conscience, a new ability to discern what your Holy Spirit is doing and a new ability to meet with you Lord. I long to hear your voice, to commune with you and to know you more intimately. You promised that the pure in heart can see God; make me pure in heart.*

Please forgive me *for being unable or unwilling to live the life you've given me and for running from your plan instead of running into your arms for strength and courage. Set me free to choose to be in the center of your will. I choose to receive the joy of my salvation, of interaction with you Father God and of being your love and power to others.*

I confess to judging my parents and others for *not providing spiritual nurturing and teaching in my childhood. Because I blamed others for my shortcomings, I reaped a harvest of indifference, unable or unwilling to feel what others feel or reach out to help them. For these wounds, I am deeply sorry.*

Forgive me for failing others *or my own children by not providing a godly example for them, for not building strength of character into their young lives because of my slumbering spirit. Father, I don't know how to properly nurture their spirits or teach them values, but I want to learn how to carry them in my heart as you do.*

I forgive myself for allowing my spirit to fall asleep, for not responding in love to others and for letting my spirit lie dormant and not useful to you.

Lord, by the power of the resurrected Christ and because of His blood poured out for me, I choose life and want to obey your plan. I ask you to awaken my spirit, cleanse me and remove the cobwebs from my consciousness that I may be of better service to you and others. Free my spirit from the prison of apathy. Let your river of abundant life flow through me, refreshing and enlivening every part, like a dash of cold water on the face.

Breathe life into my slumbering spirit. I bring myself to you and to the Cross, asking that you bring to death my indifference, my unwillingness, and my tendency to flee from your plan and the life you've given me. Resurrect me to full consciousness. Strengthen and discipline me to respond quickly to your voice and to the needs of others.

Thank you for not giving up on me. Like in Jonah's life, a fresh opportunity has been granted. Don't let me waste it! Help me sense your presence, your Spirit within me, calling me to new creativity and awareness. Make me accountable, vulnerable, and responsible, a true child of God. I receive your Spirit to be one with my spirit, Lord.

Teach me how to find my tribe and the greenhouse of growth you have prepared for me. Open my spiritual eyes and ears to discern your vision and missions for me. I choose to believe that you will bring people who will consider it an honor to support me and my vision and to invest in my vision and mission.
Amen.

Strongholds: Corporate and Personal

"For the weapons of our warfare are not carnal, but mighty through God to the pulling down of strongholds, casting down imaginations and every high thing that exalts itself against the knowledge of God and bringing into captivity every thought to the obedience of Christ" (II Corinthians 10:4-5).

A personal stronghold is an automatic, practiced and habitual way of thinking and behaving sinfully that we know is not godly but we feel hopeless to change. Common personal strongholds are related to illness, bitterness, anger, separated thinking, jealousy, doubt, unworthiness, self-pity, performance-based acceptance, rejection, fear, intimidation, accusation, witchcraft, religious control and pride.

A stronghold often begins when we react sinfully to personal hurt or trauma. God created us with lives and wills of our own, but the automatic sinful reactions that we create also have a life of their own. This is manifested in habits, fantasies, addictions and wrongful ways of thinking. The strongholds and sinful reactions that we developed before we knew Jesus can resurrect and maintain lives of their own even after we receive Christ into our lives.

Although we might originally have thought it was good for our minds to be in control, the Bible says that "a mind set on the flesh is death, but the mind set on the Spirit is life and peace" and "the mind set on the flesh is hostile toward God; for it does not subject itself to the law of God, for it is not even able to do so" and "those who are in the flesh cannot please God" (Romans 8:6-8).

Strongholds, personal and corporate, are obstacles to our own healing process because we defend our right to react and behave sinfully rather than yield to the conviction of the Holy Spirit.

Mental strongholds have an "auto-drive" of their own and our minds play a big part in blocking our relationship with the Lord because mental strongholds war against the Spirit of God. Our carnal mind does not want to give up control (Hebrews 2:15). The primary function of the baptism of the Holy Spirit is not how many gifts are functioning, **but rather who or what is in control.** We can choose for our spirits to be in control and command our minds to bow down to our spirits which can be one with Christ (I Corinthians 6:17; John 17).

In spiritual warfare, we must hurl the Word of God against the walls of the strongholds in our mind. Truth breaks down walls and takes every thought captive. Our most important warfare is against the ungodly sinful reactions and behaviors in our own lives.

Think about it: the first sin was a mental sin setting up a stronghold. Adam and Eve chose to agree with Satan's thinking rather than God's truth. Think again: when Jesus gave His life for us, He was crucified on Golgotha, which means "the skull," the residence of the brain or the mind.

Romans 12:2 commands us to "be transformed by the renewing of our minds, that we may prove what the will of God is, that which is good and acceptable and perfect." Warfare against mental strongholds is Biblical. It is not simply casting out demons, but rather the act of destroying speculations, pretensions and every lofty thing raised up against the intimate knowledge of God, taking every thought captive to the obedience of Christ (II Corinthians 10:5).

Before I started praying scripture, I couldn't see that I had the most common strongholds of bitterness, jealousy, self-rejection and fear. After I had been encouraged to pray scripture for two years, I finally began to do what Jesus did. Jesus prayed, "It is written...," swinging the Sword of the Spirit during His forty days of warfare in the wilderness (Matthew 4). Jesus gave us a model for entering into warfare against the personal strongholds that hold us captive as individuals or corporate strongholds that can captivate entire nations. He showed us how to wear the armor of God and to use our offensive spiritual weapons to win as we swing the Sword of the Spirit, the Word of God, and pray in the Spirit (see Ephesians 6).

What is the difference between a personal and a corporate stronghold?

A corporate stronghold is a practiced, habitual way of thinking that we share with the common mentality of a group or mankind. It is a type of tradition or philosophy actively controlling churches, groups, masses and nations (Colossians 2:8). We may call ourselves free thinkers, but actually, we have lost our freedom and have become captives to a mental stronghold preventing our knowledge of God.

Examples of corporate strongholds would be racism, sexism, addictions, abortion, sexual immorality, pornography, liberalism, modernism, humanism or Aryan superiority (as resurrected in Aryan gangs today.) Religious strongholds deny the manifestations of the Holy Spirit, quench the new moves of the Spirit of God and even blaspheme by attributing the work of the Holy Spirit to the devil.

In order to control us, strongholds rob us of free will and spiritual power, of the ability to respond to the Holy Spirit, our destiny and an intimate relationship with Christ. Corporate strongholds block the Word of God and the workings, guidance, direction and conviction of the Holy Spirit for whole churches, cities or nations. The purpose of a corporate stronghold is to distort the Word of God, block our spiritual discernment and to bring to us to destruction (II Peter 3:16).

By definition, a stronghold is a blind spot that we defend instead of receiving conviction. If you hear yourself saying, "This sin isn't so bad; I deserve a little fun" or "Everybody else thinks this way," that is the stronghold talking.

Believers must learn how to recognize and overcome personal and corporate strongholds. We need to understand how to use our armor and offensive weapons, that we must pray and fight in teams and know our prayer assignments. For example, our church united in prayer to tear down the stronghold of greed in our area. We prayed the same scriptures and did prayer walking in strategic areas of our counties. Eventually, our area became the hottest real estate market in the south.

It is important to know when to minister to someone with strongholds, when they are ripe, truly repentant, how to discern spiritual roots, what hurts need to be healed and how to free the captives with the two-edged sword of God's truth in His Word.

This is my paraphrase of Isaiah 61:1 and 7: "The Spirit of the Lord GOD is upon me; because the LORD has anointed me to bring good news to the humble; he has sent me to heal the brokenhearted, to <u>proclaim liberty to the captives, and to open the prison for them that are bound</u> . . . For your shame you shall have a double portion; and instead of being confused, you will rejoice in your double portion: therefore in your land you shall possess double and everlasting joy shall be yours."

Prayer to break the power of corporate and personal strongholds

Father, I thank you for revealing the presence of this stronghold *in my life and for showing me that I am not helpless to change it. you have shown me how it was built long ago and now lies deeply embedded in my soul. I thank you for your faithfulness, for you have also opened my eyes to how this thought pattern, pretense or imagination is blocking my own healing, hindering me from knowing you, Lord, and believing your truth (II Corinthians 10:3-6). I receive your true discernment of the thoughts and intents of my heart (Hebrews 4:12-13).*

This ungodly mindset and behavior *used to make perfect sense to me, but now I understand how illogical and destructive it is. I repent of defending my right to react and behave this way when you tried to convict me in the past. I want to be free from its power but I need your help and your strength to break free. Please free me now from my fleshly structures of _____.*

For the way I judged others *in condemning them for not agreeing with my principles, I ask your forgiveness and pray they will forgive me for the hurt I caused them as well. Help me restore the relationships with my family and friends that have been damaged or lost because of my sinfulness. I loose myself and them from all that is not of God and bind me and them to all that is of God.*

Please forgive me for becoming a part *of this stronghold on a corporate level too. I forgive other people who lured me further into this destructive stronghold by their example of ungodly minds set on indulging the flesh. Bring them to the insights you've given me, Father, that they may be saved from themselves and enlightened by your holiness.*

As for my participation in this stronghold, I forgive myself *for allowing it to take control of my thoughts and behavior. I finally give you access to the unhealed hurts that gave the enemy access. The cost is too great for me to continue on this path. Lord, show me how to identify the bitter roots in my life, which opened the gateway for this stream of thought and behavior. With the strength of Holy Spirit within me, we will tear down the walls of this stronghold so that not one stone is left.*

From this moment on, I commit myself *to the defeat of this stronghold as I come into true agreement with your scriptures. I commit myself to put on the whole armor of God (Ephesians 6) and to swing the Sword of the Spirit, as Jesus did in Matthew 4. Through the power of the blood of Christ, it will no longer dominate me. In the mighty name of Jesus Christ, I bind this stronghold to the Cross, asking you to put it to death. Renew my mind by your resurrection power within me. I receive your strength to submit myself to God, to resist the devil, to stand against the enemy and to be single-minded (James 4:7-8).*

Because of your love, *your grace, and the blood of Christ that washes me clean, I am loosed from the seduction of this thought pattern. I renounce all sinful behaviors attached to it. I choose to submit my mind and my will to the working of the Holy Spirit. May my life reflect the beauty and the holiness of my Savior, Jesus Christ, as I finally make Him Lord of my life.*

Send me people who will walk with me *on your righteous path, who will help me submerge myself in prayer, in your Word and in reverence before you. I choose to build my life on the foundation of living faith, not on old habits and automatic ways of thinking. Help me to enlist prayer support that will hold me up before your face as I learn to replace the old ways with new ways gathered from spending time with you and your people.*

I choose to be an overcomer *who walks in your resurrection power and your authority and to present myself as a living sacrifice. As you transform my mind, I will fight with spiritual weapons and partner with you to free other captives. Thank you, Lord. Your Truth makes me free indeed. Amen.*

Suicidal Intents

Most suicide attempts are expressions of extreme distress, not harmless bids for attention. A person who appears suicidal needs immediate professional help. ***If you think someone is suicidal, do not leave him or her alone.*** Try to get the person to seek immediate help from his or her counselor, doctor, the nearest hospital emergency room, or call 911. Eliminate access to firearms, weapons or other potential suicide aids, including unsupervised access to medications.

Besides straightforward or "sideways" comments about not wanting to live any longer, some of the red flags that a person has a high risk for self-harm include acquiring a weapon, making or changing a will, giving away personal belongings, mending grievances, checking on insurance policies, withdrawing from people and not frequenting usual places.

Suicide risk is higher if people have recently experienced any of the following extremely stressful life situations (this is certainly not a comprehensive list): loss of a significant relationship or death of a loved one, diagnosis of a terminal illness, loss of financial security or job, loss of home, inability to work, or aftereffects of abuse, rape or other serious emotional trauma.

People sometimes become more suicidal as they begin the climb up out of depression. Sudden withdrawal from antidepressant drugs or the relief during the first three weeks of taking antidepressant drugs can increase suicide risk. One of the reasons for this is that as their lethargy lifts, they can more easily find the energy to carry out a suicide plan. Another possible reason is that they might feel more in control and therefore at peace with their situation once they have made the decision to end their own life. This is important to keep in mind because people may appear as if they're getting better when in fact they are more at risk.

Antidepressants are far from harmless and their use must be managed by a professional so their use will not contribute to suicidal intents. They are also linked to many serious health problems, such as interfering with the immune system so the body cannot fight off infection or pain. Sudden withdrawal from antidepressants can also bring on thoughts of suicide or violent behavior.

Regular exercise is one of the secret weapons in overcoming depression and suicidal intents. It works by helping to normalize insulin levels while boosting the feel good hormones in the brain. This doesn't necessarily mean joining a gym and working out until every muscle aches. A brisk half-hour walk at least three times a week is sufficient.

Foods have an immense impact on your body and your brain and eating whole foods will best support both mental and physical health. Avoiding sugar and grains will help normalize your insulin and leptin levels, which is another important aspect of depression. Grains, especially processed ones like white flour, are quickly converted into sugar in the body, although whole grains are converted at a slower rate that doesn't spike blood sugar quite so quickly. Sugar causes chronic inflammation, which disrupts the body's normal immune function and can wreak havoc on the brain.

Have you ever noticed how great it can feel to spend time outdoors on a sunny day? Well, it turns out that getting **safe sun exposure**, which allows your body to produce vitamin D, is great for your mood. Research has shown that vitamin D levels drop during winter months or extended periods of rainy weather. This correlates with times when suicide rates increase. You can optimize your vitamin D either by sunlight exposure or by using a safe tanning bed, or by taking a high-quality vitamin D3 supplement.

A person who is suicidal is focused on their current unbearable circumstances and any future seems impossible to endure given the overwhelming pain of the present. Although the hurting person may feel suicide is the only way to escape, he or she doesn't always take into account how this may affect others. The intent to take one's own life is a death stone that sends out ripples of pain into the lives of friends and family members.

Someone told me about her struggle to overcome her suicidal intents. She had come within minutes of a successful suicide. All her possessions were laid out. Her will was completed. Correspondence to family and friends was finished. Even her funeral wishes were on paper. It was at that precise moment she decided to get help. She came for several sessions of **restoration prayer ministry**.

I'm happy to say she chose to live that day and chooses to surrender her life to God each morning. What a turnaround! Once she finally believed the truth of who God said she was in Christ, she began noticing little "God-surprises" popping up every day, to remind her of His constant presence and abiding love. It wasn't a quick fix, but her life change was nothing short of a miraculous supernatural healing of her soul. Now she listens to God's voice instead of demonic suicidal voices.

God promises us grace sufficient for today. He assures us He will provide a way to escape or to endure all our temptations and trials. His rest and inexhaustible grace are available each day, no matter what we face. He is always with us, whether or not we "feel" His presence, because He promised to never leave us or forsake us.

In the depths of despair, we can talk to God and tell Him everything that's on our minds. He already knows our innermost thoughts and secrets, and it's safe to let Him hear our anger, our turmoil and our frustrations. He loves us with an everlasting love that just won't quit. He is our shelter in the time of our worst life storm. When we're finished raging and are quiet inside, we can be still and listen for His still, small voice, sending assurance of His healing love to our wounded souls.

Believing these truths from the heart and concerned friends will melt away suicidal intents.

Prayer to choose life

Lord, you know all about my downward spiral *of despair, anger, stress, blaming, bitterness or self-centeredness that ultimately led me towards suicide. You know because you were there with me all along, waiting for me to leave the shadow and come into your light. Because I now believe the truth of who you are and who I am in you, I no longer wish to end my life. Instead, because of your love and the sacrifice of Christ, I choose to embrace life and the destiny you have in mind for me. Teach me to dare to trust you, so that trust will take root and grow. I turn my spirit toward your light; I have walked in the darkness of my own making for too long.*

In the past, I admit I've been angry with you, Father*, because I believed the enemies. The enemy whispered that you didn't care about me or the pain I suffered. I wanted to end my life because I couldn't bear the thought that no one cared, not even you. I'm so sorry for all the times I whined, complained, and accused you of all sorts of things you were not guilty of. I release you from any blame I hurled at you in my despair when you wouldn't answer my prayers in the way I wanted. I cannot control you; I can only control my attitude and even that has to come through your power within me.*

I confess that I have judged other people *for wounding my spirit or supporting my sinful self-pity. I viewed them, and even my doctors, as just as deficient and uninformed as myself. In sowing dishonor and disrespect to them, I reaped a harvest of self-loathing in my own life. I have sown weeds of damage in the lives of others. Let my repentance somehow help them; show me what I must do to bring healing to those whom I defiled. Help them to see your truth that sets them free.*

I forgive myself for wallowing in misery*, much of which was my own making. I regret the many opportunities I wasted while contemplating the destruction of my life instead of running to you to rest and rejoice in your love for me. I'm sorry for all the ripples of hurt and worry I caused those around me. In faith, I choose instead to be grateful for my life, to accept myself as a blessing that will bring glory to you and be a help to others. I am your precious asset, not a liability.*

You promised to give peace in the storms of life*, but I realize now that my choices and my attitude are my responsibility.* ***Through the power of your Spirit****, I chose to be thankful for opportunities to run to your great heart for comfort, courage, wisdom, peace, and anything else I need for life. Thank you that you are in control. Father, open my eyes to your power within me. I invite your Holy Spirit to fill every part of my body, soul and spirit. Let your abundant life flow through me, bringing joy in knowing you and accepting that I am redeemed by the blood of Jesus, who loved me and gave Himself for me. Amen.*

Unforgiving Attitude

The number one reason people do not reach their potential in life is not the choices that other people make, because of circumstances beyond their control or even because of their own lack of ability. (Thank God that the choices that other people make cannot prevent God from being faithful to us.)

The main reason they can miss their destiny is that they have not chosen to completely forgive those who have offended them. In essence, they begin collecting emotional IOUs for debts they think are owed to them. In holding onto these unresolved grievances and so-called "debts" they stunt their own emotional and spiritual growth and develop a root of bitterness that taints all their relationships. They cannot move forward because they are stuck in the rut of focusing on how badly they've been treated or on other people's sins.

Prayer ministers can help people with unforgiving attitudes to let go of the IOUs and to give them to God for vindication in His own way and in His own time. Once people stop accumulating debts they feel are owed to them, they can focus on letting God heal their damaged emotions and correct their own sinful reactions to past issues and old wounds.

What does forgiveness mean? Handing over emotional IOUs to God doesn't mean that anyone has "gotten away with" anything. Forgiving means only giving up your right to get even for something you feel is unfair or "owed" to you. When we give up that right and instead relinquish our IOUs to God, He becomes our Heavenly Judge in charge of judging our case and collecting on those debts.

When we forgive both offense and offender, the right of vengeance transfers to God (Romans 12:19). Our offenders no longer owe us a debt; they owe God. Since we will all stand before God someday to give an account of our lives, it is wise to be sure we harbor no unforgiving attitude and hold no IOUs. We stand cleansed and whole before God only through our faith in the righteous work of Christ on the Cross and by His grace alone.

God has impressed me to press in further to my potential by pressing in to His riches in GRACE FOR OTHERS. He has impressed me that the higher levels in Him are full of absolute grace for others, like the grace that I have requested for myself, having been the "chief of sinners."

Father God has required me to submit to a more stringent test that I would like to share with you because the freedom found in accomplishing forgiveness is awesome. The pure in heart see and know the awesome grace of God's forgiveness.

I want the very best for you, and also for myself and our offenders. But am I willing to pray for God's unlimited grace for myself and others? Am I willing to advance that grace to my offenders who "do not deserve it?"

Read the following list and see if any seem familiar in your own life:
- Do you still give in to the temptation to tell someone how they hurt you?
- Do you hope that they feel bad or uncomfortable around you?
- Do you still avoid them or just happen to leave them out?
- Do you still claim your rights to an apology, vindication or restitution?
- Do you still hope that they will be exposed and punished?
- Do you still rehearse what you could have said or done to retaliate?
- Are you surprised when God chooses to use them in His service?
- Have you lost spiritual power or hear God less clearly than you did before?
- Do you have physical problems, aches and pains that have no cure?
- Is your sleep disturbed? Not restful? Troubled with dreams?
- Are you still justifying your defenses and fleshly self-protection?
- Are you keeping a better record of their wrongs than of your own unforgiving reactions?

If any of the above behaviors or attitudes sound like you, it's time for a soul-searching session with God. Write down your areas of unforgiveness and using the Cross Walk Prayer in the appendix, pray through them. Forgiving others may be a key to open your doors of opportunity. Asking for forgiveness in five ways will set you and your offenders free and place you on the road to your spiritual recovery.

The familiar Lord's Prayer includes the truth that God forgives us as we forgive others. In other words, what we choose not to forgive becomes a festering wound that defiles our Christian walk and stunts our growth in faith and interferes with a close relationship with our Heavenly Father.

Read Romans 12 for a beautiful word picture of the one who truly forgives, and have confidence that Jesus will accomplish that same level of forgiveness in you. Believe that you will be without hypocrisy, clinging to good, hating evil, kindly affectionate, humble, preferring that the other be blessed, etc. Pray that you will be willing to feed them, give them living water, invest in their future, rejoice when they are promoted over you—and that you will overcome evil (in your own heart) with good.

May I encourage you one more time! Choose to receive the inexhaustible fullness of the grace of God for them and also for yourself. Forgive as you have been forgiven—not because you deserve it, but because it has been paid for by the blood of the very Son of God.

Prayer to dissolve an unforgiving attitude

Lord Jesus, I surrender to you, the judge of all the earth! I ask you to forgive me for withholding forgiveness, for trying to take your place as Judge, for doubting your fair justice and for my own sins. I forgive myself for my own hypocrisy. Teach me how to forgive others in the same way that you forgive me.

Why Do We Train Restoration Prayer Teams?

I believe God is allowing the body of Christ to come to the place where we will have to rise to our calling to minister restoration. Do you believe that believers can be taught, trained and equipped to have a significant part in restoring individuals, small groups, churches, cities and nations? Who will minister restoration prayers to the great harvest?

Do you believe you can be a part of a new generation of restoration ministers? If you had an opportunity to be trained to be on a restoration team or to train up restoration teams, would you be interested? For many believers, this is radical thinking. The Bible says that if you have Christ in you, you have everything you need for life and godliness. Christ in you has all you need to fulfill your destiny but most people may not know how to release this life-changing power. Believers have His unlimited power within to be all He has called them to be. He has made unique deposits into each believer's life and has been preparing us for a unique gifting, a unique calling and a unique anointing.

I believe that many Pastors and Priests would be interested in training up restoration teams if they saw this book. Why? Because they are accountable for how their members minister and they need a protocol and guidelines to define what a restoration team does. With the manual in hand, they can define what tools are to be used:
1. Clear definitions of what each issue is about
2. Approved prayers asking forgiveness five ways
3. Scripture prayer strategies to define "biblical"
4. Helpful handouts and self-tests
5. Relevant books, articles and teachings

Do you share my vision of churches raising up restoration teams who will minister to the great harvest of new believers, prodigals and even the fallen? God has already given revelation and spiritual insights that enable believers to partner with Him to heal the broken hearted and minister freedom to the captives. The big question is how to equip members to minister healing, freedom, activation in the spiritual gifts and to be demonstrations His love and power.

Manual One and Manual Three

I think of this book as Manual Two. *Restoration Prayer Ministry Manual One* was written to provide you with insights, scriptures, resources, tools and prayers for ministry to issues that are common in prayer ministry. It also includes instructions and handouts to do Issue-Focused Prayer Ministry. It is necessary to master the ministry guidelines in Manual One before you study the complex issues in Manual Three. It will have advanced teaching and ministry helps. If you sense a call to begin a Restoration Prayer Ministry of your own, you will appreciate the forms and advanced resources in Manual One.

Manual Three will include insights, resources, tools and prayers for more advanced issues. It is absolutely critical that you have received our 18 hour Restoration Prayer Ministry yourself before you attempt the advanced ministry in Manual Three. It will be a priceless asset to those who have studied to show themselves approved and prepared by applying the insights in Manual One.

Part 4: Exhibits and Opportunities

Cross Walk Prayer

Dear Lord Jesus,

I have a negative pattern in my life, that is not Godly and I cannot get rid of it by myself. I know that a bad fruit has a bad root. I don't want this pattern of _____ any longer. I don't want to reap this in my own life or in the people around me. Please show me the spiritual root of it and how to deal with my part of this problem (even if I am only 10% of the problem.)

Did I sow this and now I am reaping it, more and later?	Galatians 6:7-10
Did I dishonor my parents or authorities in this area?	Ephesians 6:1-3
Did I judge someone and now I draw that thing to me?	Matthew 7:1, Romans 2:1-4
Did a bitter expectation spring up in me, defiling others?	Hebrews 12:14-15
Did I make an inner vow in not to be like them?	James 5:12, Matthew 5:37

1. **I RECOGNIZE** that the reason this problem of _____ is now a pattern in my own life, is because of my sinful reaction of (dishonor, judgment, sowing the sin myself, inner vows or bitter root expectation.) The fruit is that I am reaping similar problems in others and myself according to the LAW of sowing and reaping. I am reaping this crop because of my sinful reactions to their sin. I am reaping from the sinful seed that I have sown - not from what they have sown.

2. **I REPENT** and ask forgiveness in five ways. Please forgive me:

   1. for not asking others to forgive me
   2. for judging others and not forgiving others
   3. for sowing my own sin / sinful reactions
   4. for blaming or doubting you God
   5. and for not forgiving myself

3. **I RENOUNCE** my sin of dishonor, judgment, sowing the sin myself, bitter root expectations or fleshly inner vows. I choose to forgive them, releasing them to you, the Judge of all the earth.

4. **RELEASE** me from reaping this crop that is now mine to reap because of my sinful reactions to others.

5. **I RECKON** dead on the cross all flesh that identifies with this reaction and all automatic reactions that I have developed with it. I ask you Jesus, to bring it to death, because I cannot. Create in me a pure heart that agrees with your responses.

6. **RESURRECT** your likeness into every area that you have brought to death.

7. **RESTORE** all the years that the locusts have eaten while I was disobedient.

8. **I RECLAIM** all the spiritual blessings that my family and I have missed.

9. **REWARD** us for generations to come, as we sow true discernment, grace and mercy. Thank you, Lord, for the forgiveness you have provided for us on the cross and all the blessings that we are free to walk in now. We believe you for them! Amen

Circles Diagram

Body, Soul and Spirit diagrams adapted from "Exchanged Life" by Charles Solomon

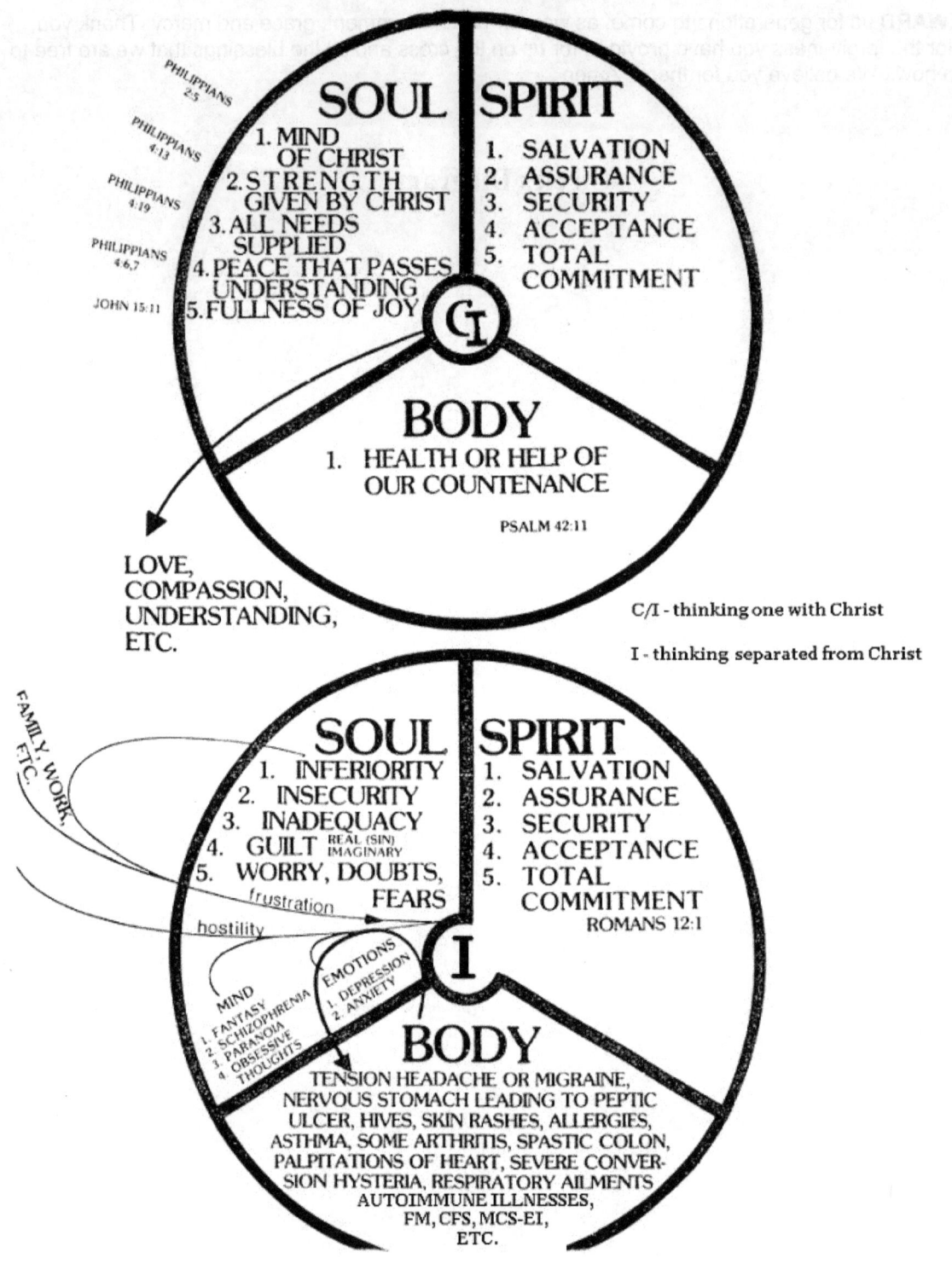

Probably one of the biggest challenges we have is to understand the love of God. Don't ask me, "Why does God love us?" He is love, and He does. Let's pray and ask Father God to expand our hearts so we can receive our Father's Love Letter, His love and His unconditional acceptance. It is truly more humble to receive God's love than it is to refuse it. Pray that you will be able to run to His arms with abandon when you begin to see Him waiting for you. You will find incredible peace sitting in His lap.

Love Letter
Adapted from the Father's Love Letter - free downloads at www.fathersloveletter.com

You may not know me, but I know everything about you. Psalm 139:1
I know when you sit down and when you rise up. Psalm 139:2
I am familiar with all your ways. Psalm 139:3
Even the very hairs on your head are numbered. Matthew 10:29-31
For you were made in My image. Genesis 1:27
In Me you live and move and have your being. Acts 17:28
For you are My offspring. Acts 17:28
I knew you before you were conceived. Jeremiah 1:4-5
I chose you when I planned creation. Ephesians 1:11-12
You were not a mistake, all your days are written in My book. Psalm 139:15-16
I determined the exact time of your birth and where you would live. Acts 17:26
You are fearfully and wonderfully made. Psalm 139:14
I knit you together in your mother's womb. Psalm 139:13
And brought you forth on the day you were born. Psalm 71:6
I have been misrepresented by those who don't know Me. John 8:41-44
I am not distant and angry, but the complete expression of love. 1 John 4:16
And it is my desire to lavish my love on you. 1 John 3:1
Simply because you are my child and I am your father. 1 John 3:1
I offer you more than your earthly father ever could. Matthew 7:11
For I am the perfect father. Matthew 5:48
Every good gift that you receive comes from My hand. James 1:17
For I am your provider and I meet all your needs. Matthew 6:31-33
My plan for your future has always been filled with hope. Jeremiah 29:11
Because I love you with an everlasting love. Jeremiah 31:3
My thoughts of you are countless as the sand on the seashore. Ps 139:17-18
And I rejoice over you with singing. Zephaniah 3:17
I will never stop doing good to you. Jeremiah 32:40
For you are My treasured possession. Exodus 19:5
I desire to establish you with all My heart and all My soul. Jeremiah 32:41
And I want to show you great and marvelous things. Jeremiah 33:3
If you seek Me with all your heart, you will find Me. Deuteronomy 4:29
Delight in Me and I will give you the desires of your heart. Psalm 37:4
For it is I who gave you those desires. Philippians 2:13
I am able to do more for you than you could possibly imagine. Ephesians 3:20
For I am your greatest encourager. 2 Thessalonians 2:16-17
I am also the Father who comforts you in all your troubles. 2 Corinthians 1:3-4

When you are brokenhearted, I am close to you. Psalm 34:18
As a shepherd carries a lamb, I have carried you close to My heart. Isaiah 40:11
One day I will wipe away every tear from your eyes. Revelation 21:3-4
And I'll take away all the pain you have suffered on this earth. Revelation 21:3-4
I am your Father and I love you even as I love My son, Jesus. John 17:23
For in Jesus, My love for you is revealed. John 17:26
He is the exact representation of My being. Hebrews 1:3
He came to demonstrate that I am for you, not against you. Romans 8:31
And to tell you that I am not counting your sins. 2 Corinthians 5:18-19
Jesus died so that you and I could be reconciled. 2 Corinthians 5:18-19
His death was the ultimate expression of My love for you. 1 John 4:10
I gave up everything I loved that I might gain your love. Romans 8:31-32
If you receive the gift of My son Jesus, you receive Me. 1 John 2:23
And nothing will ever separate you from My love again. Romans 8:38-39
Come home and I'll throw the biggest party heaven has ever seen. Luke 15:7
I have always been Father, and will always be Father. Ephesians 3:14-15
My question is, "Will you be my child?" John 1:12-13
I am waiting for you. Luke 15:11-32

Love, your Dad, Almighty God

A PROTECTION PRAYER FOR EVERY DAY

We plead the Blood of Jesus over us, our loved ones, pets, possessions and property, everything and everybody we care about. In the Name of Jesus Christ, Son of God Most High, we bind all evil spirits within or around us and cancel every assignment of the enemy against us or them! In the Name of Jesus Christ of Nazareth, Son of God Most High, we command all demonic spirits to go to the dry, uninhabited places and never come back!

We take the Sword of the Spirit and in the Name of Jesus, we cancel and break all witchcraft practices and prayers, curses, hexes, spells, circles, triangles, incantations, any mind binding or mind control actions taken against us and our loved ones! In Jesus Name, we cancel every assignment of area covens, familiar spirits, watchers, interjects and astral spirits! We place a wall of fire and a hedge of protection around us that no spirit can astral project over and if they attack us on purpose, their human hosts will be literally burned. We bless them that continue to try to curse us and bless them with the knowledge that the love and power of Jesus Christ is stronger.

In the Name of Jesus Christ the Anointed One of the Most High God, only the Holy Spirit can affect us and no other spirit can see or hear what is happening on our properties or any of our communications. In the Name of Jesus Christ of Nazareth, we bind and crush every evil source of every evil activity and loose the Spirit of Truth on those who practice it, that they may come to know Jesus Christ is Lord and Master of ALL!

PROTECTION PRAYER AS WE MINISTER

In the Name of Jesus, we trust you, Lord, to undo all assignments of the enemy and all knowledge of who we are, what we are doing, our sessions and the work of Holy Spirit. We trust you to hide us in a place that is safe from attacks from demonic spirits and to establish genuine trust between us and our prayer receivers. We believe for your discernment to know your prayer strategies to destroy the works of the enemy.

We ask you, God Most High, to rebuke or bind any being from realms of darkness, making them deaf, dumb and mute, canceling all their plans for backlash, back up forces, back up curses or retaliation of any kind. We call every part of our own hearts to come into alignment with Father God's Truth so they can receive healing and freedom.

We swing the Sword of the Spirit, pray in the Spirit, speak the will of Almighty God and call God's holy warrior angels to fight against the enemy (principalities, powers, rulers and wickedness in high places (Ephesians 6:12) with swords of fire! We ask you, Lord, to rebuke all cosmic interference from the second heavens and even from outside of time.

In the Name of Jesus Christ, the Anointed One, we ask you Oh Lord, to dismantle spiritual structures of hierarchies of darkness, mind control and programming, as you see fit, in your will, way and timing. We release your mighty angels to execute your will and empower them as we speak your Word. We thank you for making us and your ministry through us invisible to enemy forces and for making a way for believers to "step out" of captivity into true freedom in Jesus Christ, our blessed Lord and Savior. We choose to believe you are transforming us and making us one with you. We rest in your supernatural power.

We trust you to cleanse us from any doubts, worries, fears, demonic attachments or transferences, to purify our hearts, making us true expressions of your heart, in your love and power, so we can serve you, wholly given to you. Amen

Opportunities

18 Hour Restoration Prayer Ministry Works!

You can't heal your heart with your head; you can't heal spiritual problems with analysis. What we do is not talking it to death, rewriting history or behavior modification. God has shown us how to offer an integrated ministry, which includes His revelations to many ministries. Restoration Prayer Ministry is **over 18 hours of integrated ministry,** praying over issues from your whole life. We offer follow-up appointments and mentoring. Our alumni can continue a growing lifestyle with a godly strategy for mentoring, training, activations, ongoing education and residential internships.

We begin with a strong start in cooperation with the supernatural power of God. We take a six-hour history of the patterns and blockages in your spirit, soul and body. We hear God's voice for the **root symptoms and causes** and His strategies.

We partner with God to break the power of long-standing **destructive patterns.**

1. We renounce the **deceptions and ungodly beliefs** blocking your true identity.
2. We break the power of **word curses, bitterroot judgments and expectations.**
3. We invite Holy Spirit to heal **hurts and memories** that have been suppressed.
4. We minister **lasting deliverance** from bondages and spiritual oppression.
5. We bring alignment of your **identity, personal purpose and the power** of God.

Restoration Prayer Ministry is NOT a one-time fix; it's a lifestyle of growing in freedom. Once you are healed and free, you will be ready for mentoring and training. You may come in person or make appointments by phone or free Skype.com or ooVoo.com.

First steps to apply: Go to http://www.restorationprayerministry.com/restoration.html

- Read the four articles about RPM
- Ten-page application and costs
- Request a phone interview
- Agree on appointment times
- Make reservations by donating
- Sign and send the ten-page application
- Read *Restoration Prayer Ministry Manual One*
- Prepare your heart in prayer

I am usually booked one-two months ahead of time. Be sure to call ASAP!

Mentoring Opportunities and Resources

We are delighted to offer mentoring by phone, Skype or in person at your site or ours. Mentoring is important for those who are called to the ministry and to those who are called to include ministry in their business, education, media, government and the arts.

Our purpose is to provide a place for you to receive unconditional love, wisdom and insight so that you will develop such an intimate relationship with God, that you will be able to impart His restoration and transformation to others. You will gain the tools to help others to better fulfill their callings. This is possible through adequate healing, freedom mentoring and training.

We are available to be a Christian mentor for you or your ministry teams, on-site at your ministry or with ministry internships here at Cross Walk Life. If you have ministers or team candidates who are called and gifted to minister, we are available to train them, if they meet the pre-requisites. See our requirements for mentoring and internships on our main mentoring pages at **www.CrossWalkLife.com.** You can host a seminar or webinar for your small group or teams whether they are small or large.

Most people begin mentoring with follow up appointments after receiving RPM. They continue to submit issues and ungodly beliefs for healing and deliverance. They learn to tear down personal strongholds using our audio course and CD manual. As they begin attending NowFaith.TV, they send in a paragraph of testimony homework after viewing each video and I reply in writing or in phone appointments. They participate in our conversations and testify on Facebook and on Cross Walk Talk Radio, our online talk show. You can host a seminar or webinar for your small group or teams whether they are small or large.

We are happy to offer MEGA Weekend training and activations for your teams. See the form to apply to be a training host on our main seminar page.

Your eight-step mentoring plan:

- **Restoration Prayer Ministry** - Six three-hour sessions to get healed and free and to identify your mentoring plan
- **Mentoring follow-up appointments** - learn to use your new tools as a lifestyle of overcoming
- **Tearing Down Personal Strongholds** course and manual on computer CD
- **Resources** - Courses and whole seminars on CDs, DVDs and as downloads
- **NowFaith.TV Video Training School Online** - Interactive mentoring using videos, audios, articles, prayers, emails and appointments
- Participate on **Facebook** and our live call-in program **Cross Walk Talk Radio** online
- **Seminars and webinars** - Host your own or attend a MEGA Weekend or sizzling Saturday of training and activation.
- **Internships** - Requirements and applications for one-two or three-six months of residential internship

Join NowFaith.TV Training School - Online - Any time
Videos, audios, articles, prayers
Live ministry demonstrations
Hot Cutting Edge Interviews
Whole video training seminars
Pastoral Prayer and Counseling
Earn a Certificate of Attendance

TO ENROLL: Go to www.NowFaith.TV and click JOIN

1. Read our NowFaith.TV Covenant
2. Introduce yourself to us
3. Be a blessed contributing member
4. Fill out the interests questionnaire
5. **Click Schools - Ministry archives**

REQUIRED READING TO EARN A CERTIFICATE OF ATTENDANCE

FIRST SEMESTER:

Transformation of the Inner Man by John and Paul Sanford. *Restoration Prayer Ministry Manual One* to learn how to minister restoration.

SECOND AND THIRD SEMESTER:

Healing Women's Emotions (Every minister will minister to women. *The Bait of Satan* is a must for all Christians to maintain their own freedom. *Breaking Intimidation* key to walking the walk in faith, free of intimidation. *Search for Significance* with a workbook for renouncing ungodly beliefs.

HOMEWORK: The homework for each class is to email a testimony of Holy Spirit's work in your life after you prayed the prayer for that class. Your testimony must be less than one page and include a balance of your ISSUE BEFORE, the PRAYER you prayed and the RESULTS after you prayed. Credit will only be given for a testimony of how God worked in YOUR OWN LIFE and the result.

MINISTRY TRIPS: We are invited to hold seminars for other ministries. Please contact us if you would like to go, can pay your own way (travel, room and board) and assist our ministry team every day, serving us and our host ministry or business.

SEMINARS: We would like to do seminars in your area. Please contact us to schedule a seminar. We are a para-church ministry and hope to be of service to you by offering healing, mentoring and training to your existing local teams or potential teams.

LEARN MORE AT **http://www.restorationprayerministry.com/schools.html**

Resources, CDs, DVDs and Downloads

Visit our online store for a great selection of resources
http://crosswalklife.com/Christian_Resources_DVD_CD.html

TEARING DOWN PERSON STRONGHOLDS
Audio Teachings plus a 70-page manual
to print as a document
Introduction to TDPS
Bitterness - Unforgiveness
Jealousy and Envy
Doubts and Unbelief
Rejection
Fears and Intimidation
Accusation
Religious Spirits
Witchcraft Prayer
Leviathan, King of Pride
+ Who I Am in Christ

As downloads or on CD

RESTORING RELATIONSHIPS DVDs
Experience transformation for your entire family as you watch this powerful **2 DVD set** together. Build a new foundation on cutting edge truth, timely for today's family issues:
Healing Our Childhood Wounds
Transforming Hearts of Stone
One in Spirit With Him
Our Differences
Importance of Fathers
Roots of Bitterness
Negative Expectations
The Law or the Spirit?

Healing Your Identity
Healing you with this 14 part DVD series
Prophet Carlotta Waldmann is invited to ministries to hold staff training workshops and to minister to the staff with individual Restoration Prayer Ministry and personal prophetic prayer ministry. This 14 part DVD series was recorded in Ga. for the staff of Cheerful Hearts Ministry and includes teachings from the workshop, two sessions of personal prophetic prayer ministry, testimonies and a skit about our new identity when we are one with Christ.
This is an IN-DEPTH menu for mature ministers.

Visit our online store for a great selection of downloads
http://crosswalklife.com/Download_Store_CWL.html

Restoration Prayer Ministry PDF Manual One, Leader's Guide and Prayer Sheets
(Restoration Prayer Ministry Manual One is also in paperback on Amazon)

Communion – Hearing God – 8 downloads

Breaking Free – 4 downloads

Breaking Powerful Roots – 4 downloads

Spiritual Gifts, Discernment and Prophetic – 4 downloads

Tearing Down Personal Strongholds – 11 teachings

Healing for Survivors – 6 audios and 2 handouts

Restoring Relationships – 8 downloads

Interview Rev Russ Dizdar: Ministry for Survivors of Mind Control – 3 downloads

Interview Rev Pat Torok: Healing for Dissociation – 3 downloads

Bibliography and Reading Suggestions

Bevere, John. *Breaking Intimidation*. Charisma House, 2006.

Bevere, John. *The Bait of Satan: Living Free from the Deadly Trap of Offense / John Bevere*. Charisma House, 2014.

Chapman, Gary. *The Five Love Languages: The Secret to Love That Lasts*. Northfield Publishing, 2010.

Gaborit, Chris, and Schultz, D. Stephen. *Mentoring and Fathering*.

Preparing the Way Ministries, 1996.

Kylstra, Chester and Betsy. *Biblical Healing and Deliverance A Guide to Experiencing Freedom from Sins of the Past, Destructive Beliefs, Emotional and Spiritual Pain, Curses and Oppression.* Chosen Books Pub Co, 2014.

McGee, Robert S. *The Search for Significance.* W Pub. Group, 2003.

Sandford, John Loren and Paula. *Restoring the Christian Family: A Biblical Guide to Love, Marriage, and Parenting In a Changing World.* Charisma House, 2009.

Sandford, John Loren and Paula. *The Transformation of the Inner Man.* Victory House Publications, 1982.

Sandford, Paula. *Healing for a Woman's Emotions.* Charisma House, 2007.

Virkler, Mark and Patti. *How to Hear God's Voice.* Destiny Image Publishers, 2006.

Waldmann, Carlotta. *Restoration Prayer Ministry Manual One.* Christian International Publishing, 2016.

Wright, Henry. *A More Excellent Way – Be in Health.* Pleasant Valley Church, 2005.

www.ingramcontent.com/pod-product-compliance
Lightning Source LLC
LaVergne TN
LVHW061309060426
835507LV00019B/2078